LIGHTHOUSE ADVENTURES

HEROES, HAUNTS & HAVOC ON THE GREAT LAKES

WES OLESZEWSKI

AVERY COLOR STUDIOS, INC.
GWINN, MICHIGAN

©1999 Avery Color Studios, Inc.

ISBN 1-892384-01-9

Library of Congress Card Number 99-C72160

First Edition 1999, Reprinted 2000, 2002

Published by
Avery Color Studios, Inc.
Gwinn, Michigan 49841

Cover photo by
Wayne S. Sapulski

Shown on the cover
Chicago Harbor Light, Lake Michigan

To My Uncle John (Jack) Fowler Sr.

As I travel around this world, I find that there are far too few people who actually live the life they preach. My uncle Jack is one of the few. His faith is exercised through his kindness and unending simple acts of giving of himself to all who cross his path. I know that if at any time, in any place, should I ever be in need of anything or any one, I can count on Uncle Jack to be there for me without question, as he is there for everyone. It is with the greatest of respect that I dedicate this text to him. Should I be able to demonstrate only a portion of the kindness that is his by example, I will become a better person.

Table of Contents

Preface

In the autumn of 1996 the folks at Avery approached me and asked if I would write a book containing a complete guide to Great Lakes lighthouses, U.S. and Canadian. As a writer of the true adventures of the Great Lake maritime industry, I knew too well the great importance of these lights as well as the tremendous interest that the public has in lighthouses and the need to preserve these historic sites. For those reasons I agreed and wrote *Great Lakes Lighthouses American & Canadian*. In keeping with the publisher's wishes, the book was structured in the form of a list and guide with accompanying photographs of each site. This kind of book was somewhat removed from my normal writing style which deals with detailed narratives of the obscure maritime events and the people involved in them. In the writing of *Great Lakes Lighthouses American & Canadian*, I discovered many fascinating tales of the lighthouses that were far too big to fit into a guide book. Those true adventure stories are content of this book.

By the time that I finished *Great Lakes Lighthouses American & Canadian* I found that there was a great hunger among the lighthouse buffs for more information. Thus, I decided that it would be a real waste not to share the material that I had accumulated while writing *Great Lakes Lighthouses American & Canadian*. There were drawings and cutaways, documented heroism and the lore of hauntings. If I did not write it... who would?

Within these pages will be found short stories, long stories, technical descriptions, shipwrecks, acts of courage, fascinating drawings, details on how things worked, maps of where things are and were, photos, and generally something for everyone. There will be quick reading for the days that you desire just a taste of lighthouses, and long, detailed adventures for the times when you want to be transported to another place and era. You will read the fascinating details on how some of these lighthouses were constructed in projects that are still considered as feats of ingenuity. Technical and cutaway drawings from the United States Lighthouse Board will be found within these pages, reproduced from the original reports of more than a century ago. Along this path of discovery you will become acquainted with people and places that were our neighbors and neighborhoods long forgotten. In short, this text contains a wide range of lighthouse adventures from construction to shipwrecks to ghosts and hauntings.

As with all of my writings of the Great Lakes, each one of these stories is completely factual and the result of detailed research. There is absolutely no fiction here; the adventures that you will be reading actually happened, the people named actually existed and their trials and tribulations really took place. This is not a docu-drama, because the actual events listed are so fascinating in their reality that no embellishment is needed. Additionally, when dealing with lore and hearsay, the text will state exactly that. Considering that so much of lighthouse history has been lost, sometimes all that we have is legend. As always when working in the form of historical narrative, the flow of my stories requires a small departure from the above rule. Some dialogue is synthesized and or mixed with documented dialogue to maintain syntax integrity. Also what will not be found in this text are the numbered notes and footnote distractions that so often appear in history texts. In that case direct those who crave such references to the "Sources" bibliography section. It is my opinion that such textbook-proper notation belongs exactly there—in a textbook. This is not a textbook, but a book of factual, descriptive, historical narrative. Excess notation, in my opinion, detracts from the essence of the presentation and anyone who feels compelled to double-check my sources is quite welcome to look them up using the bibliography. There is only one area where I have constructed a chapter, but have no documentation, and that is the story of the lady who takes care of the Pointe aux Barques Lighthouse. The problem there is that the lady is a ghost! No one has officially documented her presence and we are left with only the account of the person who saw her. Fortunately, the story of this lost lightkeeper is just too much fun to leave out, so I wrote it using what little we do have. In that case, the reader is told up-front that we are dealing largely with a first-hand sighting. No matter what part of the text the reader deals with, they may be assured that the material contained within this book is true and I have done my best to keep it that way.

In writing about Great Lakes maritime history, the author has already forged more than a quarter of a million words, and no detail has ever been too small to be included. The same method has been used in the writing of this text. Considering that there are as many ways to tell a story as there are stories to tell, some who read this text may wish to disagree with my work. The author is not above error and typos. In this era of computer-checked text, errors do still occur. So, even if you find areas of disagreement, my hope is that you can read and enjoy the writings. In the final analysis, that is why the book was created.

It is worth noting that attempting to gather information on lighthouses is far different than assembling stories of shipwrecks. There is a large quantity of firsthand information on the shipwrecks of the Great Lakes that has yet to be uncovered, and almost every effort at research results in new data. Researching lighthouses, however, is roughly equivalent to attempting to squeeze a rock in order to obtain water. Much of the documentation of these historic sites has either been lost, destroyed or hoarded. At one point while researching this text, I spent two full days at the National Archives and came away nearly empty-handed. It seems odd that a few weeks of work on a forgotten shipwreck can yield a folder of information that is an inch thick, yet a full year of working on a lighthouse which is currently operational can yield just a few scattered documents. When these documents are found, however, it is a greatly gratifying experience.

My adventure in writing this text has lead to many events that some readers may think insignificant, yet I feel in awe of their importance. In one case while working on a story concerning the Pointe aux Barques Light, I found myself in the research room at the National Archives in Washington D.C. actually holding in my hands the original deed to the property on which the lighthouse is constructed! In pursuit of that same story I stood upon the property of the lighthouse, now closed for the season, and took account of pieces of wooden shipwrecks that continue to wash up on the nearby shore. As I have said before, the readers get to enjoy the books, but it is the author who gets to have the most fun!

Acknowledgements

It is always the name of the author that appears on the cover and binding of every book, yet without many other people lending assistance and contributing facts, no single book of nonfiction could ever be successfully produced. Fortunately, the publishers are kind enough to allow each author the opportunity to give credit where it is due. Since the assembly of a text such as this takes years, and often individual chapters are started, stopped and restarted, it is likely that some people who have helped could be easily overlooked. However, I have done my best to make sure everyone is mentioned.

Persons who guard, manage and tend to the lighthouses are essential in the making of a book such as this. People such as Ray and Martha Janderwski of the Pointe aux Barques Lighthouse were very helpful in the construction of chapters involving that site. Bernard Hellstorm offered much insight on the needs of abandoned lights. Thomas Taylor, the Ponce DeLeon Inlet Lighthouse historian, was more than helpful in his inside tour and expert information on the restoration of lenses and nearly every other aspect of lighthouse preservation. Mark Fowler, who also happens to be my cousin, was helpful with his information on the restoration of Round Island Light. B.M.C. Smith at the Tawas Point Light deserves thanks for his help. Importantly, no book of Great Lakes lighthouses can be produced without the acknowledgment of one of the deans of lighthouse historians on the freshwater seas—Jack Edwards. One can learn more about the lights of the lakes by simply chatting on the phone with Jack than by accessing the accumulation of every text in the lighthouse section of any bookstore.

Those who take the photos and lead the pack in the admiration of these historic sites are also important in the making of books such as this. At the top of that list is Pat Snider, who has a love affair with the Point Marblehead Light, and her stunning photos show it. Additionally, there is Randy Beebe, who was very encouraging along the way. Jack Miller's Schoolhouse Gallery in Marblehead, Ohio, did much to inspire this text.

Historians of the Great lakes in general also played a major role in the production of this book. Dave Swayze is always just a few computer keystrokes away, and often provides important information at the speed of light. Likewise, Richard Palmer can be counted upon to provide answers to anything that can be asked concerning Lake Ontario. The reclusive but highly respected Ralph Roberts is one of the best sources on the planet for needed history. Fellow lighthouse author and dean of shipwreck authors, Fred Stonehouse, is always there to share information. Ann Sindelar of the

Western Reserve Historical Society in Cleveland was more than kind when dealing with this author's questions. Research divers Roy Pickering and Cris Kohl did their best to help with making the details clear, and lighthouse author Betty Neidecker was simply charming to meet and has written a terrific book herself. Thanks must appropriately go to Rick Peuser and Rebecca Livingston of the National Archives. Thanks are also due to Suzette Lopez and the staff of the Milwaukee Public Library. Special thanks go to Noel McFarland, and Carla LaVigne of the Great Lakes Historical Society, Vermilion, Ohio, for their quick response to my calls for help.

There are also the staffs of the libraries that have tolerated my endless sessions at their microfilm machines. For all of the times I ran them out of paper and toner I wish to thank the people of the Bay City Branch Library, Port Huron Public Library, Hoyt Library, Annapolis Public Library, and most of all, the staff and director of the Nimitz Library at the U.S. Naval Academy.

Lastly, there are the people around me who put up with my writers' eccentricities on an hourly basis. At the top of that list must be placed my wife, Teresa, who somehow manages to tolerate the hours of research, and verbalized pondering that is a part of every writer's makeup—yet who still thinks that cleaning the bathroom is a far greater accomplishment for a spouse than is the publication of books. I seem to have the books part down pretty well, but need to work harder at housecleaning. Next on the list of those who need thanks are my Dad, Walt, and my Mom, Sue. I will probably never need a publicity agent in the Great Lakes region as long as these two are at work. My sister, Jeanine, is likely responsible for increased sales because every time she visits a gift shop or bookstore which carries my work, she secretly makes sure that the books are repositioned on the shelves so that they are displayed at eye level and cover out, rather than binding out. The publisher just loves that! My sister, Karen, whom I hear from too infrequently, keeps me in her prayers which provides help and strength that I can never fathom. My brother, Craig, who is also one of my best friends, is always there with educated support and an ability to point out when I have written a run-on sentence. He is always prepared to cast the fragile being of my work into the temporal vortex of literary perplexity using only the enormous powers of his mind. Either that, or he just sends me a really cool e-mail joke!

Lastly, there are you, the readers. Often, I get deep into my research and find myself working on a text that will not reach the bookstores for years, and I forget that folks actually read the stuff. When I go to a book signing, however, and get the chance to meet you, I find the event to be energizing and inspiring. Those who are the "lighthouse people" are among the best of folks with whom to meet and chat. To you I offer both recognition and thanks.

To all that I have mentioned, and to anyone who I may have missed, I offer my gratitude for your input and aid in the making of this book.

Introduction

Details and True Tales

When the average lighthouse buff visits a remote yet romantic old light-station, they tend to ponder many of the same questions:

"When was it built?"

"How was it constructed?"

"What about the people who lived here?"

"What kind of adventures took place here?"

"Was there ever a shipwreck nearby?"

Surely, there are countless answers to these questions depending on which light you are considering. In fact, there are many more stories than can be contained in any single text. The problem is that, normally, the lighthouse buff has to travel great distances to visit a lighthouse and then hope that they stumble upon some expert on that particular site in order to get the story. This book will help to solve that dilemma.

The purpose of establishing any lighthouse is to guide and warn mariners and the vessels that they operate. Other than that single function, lighthouses would not have existed in the first place. Yet, oddly, for that same reason shipwrecks and lighthouses are very often intertwined. Thus, many of the adventures that the reader will find in this text also involve lake vessels and often their wrecks. It seems strange that the very thing that the Lighthouse Board intended to prevent by establishing a light would turn out to be the same thing that distinguishes the lighthouse and its people.

The reader will be transported through distance and time to experience the true adventures of the lighthouses of the Great Lakes without ever having to leave the comfort of their favorite chair. Be prepared to learn, however, because in this text are the details and true tales of nearly every aspect of the lights, vessels, and people of the Great Lakes, that you can not imagine to find anyplace else. You will be reading history, but it will simply seem like entertainment.

When you read of people such as Catherin Hazen, Lillian Bassett, Edward Peterson, Mary Muellerweiss and Andrew Shaw, it is important to keep in mind that all of these people really existed. They all had families, friends, bills to pay and a life that each person actually lived. In this text we are often focused on one episode in their lives.

With this book as a guide, the reader can choose to actually travel to some of the sites described and ponder, firsthand, the people who experienced the adventures so long ago. You can set foot in the same places as the persons in these stories. Sometimes, however, the sites of the adventures are too remote to allow the reader to actually visit, or the setting of the adventure no longer exists. In these cases, the reader will be transported there by way of the story alone.

As in all of this author's work, the details are important. A good example of the difficulty in this type of writing can be seen in the writing of the tale of the Huron Island Lighthouse, and an incident involving the schooner-barge *George Nester*. As the story developed, there was some confusion as to the spelling of the name of the vessel's captain. The name could often be found as "George Debeau," but was also found as "George D. Bau." With the help of C. Patrick Labadie of the Canal Park Museum in Duluth, the 1906 *Ship Master's Directory* and 1907 *Great Lakes Red Book* were checked. These normally highly reliable sources gave the good captain's name as "George DuBeau" and "George DeBeau" respectively. Additionally, the *Sault Evening News*, which used the spelling "D. Bau" listed the captain's hometown as "Algoma" while the *Duluth Evening Herald* lists him as Captain "Dubeau" of "Algonac" and later as Captain "J. DeVoe" of that same city. To increase the confusion, the 1906 *Ship Masters' Directory* says that Captain "DuBeau" was the master of the schooner-barge "*Thos. Nester*" rather than the "*George Nester.*" By the time that the research on this single point of fact was well underway, there were six names, two hometowns, and two vessels given for the same person! Likewise, the name of the Captain of the *Nester's* towing steamer was found spelled two very different ways. The Marquette *Daily Mining Journal* gave the name as Captain "Brassa" in its May 3rd edition, but four days later cited a letter written by the same captain as being penned by Captain "Bourassa." Oddly, it began to appear that the more this story was researched, the more the facts became frazzled.

So, how does one resolve such an issue? In this case running down the captain's hometown seemed to be the answer. Since two hometowns were listed, Algonac and Algoma, I elected to take a 50/50 shot and try Algonac first. The Port Huron newspapers would cover that town and the news of its residents, so I sourced the *Port Huron Daily Times* for the proper time frame. Indeed, three of the crew were from the town of Algonac, including the captain. In the news piece detailing the loss, however, the captain's name is printed as "De eau" with one letter apparently missing from the hand-placed type of the time, and then as "De Baul" all of which adds to the confusion by now giving a total of seven spellings of the luckless captain's name. The vessel's incident did not take place within the scope of the United

States Lifesaving Service, so the event was omitted from their records. The next step was highly unscientific—I looked in the Algonac telephone book to see if the name was listed. This often works, as descendants of the person in question may still reside in the area. Normally, in the Great Lakes region, people are friendly enough to tolerate a meaningful phone call from a serious researcher. In this effort I did manage to locate a "Dubeau" in the Algonac region and managed to connect that spelling as my best selection for the name of the lost captain. If, upon reading this, however, some other direct descendants of this lost lakes captain should discover this usage to be in error, I urge them to contact the author through the publisher so that the name can be corrected once more.

Additionally there will be the "trivia" that you, the lighthouse buff, can use to annoy your friends who have a similar interest. For example, the records state that the Detroit River Lighthouse was first activated and manned on August 20, 1885. In reading the chapter on the Detroit River Lighthouse, however, you will discover that the very first lights placed on that site were two red warning lanterns installed upon the new crib in the spring of 1884, and two men were quartered in a makeshift shack on that same spot to tend to the lanterns. Thus, the site was actually manned and lighted in the spring of 1884. A word of caution, however, as only the true lighthouse buff—when armed with such knowledge and this text—should use it to annoy their lighthouse friends.

I

KEEPER MARSHALL'S ITCH

It would be safe to say that June 7, 1883 was a proud day in the lives of Joseph and Alfred Cardran. A month later, on Tuesday, July 15, another proud day of ceremony made the event official. This apex in the lives of these two individuals had its foundation in an act of Congress passed on the 20th day of June, 1874. This same act was renewed on June 18, 1878 and again on May 4, 1882. It granted the Secretary of the Treasury the power to award medals of valor through the United States Lifesaving Service for acts of lifesaving both service and civilian related. These medals were in two forms, silver for acts of courage or assisting in acts of bravery, and gold for acts of exceptional valor. On that memorable July Tuesday of 1884, the two Cardran boys were each officially awarded a gleaming gold medal from the United States Lifesaving Service for an act of rescue involving a "...heroic and persistent effort... at the imminent risk of his own life." To say that this was a big event on the Cardran's home of Mackinac Island, Michigan would be an understatement.

Oddly, the whole story of the Cardran boys' valor does not take place on their island home of Mackinac. Rather, the saga begins a dozen miles down Lake Huron at Bois Blanc Island. Pronounced "Bob Low" by some (closer to the original French pronunciation), and assorted ways by others, Bois Blanc Island is the isolated home of a few fishing docks and a single lighthouse. The light, located on the northeastern tip of the island, warns of the shoals that lurk nearby and also helps to mark the course that vessels need to follow in order to enter the narrow Straits of Mackinac. The original light on this island was destroyed in a January gale of 1838. Constructed as a "schoolhouse style" structure, the next Bois Blanc Lighthouse was made of buff-brick and probably resembles the original structure. Even in modern

Bois Blanc Island Lighthouse, Lake Huron. (Wayne Sapulski photo)

times, this is an isolated place, and it was much more so in 1883. Normally, the only company that the acting lighthouse keeper, Lorenzo O. Holden, would have would be an occasional local fisherman. Interestingly, the official records show that Keeper Holden was assigned the position of "acting" keeper on the 15th day of July, 1881 while the Lighthouse Board decided on someone to be appointed permanent keeper. Apparently, there were few candidates stepping forward to take the job, because a full decade went by and Holden remained the acting keeper. He, in fact, was not appointed as the permanent keeper until June 13, 1891! Part of the reason why the job as keeper of the Bois Blanc Island Station was somewhat less than desirable may have been the pay. This offshore station offered a compensation of only $560 annually. Other offshore stations in the upper lakes during the same era paid a standard $800 annually. Perhaps the lighthouse board figured that island stations were easier to tend than were the shoal stations such as Spectacle Reef and Stannard's Rock which both carried the $800 salary for their keepers. Yet the records indicate that Holden tended the light alone, and without an assistant keeper, so his position must have been lonely and ill-paid.

Usually, the ice on the Great Lakes keeps the Detroit and St. Clair rivers as well as the Saint Marys River and Mackinac Straits, blocked until late April. For that reason, there was no real "engraved in stone" deadline for the keepers to get to their lights. Rather, the lightkeepers of the 1880s were obligated to get to their lights as soon as the ice would allow. Among the lights that were activated early in April of 1883 was the Bois Blanc Island Light. Surrounded by the thick woods of the island, the light was the only significant man-made structure to be found in any direction. The grounds surrounding the light were still a muddy mess left over by the spring thaw, and the gray clouds hung overhead as if winter was refusing to release its grip. Out on the lake, cakes of ice tossed with the waves in their own effort to keep a wintry hold on Lake Huron. Leaves had yet to bloom on the trees and the early spring winds howled through the bare branches with a lonesome moan. On Saturday, April 15, 1883, however, Keeper Holden was not as lonely as usual. He was in fact being visited by a group of local fishermen who were at the lighthouse in quest of shelter from the rude weather that was blowing out on the lake. All of the fishermen were residents of Mackinac Island and among them were Joseph and Alfred Cardran. As the fishermen relaxed in the warmth of the lighthouse and waited for the gale to abate, they had no idea that the events of peril and valor were forming just north of their location. Likewise, Keeper Holden had no hint that he would soon be visited by another group of unexpected guests including his old friend and keeper of the Spectacle Reef Lighthouse, William Marshall.

Records indicate that William Marshall took charge of the lighthouse as its keeper on August 20, 1881, when Keeper Lorenzo Holden was transferred from the Spectacle Reef Lighthouse to the Bois Blanc Island Lighthouse. This appointment was probably fully expected, because the Marshall clan of Mackinac Island were a family of lightkeepers. Scarcely can the records of keepers listed in the Mackinac Straits region than the name of a Marshall is not seen in the listing, and William Marshall was indeed following in the family business. Starting out as a third assistant keeper on the Spectacle Reef light on October 13, 1877, William Marshall had begun his lighthouse career working under Lorenzo Holden. When the 1881 season opened, however, Marshall was offered the opportunity to take the position as keeper at the Bois Blanc Island Lighthouse, and was appointed as acting Keeper at that station on May 21st of that year. Marshall apparently had left Spectacle Reef and Lorenzo Holden in order to get his first command, but then a strange occurrence took place. For reasons that are today unrecorded, Marshall and Holden suddenly swapped stations! Just under two months after Marshall had taken charge of the Bois Blanc Station, he switched to become keeper of the Spectacle Reef Lighthouse, and Holden took charge of Marshall's light. For Holden it was a significant cut in pay, but he was on an island with no one under his authority. For Marshall, it was an enormous pay raise, and he took command of a crew of assistant keepers. Perhaps the circumstances of both situations fit both keepers better. After all, Lorenzo Holden could actually have his family living with him at the Bois Blanc Station while he was on duty, and no such opportunity was afforded those serving out on Spectacle Reef.

On that stormy Saturday in mid-April of 1883, while Keeper Holden enjoyed the momentary company of the local fishermen, Keeper Marshall was having a much worse day. Standing on the shores of Mackinac Island, he knew well that if the ice in the straits was on the move that meant that surely the waters down by Spectacle Reef were opening. For the past several weeks, Marshall had been itching to get back on the light and had chartered a steamer to take him there. At the last minute, however, the steamer had suffered a mechanical failure. Now the itchy lighthouse keeper would have to wait an indefinite length of time before he could get to his duty. This turn of events did not sit well with Keeper Marshall, not well at all. The Spectacle Reef Light was calling him and his obligation to the light began to grow to an obsession. When his chartered steamer broke down, the hope of satisfying his obsession to get out to his lighthouse was shattered. Keeper Marshall was beside himself. His overwhelming itch to get out on the light now sent him prowling around the waterfront in search of a vessel. He would find another way to get to his lighthouse, and that was certain.

Located 23 miles east, southeast of Mackinac Island, Spectacle Reef is also more than 10 miles from the Michigan mainland. The reef itself is part of a short series of post ice age outcrops that are simply a part of the island chain that includes both Mackinac and Bois Blanc islands. Spectacle Reef and nearby Reynold's Reef just happen to be low enough to remain submerged and thus being robbed of the title of "island." These "reefs," however, are much more than simple shallow spots in a lake, rather they are underwater mountains in a freshwater sea. Spectacle Reef taxes the imagination when thought of in this manner. If you could stand on the bottom of Lake Huron, three and one-half miles to the northeast of the reef, you would see a mountain of rock that rises 378 feet in front of you. If you then climbed the reef, on the other side you would find a cliff that drops off 126 feet. Indeed, Spectacle Reef is no ordinary shoal. To make the matter worse, soon after the lakes' maritime industry began to come into its own, the course that vessels used getting from Lake Huron to Lake Michigan was drawn dangerously close to this reef. Then, with the opening of the first locks at Sault Saint Marie in 1855, the vessel traffic expanded rapidly in northern Lake Huron and lakeboats bound from Lake Superior into Lake Michigan crowded very near Spectacle Reef. By 1870, it had been decided that, in order to insure the safety of vessel traffic in the area, a light was needed on the reef.

Construction of the light was truly a marvel of marine engineering for this era. The site was a considerable distance from the mainland and an even greater distance from civilization. For that reason, a base camp was established at a place called "Scammon Harbor" on Drummond Island. From that spot the pieces of the lighthouse were to be pre-fabricated and boated out to the reef. A fleet of lakeboats had to be chartered by the Lighthouse Board to work the project. The tugs *Champion*, *Stranger*, *Hand* and *Magnet* plus the

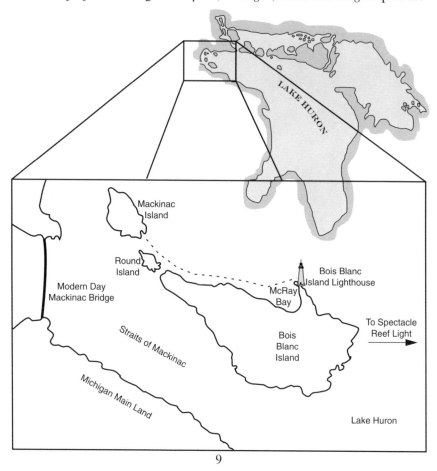

The Lighthouse Board's idea of what the Spectacle Reef Light should look like.

schooner-barges *Table Rock, Belle, Ritchie* and *Emerald* were all hired into government service. On July 18, 1871, led by the lighthouse tender *Warrington*, the whole fleet set out for Spectacle Reef. Only the *Table Rock* was left behind holding a load of 310 tons of "reserve stone." The *Warrington* was towing the *Belle* that Tuesday morning, and aboard the two boats was a combined labor force totaling 140 men. They were on an all-out assault on the reef.

A giant wooden cofferdam was also constructed upon the shoal in the spot where the lighthouse foundation was to grow. Measuring 82 feet in circumference and 15 feet tall, the cofferdam was sunk on the desired spot and then hard-hat divers were dropped in. Along the uneven spaces below the dam's walls, the divers filled the gaps with oakum and Portland cement. The dolomitic limestone of the reef was very rough and uneven and needed to be leveled in order for construction to begin. Once the cofferdam was sealed, pumps with a capacity of 5,000 gallons per minute were used to pump it dry. Then, the labor crew went to work leveling the bedrock using the most advanced technology of the day... picks and shovels. It took three months to build the cofferdam and only 14 days to level the rock. Rock and concrete were used to fill the crib and form the foundation for the lighthouse. The biggest hang-up did not come in the logistics of moving labor and materials across 26 miles of stormy Lake Huron, but in the failure of a contractor. Originally, the stone blocks that were to be used in the construction of the tower were supposed to be supplied from a Duluth granite quarry. That contractor, however, had made "...a trifling effort to quarry the stone" and abandoned the contract. When it came time to build the tower, there was no stone. The Lighthouse Board then turned to the limestone quarry at Marblehead, Ohio. This contractor was well able to supply the needed stone and the light was constructed using it. Finished with a focal plane of 97 feet above the lake's surface, the light went into operation in 1874. At a cost of more than $406,000 the site was boasted as being one of the most expensive of the Lighthouse Board's undertakings on the Great Lakes. With the beginning of the 1883 season, and thanks to Light Keeper Marshall's impatience, the price of the Spectacle Reef lighthouse was about to get higher.

When Keeper Marshall got the word that his hired steamboat was out of commission, his compulsion to get to his lighthouse must have overwhelmed him. In fact, his actions indicate that he was driven well past the point of good sense. A fresh southwest wind was blowing and cakes of ice were thrashing in the straits, but the itchy lighthouse keeper decided that he would pack up and head out by the use of a small sailboat!

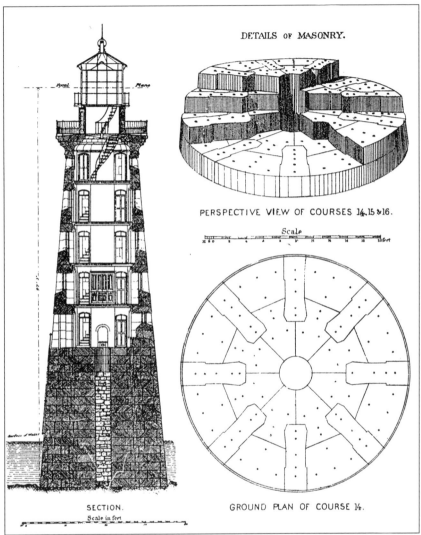

Cutaway drawing showing the interior of the Spectacle Reef Light. From the Lighthouse Board's 1894 Annual Report.

Early on the morning of April 15th, the entire crew of the Spectacle Reef Lighthouse worked at loading a small one-masted sailing boat for the trip to the light. Aboard were loaded several weeks provisions and a full season's clothing for the entire crew of four men. Then, following Keeper Marshall, First Assistant Light Keeper Edward Chambers, Third Assistant Keeper Edward Lasley, and Second Assistant Keeper James C. Marshall, the son of the lighthouse keeper, all piled into the overburdened sailboat. This would be Lasley's first season on the Spectacle Reef Light, and he had actually not yet been officially appointed to a position as third assistant. Apparently, Keeper Marshall had transmitted his letter of request during the previous month, but the Lighthouse Board had not yet replied. The previous second assistant keeper, Frank Kimball had been transferred on March 30th, and that left the lighthouse short-handed. Using his authority as keeper, William Marshall had decided to take Lasley out to the light and they would wait for the official appointment while he served the time there. It was the kind of last minute confusion and shuffling that only added to a lightkeeper's itch prior to opening a station for the season. Casting off the lines, the crew's progress toward Spectacle Reef was immediately thwarted by the ice. A good indication of just how bad the ice conditions were at the time is indicated by the fact that it took the efforts of a large group of islanders working from the early morning time that the sailboat left the dock until 2:30 in the afternoon to get the boat into open water. From that point on, the four light keepers would be on their own amid the spring ire of Lake Huron.

Considering the southwesterly blow, Keeper Marshall elected to run hugging the east shore of both Round Island and Bois Blanc Island. The land masses of the two islands would do much to block the stiff wind and the

Spectacle Reef Light as it appears today. (Mark Fowler photo)

13

waves would not be able to take advantage of the little sailboat. Although this sounds like a reasonable scheme, it is akin to madness. The lee of the islands would provide only about nine miles of sheltered sailing before Keeper Marshall would be forced to turn the boat out into the open lake. Once rounding the hook of Lighthouse Point on Bois Blanc Island, he would have to negotiate 14 miles of thrashing Lake Huron to get to his own lighthouse. Certainly, most people would consider an open sailboat, stuffed with cargo and passengers, to be easy prey for the big lake. Keeper Marshall, however was itchy to get to his light, and the thoughts that the lake would swallow him was completely overpowered by his obsession to get to Spectacle Reef.

The Great Lakes have always been extraordinarily unmerciful to those who lose respect for their size and power. Since the beginning of recorded history, man's arrogance and lack of respect for the lake have been repaid with death and bitter cold suffering. The waters on which Keeper Marshall now ran his little sailboat were near freezing. A human body immersed in this early spring ice water would become cramped, numb, and sapped of its life in a matter of minutes. Such reality seemed far from Keeper Marshall's mind as he drove the boat ahead in the lee of Bois Blanc Island. His plan apparently was to push as far south as he could into McRea Bay and then turn nearly due east and cut close to lighthouse point before turning southeast once again and hauling for Spectacle Reef. Just what he intended to do about the next 14 miles of the enraged lake once he had passed Lighthouse Point, no one can guess.

Like all of those who take the freshwater seas for granted, Lake Huron made quick work out of Keeper Marshall and his crew. As the sailboat was brought around on an east course to head for Lighthouse Point, a sudden gust of wind blasted down upon them and fast as a wink the sailboat was capsized. An instant later all four men felt the numbing sting of Lake Huron's ice water vengeance. The shock was that of being hit every place at the same instant by a baseball bat. Instantly benumbed the startled lighthouse crew regained the surface and clawed toward their overturned sailboat. Young James Marshall happened to be in the worst spot when the boat capsized and it rolled right over on him and kept him submerged. He was the last one to reach the surface and nearly had the life sapped from him. Fighting to get up and out of the lake, all four men regained the upside down vessel and attempted to breathe once again. They had not even gotten halfway across Mc Rea Bay, and already they were shipwrecked.

Teeth chatter and bodies shiver without control after such a dunking, because the body attempts through such motion to regenerate the heat that has just been lost. And so it was that the shivering lighthouse keepers lay stretched across the bottom of their boat. With tiptoes on the keel and fingertips on the gunwale they tried desperately to grip onto the turtled boat. Wave after wave of Lake Huron sloshed over them like buckets of ice, and it was sure that no one could hold that position for very long. Next the lake reached into its bag of punishment and played another cruel trick on the luckless crew. Using its wind and waves, Lake Huron began to push the castaways out, away from land and into its open expanse of doom.

It was clear to Keeper Marshall that if the crew were going to have any chance at all, they would have to gain a better position atop the overturned boat. Thinking that what was keeping the boat turned over was the weight of the submerged mast and sail, Marshall pulled out his pocket knife and gave it to Ed Chambers who apparently was the closest to the standing rigging. The standing rigging is the series of lines that help hold the mast in an upright position and are strung from the top of the mast to the rails of the sailboat's upper hull. Holding a knife in his numb hand must have been difficult enough, but cutting away the rigging would require diving under the icy water, and that must have seemed a superhuman task. Repeatedly, Chambers did the unbearable as he dipped himself in the stinging water and slashed at the rigging, but somehow he managed to cut away the lines and the mast dropped from its step. The plan worked and the boat rolled to the point where the four men could get a good grip on the gunwale. Now, even though their position on the boat was a bit better, it was far from survivable. James Marshall was nearly paralyzed from the cold and tended to slip off of the hull. Exerting as much of his strength as he could, Keeper Marshall kept a hold on his son by finding strength that only a parent can. As the shipwrecked crew drifted across Mc Rea Bay toward open Lake Huron, it is a sure bet that the numbing cold had silenced Keeper William Marshall's itch to get out to his Spectacle Reef Lighthouse.

Some three hours after the Spectacle Reef crew had been tossed into Lake Huron's death grip, Lorenzo Holdon, the keeper of the Bois Blanc Island Light had his visit interrupted with the Cardran boys and their fellow fishermen. Faintly, cries from outside could be heard. A trip to the window revealed a shocking sight. About 100 yards out on the lake among the churning icecakes was the overturned sailboat. Atop the wreck were draped the four crewmen and they were screaming for help with their very last ounce of strength. As luck would have it, a chain from the overturned boat was dragging on the bottom and had caught a snag. This prevented the boat from being washed past the Bois Blanc Lighthouse and into the open lake.

Dashing onto the beach, it took Joseph Cardran only a heartbeat to size up the situation and devise a rescue plan. Grabbing a nearby skiff, Joseph shoved it into the breaking surf and tossing cakes of ice and leaped in. Pulling at the oars he set the boat on end as he met the breaking waves, but kept working his way toward the wreck. Perhaps it was skill, or perhaps it was just the fact that the young fisherman had respect for Lake Huron, but for whatever reason, the lake allowed him to make it to the capsized sailboat. Arriving, he found James Marshall almost dead, and everyone agreed that the keeper and his semiconscious son should get into shore first—everyone except James. Begging his father to save himself and leave him behind James attempted to stay so he wouldn't overload the skiff. Both James and his lightkeeper father were loaded aboard the skiff and Joseph shoved off and headed for the beach. The problem was that a skiff is in no way designed to ride the breakers onto a storm-swept beach. Shaped much like a bullet and having a flat bottom, this type of boat is unstable in the waves and vulnerable to swamping from behind. So, when the skiff was tantalizingly close to salvation, the breakers began to roll in over the stern and fill the boat like a tub. Next, Joseph lost directional control of the tiny boat and the waves instantly took advantage and flipped the skiff end-over-end.

Miraculously, all three men resurfaced and got hold of the skiff. Joseph could see right away that the little boat would not support all three men.

"Hold on!" he shouted and he set off in a swim for the beach.

Shortly after Joseph swam away, William Marshall watched in a daze as his son James let go his grip on the skiff and vanished into Lake Huron's grasp. He wanted to reach out with all of his heart as save his boy, but his hands were paralyzed in a grip on the yawl by the numbing cold. A moment later and the lightkeeper himself fell into unconsciousness. Joseph, meanwhile, was being bashed among the ice cakes in his swim for the beach. Just short of safety, he too blacked out. Dashing into the surf, his fellow fishermen dragged him clear of the water and flopped him on the beach like a net full of perch. Soon after, the skiff washed in close enough that they could grab it and keeper Marshall too. We can only imagine the sight as 18-year-old Alfred Cardran knelt next to the motionless forms of his brother and William Marshall on the beach. A moment later he looked back at the ice studded waves and the helpless men on the capsized sailboat beyond. Most people would give up in the face of such a hopeless and apparently deadly situation, but not Alfred Cardran. Something inside him burned and he fearlessly strode over to the waterlogged skiff. Emptying the boat of its water, Alfred shoved it into the surf and ice just as his brother had minutes earlier.

Jumping aboard, Alfred pulled for the wreck. Sitting backward at the oars he could see, surrounded by his friends, the bodies of the two men that the lake had just expended. At his back he could feel and hear the massive cakes of ice as they smashed into the wooden peak of the skiff, and all around the surf roared in a deafening protest at his invasion. With the toiling respect for the lake that only a professional fisherman can have, Alfred reached the wreck. He decided not to repeat his brother's error and to only take one crewman this time. Ed Lasley got aboard and Alfred headed back toward the beach. We can only imagine the thoughts of Ed Chambers as he was left behind on the capsized sailboat. If the skiff floundered this time, who would come out to save him? Surely, he would then be doomed to perish right where he was.

Skillfully, Alfred maneuvered the skiff into the breakers and hanging on the edge of each whitecap he made dry land with his passenger aboard. Depositing his human cargo on the island, he set his sights on rescuing the last survivor. Once again he launched the skiff and pulled for the wreck. This time he had the feel for the trip and in short order he had Ed Chambers aboard and was pulling for the beach. Gliding in the surf he made it look easy as he transported the last member of the Spectacle Reef Lighthouse crew to safety. As they landed the men were just bringing his brother back to consciousness. The other three survivors were in far worse condition. They had spent three hours in conditions that should have taken their lives in just a

Spectacle Reef Lighthouse as seen from the air. (Penny Story photo)

matter of minutes. All of the other survivors had to be dragged into the shelter of the Bois Blanc Island Lighthouse and the warmth of its big iron stove.

Chambers and Lasley recovered rapidly, but it took five hours to bring Keeper Marshall around. His haste to get to his lighthouse and his lack of respect for the big lake had cost him dearly. His son was taken as payment on the caution that he had lacked and the itch that he had let possess him. The result was that both the keeper and his crew would be sorrowfully tardy in getting the Spectacle Reef Light opened for the 1883 season. Interestingly, the record shows that during that delay, which was far greater than the wait for the steamboat would have been, not a single vessel ran onto Spectacle Reef and was shipwrecked or stranded. There was no reason for Marshall's haste.

Ed Lasley's appointment as an assistant keeper did eventually come through on the 30th of April 1883. That was the same day on which Marshall's appointment was officially vacated and the word "Deceased" was penned on the line in the record book that contained his name. On the 9th of July of that same season, Lasley was promoted to another lighthouse and his place was taken by Walter Marshall—yet another member of the lightkeeping Marshall family. Lorenzo Holden, the "acting" keeper of the Bois Blanc Lighthouse remained on the records as an acting keeper until June 13, 1891 when he was finally promoted to the position as the permanent keeper, at the same rate of pay—of course. Keeper Holden only enjoyed that status for two years. On September 2, 1894, he died while on duty on Bois Blanc Island.

Looking back we can not fault Keeper William Marshall too much for his itch. Lighthouse keeping was a true calling, and unlike vessel mastering, lightkeepers always seemed to become mated to their stations. They seemed almost possessed by the calling and often have gone far beyond their prescribed job description to maintain their beacons. While some of us may look back and see Lightkeeper Marshall's venture in 1883 as a deadly folly, he looked out onto the lake that day and saw it only in terms of his duty. The Cardran brothers looked out onto Lake Huron that day and saw people in need, they put their own self-interest aside and rushed to the rescue, becoming true heroes. For us today, living in a time when a person needs to do little more than sink a basketball, or toss a football, or play a likable character on television, or make empty political promises, or simply have a good "spin doctor" in order to attain hero status, it is good to spend some time with people who lived their lives based on duty and without self-interest. It is good to spend a few pages with the Marshalls and the Cardran brothers.

Today, the Spectacle Reef Lighthouse, where William Marshall spent endless hours of heartbreak and care, is little more than a shell. The ornate glass of its lamproom is gone and only the skeletal remains of the framework can be found. The second order Fresnel optic that Marshall once tended with the greatest sense of duty is also gone. In place of the original optic, a plastic lamp shines, powered by solar energy and in no need of a keeper. The stone tower that once housed the crew of four through a whole season is boarded up and at the mercy of the elements. Although the lighthouse itself is far out on Lake Huron, this lighthouse's original optic can be visited, as it is now on permanent display at the Great Lakes Historical Society's fine museum in Vermilion, Ohio. Meanwhile, the Bois Blanc Island Lighthouse has been purchased by private individuals and serves as a residence. It is possible that those who reside in the former lighthouse have little knowledge of the details of the events that transpired on their beach and earned two fishermen from Mackinac Island the nation's highest award for lifesaving. The light itself has been replaced by a lamp on a post located a short distance from the original lighthouse. This light, like the one out on Spectacle Reef, is solar powered and does not require a keeper and crew. All of the persons in this story have passed on long ago and the story of their plight and valor has faded with the passing years. Oddly, there are few people in the tightly knit community of Mackinac Island who recall the heroic Cardran brothers. Additionally, their gold medals are nowhere to be found. Thus, the only complete recall of the people and events of that day in April of 1883 is here in your hands, as is the legacy of Keeper Marshall's itch.

Seen here from an aircraft, the Spectacle Reef Light rarely has visitors other than seagulls. (Penny Story photo)

II

IT WAS CALLED "STANNARD'S ROCK"

Every true Great Lakes lighthouse buff will be able to sit down and rattle off the names of every light on the lakes with a great deal of accuracy. When reading any text of the lights of the lakes, the lighthouse devotee scans each page searching for any tidbit of new knowledge or any hint of error. Thus when reading this chapter about the Stannard's Rock Lighthouse, the light aficionado may have already stopped to exclaim about the author's blatant error.

"That's supposed to be Stannard Rock, not "Stannard's Rock," will come the knowing utterance accompanied by a casual sigh.

Certainly, that is the way that the spelling appears on modern charts, as well as in modern texts and lists, so perhaps the point is well made. In a historical perspective, however, it appears that the original name of the light has been altered with the passing of time. To those who learn the story of the discovery of this place, the decision for placement of this light, its construction and its decline, the usage of the possessive form of the name may be found to be more correct than the modern moniker.

No matter what the light station on Stannard's Rock is called, it has always carried the distinction of being the "loneliest place..." in the continental United States. Located 45 miles due north of Marquette, the nearest city of any size, the rock is more than 26 miles from the tip of Keweenaw Point, which is the nearest land. Additionally, the lighthouse and reef of Stannard's Rock are a full 13 miles from the modern shipping lanes. Considering that the lighthouse stands more than 100 feet tall with a 102-foot focal plane, it means that a vessel would be 10 miles from any mainland before the light would even be seen!

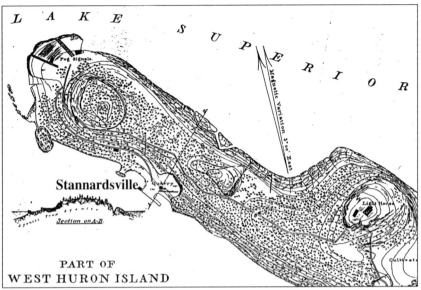

1882 Lighthouse Board map of Huron Island showing the dock and quarry where the stone for the foundation of the Stannard's Rock Lighthouse was mined.

The remoteness of the Stannard's Rock Lighthouse was clearly demonstrated on the occasion of her decline into automation. It was the evening of June 18, 1961 and a Coast Guard team of four men had been assigned to the light for the purpose of automating the station. Reportedly at about half past nine o'clock that evening a shattering explosion shook the lighthouse. Down on the pier at the base of the lighthouse tower the 1,800 gallon gasoline storage tank had exploded. Located in the boiler house, the tank had apparently leaked its fumes which had somehow been ignited. One of the Coast Guardsmen who was in the sleeping quarters was tossed to the floor and two others who were in the galley were thrown across the room as a giant fireball ripped through the lighthouse tower. The fourth member of the crew, who was said to have been working in or near the boiler house, simply ceased to exist, apparently blown to atoms in the blast. Heat from the explosion ignited the station's coal bunkers and the lighthouse at Stannard's Rock turned into a blast furnace with the lighthouse tower becoming the smokestack. Grabbing a couple of cans of beans and a few articles of clothing, the three surviving Coast Guardsmen retreated to the side of the station opposite the burning boiler house. For the next two days they remained there sheltered by a tarp while everything that could burn in the Stannard's Rock Lighthouse did burn. Proof of the station's remoteness is in the fact that on a summer's night on the heavily navigated expanse of Lake Superior a fireball fueled by an 1,800-gallon gasoline supply went up and no one noticed! Additionally, for the next two days the stone tower smoked and smoldered on the open lake, and again no one noticed! Arriving on her routine two-week supply run, the Coast Guard tender *Woodrush* found the lighthouse gutted and smoldering and the three survivors waiting to be rescued. The exact cause of the blast and fire was never concluded, and the tower stands today, gutted and supporting only an automated electric lamp. Still, this hollow stone obelisk marks a place that, although remote, has been considered a hazard to mariners since the earliest days of navigation on Lake Superior.

Captain Charles Stannard was master of the sailing brig *John Jacob Astor* in 1835, and navigation on Lake Superior was in its infancy. Charts were not committed to paper, rather the information was contained in the heads the individual mariners. This was a time when aids to navigation were

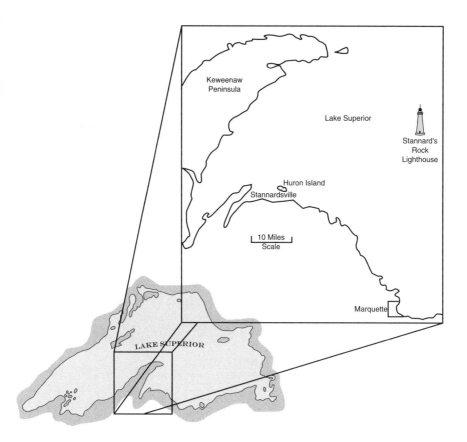

very few on the upper lakes. Reportedly, Captain Stannard discovered a reef jutting about two feet above the surface in a part of the lake where the water should be hundreds of feet deep. It was the 26th day of August, and Captain Stannard immediately saw the rocks to be a danger to navigation. The reef itself is actually a series of rock out crops that stretch a distance of about 3,000 feet on a north-south heading. They are a part of the ancient topography of the lake bottom which ranges from grand underwater canyons to peaks of submerged mountains with an aquatic petrified forest thrown in for good measure. Knowledge of the reef's existence was originally spread by word of mouth around the tightly knit Lake Superior maritime community, and the obstruction was naturally referred to as "Stannard's Rock" After all, he found it and he knew its location better than anyone else, so why shouldn't he own it—metaphorically of course.

Officially, the first mention of Stannard's Rock to the Lighthouse Board came in the form of a letter written by General W. F. Raynolds of the Army Corps of Engineers and dated November 21, 1866, nearly 31 years after Captain Stannard's discovery. The letter stated:

Stannard's Rock is the most dangerous shoal in Lake Superior, being about 23 miles southeast of Manitou Island light-house. The shoal is about three-quarters of a mile in extent. The rock rises 2 1/2 or 3 feet above the water and is 15 or 20 feet in diameter. The exact locality of the shoal is known to but few; being so far from land it is seldom seen and it is most dreaded by all navigators.

The increasing commerce of Lake Superior will at no distant day demand that it should be marked by a lighthouse, which will be one of the most difficult undertakings that could be presented.

General Raynolds was not overstating the dilemma of the task in the slightest. Considering the tools and technology available in that era, any lighthouse that was to be erected in such a remote location would be a huge undertaking. To survive on the wild expanse of Lake Superior, the structure would have to be placed atop a massive cement pier, and the tower would have to be made of mammoth stone blocks. All of the materials for the building process would have to be transported by water, perhaps from as far away as Ohio. A fleet of barges and steamships would be needed to transport everything used in the construction. Additionally, the enormous labor force that would be required for the job would have to be transported out to the light each day, or somehow stationed on site. Once up in the north country, the

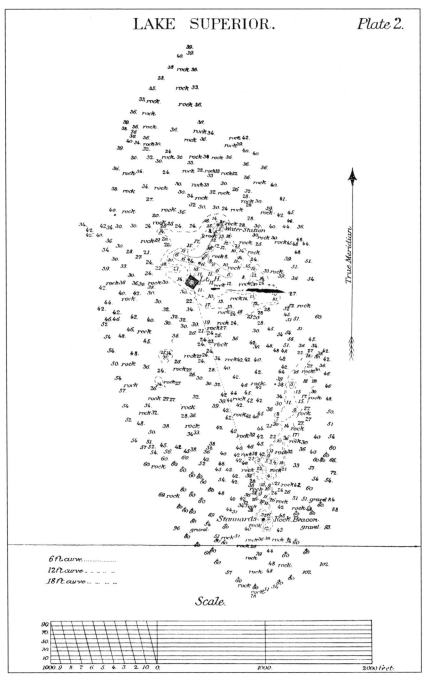

Original survey map showing water depth and type of bottom, used in placing the lighthouse on Stannard's Rock. Note the location of the day-beacon at the lower end of the map.

laborers would have be to fed, housed, and their existence fully supplied. All of these needs considered, there simply was not any such facility available in the area of Stannard's Rock in 1866. With the workmen having to be shuttled from Marquette or somehow stationed on the lake, there would be the concern of the weather. Parking a fleet of vessels and an army of laborers atop the shoal meant that the slightest blow of weather would likely result in disaster. To make matters more difficult, the season when work could be done out on the rock was extremely brief. The months from May to October would be all that could be used in the operation, and even then there would be many days lost due to weather. The reality was clear, the logistics simply did not work for the construction of a lighthouse on Stannard's Rock in the year 1866. Thus, Raynolds came up with a temporary solution to the problem, and his letter continued, "As a preliminary to this end, to render navigators familiar with its location, I recommend that it be marked with a day-beacon to be formed of a single wrought-iron shaft, not less than one foot in diameter, surmounted by a cage that would be visible not less than 5 or 6 miles."

Approval of the Raynolds day-beacon was given by the Lighthouse Board on April 4, 1868, and in June of that same year the 133-foot wooden steamer *William Cowie* headed out to mark Stannard's Rock for the first time. The

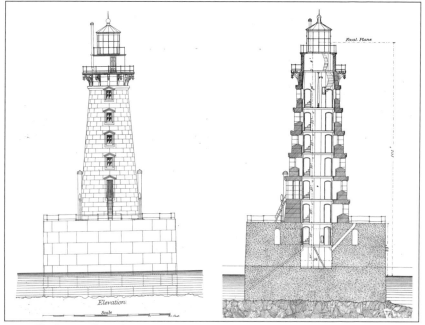

The Stannard's Rock Lighthouse,   *Cutaway of the Stannard's Rock*
Lake Superior.   *Lighthouse.*

Cowie was a spanking new vessel in her very first season of operation, and the Lighthouse Board had equipped her with additional accommodations to serve their needs. A temporary blacksmith's shop was constructed upon her deck and extra crew quarters were aboard to house the workmen. Several A-frame hoists were also fitted aboard the vessel to do the needed manipulation of the heavy materials. Although the task was as simple as mounting a wrought iron post on a rock, the work would not be easy. When the *Cowie* reached the area of Stannard's Rock, a position was taken on the southern-most end of the reef. This was the one position with the greatest amount of bedrock that was above water. In order to place the day marker, the exposed rock had to be "...brought to level." This was likely accomplished through the use of pick and shovel. Next the post on which the day beacon was mounted on the rock using nine bolts that were two and one-half inches in diameter and two feet long! The bolts were driven down into Stannard's Rock and the 12-inch diameter wrought iron spindle was secured to the bedrock. Over the spindle pipe, a frustum of cut stone in the shape of a cone was placed over the anchoring spindle and, lastly, a cage of wrought iron was placed over that. For the first time, Stannard's Rock was truly marked by means of more than just the memories of Lake Superior's mariners.

For the next decade the proposals and recommendations for the construction of a lighthouse were fluttered past the Lighthouse Board. In August of 1871, General Orlando M. Poe, the successor to General Raynolds, spelled out his concern about the Stannard's Rock obstruction. General Poe was at the beginning of his tenure as Engineer of the Eleventh Lighthouse District and involved in a career would eventually make him one of the most influential characters in the annals of Great Lakes history. So important did this man become, that in modern times the largest lock at Sault Sainte Marie has been named in his honor. His 1871 annual report to the Lighthouse Board said: "The rapid increase of the commerce between Duluth and the eastern terminus of the Northern Pacific Railroad and the lower lakes will demand at no distant day the erection of a lighthouse on this danger."

Poe then pointed out a simple correlation between the Stannard's Rock dilemma and another lighthouse project which was under way at that time. This conclusion would eventually become the solution to the Stannard's Rock logistics problem.

"The case will be similar to that of Spectacle Reef, and all the costly apparatus and machinery purchased for the latter can be made available for the former..."

General Poe was correct, the Spectacle Reef construction project had similar logistics in that the reef was located in a distant spot on Lake Huron and both labor and equipment had to be transported out to the station. The project at Spectacle Reef had been a success, but there was one large difference between that site and the Stannard's Rock site—the weather. Although Spectacle Reef is in northern Lake Huron, it is still a dozen degrees of latitude south of Stannard's Rock. For that reason alone, the season of operation for the labor force would likely be longer at Spectacle Reef than on Stannard's Rock. Laborers were able to start work at Spectacle Reef in 1871 and ended their efforts in 1874, but they could start in the early spring and work late into the autumn. On Stannard's Rock, however, the season would likely have to start in the month of June and the crews could be expected to be forced off of the site in late September or early October. Such a shortened work season would result in several years additional time spent in building the lighthouse. Additionally, there would be the times when it is absolutely impossible to navigate Lake Superior in the summer. In the 1874 season, for example, the keeper of the Manitou Island Lighthouse reported that in all of the month of June, there were only five days when there was no fog in the area of his lighthouse. Surely, the task of building the Stannard's Rock Lighthouse was not going to be a simple or short matter.

In preparation to construction of a lighthouse, a survey of Stannard's Rock was made in August of 1873 by a team led by Assistant Superintendent of Construction Henry Gillman. It was as if Lake Superior did not want a lighthouse planted upon the rock, because the summer weather turned foul and gave Gillman and his crew a bad time. In spite of the lake, the crew came away with a respectable amount of data on the reef, and then proposed a good location for the new lighthouse. A spot located north, northwest of the Raynolds day-beacon was selected. This site was said to have the most average level surface and appeared to be the most stable area on which to place the foundation of the lighthouse. Placing the lighthouse on the southwest edge of the shoal would be of strategic importance. Such location would allow access to the station in most weather conditions. Normally, most of Lake Superior's foul weather hits with winds and waves coming from out of the northwest or northeast. Vessels approaching the lighthouse in bad weather would usually be coming in from the leeward side, and would have more than 20 feet of water beneath them nearly until they reached the pier. The survey was properly reported to the Lighthouse Board, and then almost ignored for nearly the next four years.

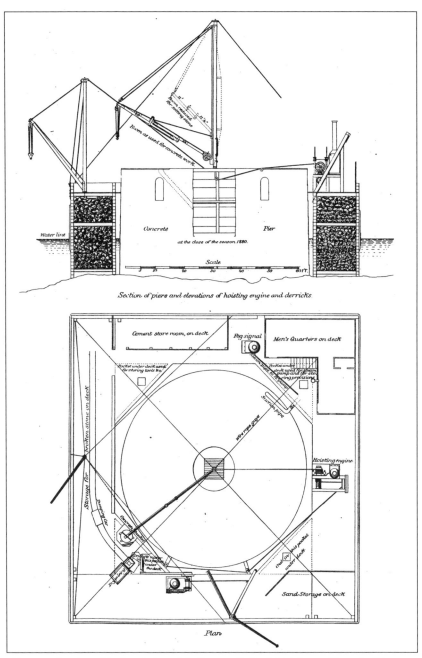

Cutaway drawing of the foundation of the Stannard's Rock Lighthouse. Note: the "dump car" and rails on the lower drawing left side, and the location of the steam power plant for hoisting on the right side.

It was not until March 3, 1877 that the Lighthouse Board won an appropriation of $50,000 to begin the Stannard's Rock Lighthouse project. Similar to the Spectacle Reef project, the workers would be stationed at a chosen base camp. Much of the stone needed for the project would also be quarried at that same location and then hauled the distance out to the reef. The tower itself was proposed to be a twin of the one at Spectacle Reef. Blocks of stone for the construction of the tower were to be cut at Marblehead, Ohio, and shipped to the site. Additional funding would be needed as the project advanced, but the initial appropriation was enough to get things started. West Huron Island would be the base camp for the labor crew, and the 33.3 acres needed for the project base was leased from Joseph Kemp for $500 or the option to retain the improvements when the project was finished. Interestingly, inspection of the billing records do not show an outlay of cash to Mr. Kemp, so we can conclude that he apparently took the "improvements option" rather than the rental cash.

On June 18, 1877, the first step in the construction of the lighthouse at Stannard's Rock was taken. This act did not take place on the shoal out on the lake, but rather was accomplished on West Huron Island. The property owned by Kemp was occupied by the force of laborers and a camp was established. This camp was appropriately named "Stannardsville." It is worth noting that even in the slang moniker of the base camp, the possessive "s" follows the "Stannard" portion of that name. After clearing the grounds, the first buildings were set up. From the Spectacle Reef project, eight rough-boarded shanties had been disassembled and transported to West Huron Island. When reconstructed the shanties made up a smith's shop, a warehouse and toolroom, a provisions storeroom, an icehouse, a cookhouse and dining room, two buildings for lodging and one office. By June 25th all was ready for the work to proceed out to the reef. Using the tug *Morse* and the lighthouse tender *Warrington*, the crew worked on the reef at Stannard's Rock driving piles into the rocky bottom. Additionally, work was started on a floating crib-like structure which was to be towed out to the reef and sunk to form the protective pier of the lighthouse. By October 23rd, Lake Superior was showing her winter temper and the operations were shut down for the season.

Work resumed on the Stannard's Rock Lighthouse on May 14, 1878 when the labor crew returned to Stannardsville. By that time it was clear that more money would be needed if the project was going to proceed, and on June 20, 1878 an additional $100,000 was appropriated for the project. In the beginning of that season, the first order of business was to complete the dock from which the stone would be loaded from Huron Island and transported to the reef. A rough log crib was constructed and then filled with stone to make up the dock. It is very important to keep in mind that this was an era and a place where heavy equipment was not in existence. The heavy stones and massive logs had to be moved and placed by hand and often the only aid in doing the work was a team of horses or a block and tackle arrangement. The work of constructing the dock went on until the last day of July. Meanwhile, work on the floating protective pier progressed. The wooden crib structure was built up to 13 feet in depth and had four different watertight compartments, and each of these compartments had an interior area of more than 1,000 square feet. In the previous season, this crib had been towed out to the reef and soundings were made to assess how the structure would sit on the rock. Now that the crib had been built up to its required depth, and fully caulked to make it water tight, 875 tons of ballast stone were loaded aboard. Next, its top was planked over to form a deck, and hatches were constructed over each of the four compartments. Two steam pumps were placed upon the deck and their suction pipes were secured in each compartment. Lastly, the hatches were covered and battened down. It was intended that the structure be towed out to Stannard's Rock, but if the tow should encounter heavy weather, the sealed hatches and steam pumps would help the crib free itself of any incoming water. At five o'clock on the morning of August 4th, the steamers *Ira Chaffee*, *Warrington* and the tug *Dudley* took the crib in tow and headed for Stannard's Rock. Hauling the crib at a snail's pace, the trip out to the reef took nearly a day and a half with the tow arriving at three o'clock the following afternoon. At half past five o'clock that same afternoon the scuttle valves, which had been built into the walls of the crib, were opened and the structure was allowed to settle into position on the reef. Only then did it become apparent that the location of the crib was such that it would not allow the lighthouse tenders to approach the site in anything but a calm sea. The shoals were far too close and the water level in the lake was more than a foot lower than it had been when measured the previous season. There was no choice, the crib would have to be moved.

Closing the scuttle valves, and activating the steam pumps, the labor crew began to remove water from the crib on the day after it was originally placed. The structure did not have to be freed of water completely, rather it needed only to be lightened enough to lift it up off of the bottom. As soon as the crib was afloat, the three towing steamers pulled it 60 feet south and 30 feet west while turning it 80 degrees in an attempt to better meet the uneven surface of the reef. Again the scuttle valves were opened and Lake Superior was allowed to seep into the crib, and again it settled onto Stannard's Rock. This time, the structure was near enough to deep water to allow the lighthouse tenders to access it, but the crib's turning had not put it evenly upon the reef. The structure had settled with the southeast corner being one foot, six inches higher than the northwest corner. To avoid more pumping and pulling, the problem was corrected by adding more superstructure of wood planking. There were still some shoals in the area, but they were removed by blasting and the work of filling the crib with stone was started.

For the next two months stone was dumped through the hatches of the crib and the structure began to fill. By the third day of October, the crib contained 4,926 tons of stone and was well suited to ride out the autumn storms and winter's ice. Again the hatches were battened and the crib was left for the season. The men who had worked the crib for these two months had been housed on the *Chaffee* and *Warrington*, but next year's plans called for quarters to be constructed upon the crib itself. As the crew departed, everyone was in hope that the structure, and all of their hard work would not be obliterated by Lake Superior over the winter. Back at Stannardsville, the work was not quite done for the season. The big Blake stone-breaking machines had arrived and were being set up and tested. That work kept up until October 26th, when Stannardsville was closed for the season and the work terminated for 1878.

Significant events happened over that winter of 1878-1879, but none of them took place out on Stannard's Rock. The tender *Warrington* was badly damaged by fire during that winter and would not be available for the upcoming season. More significantly, another $50,000 was appropriated for the project on the third day of March, 1879. On May 15th, work was again started at Stannardsville and everyone was speculating on how, or if, the crib had survived the winter. As the *Ira Chaffee*—this time accompanied by the tug *Maythem* to replace the burned tender *Warrington*—steamed out to the reef, everyone was pleasantly surprised to see that the crib was in place and in good condition. The fact was that once the winter's ice encased the structure, it shielded it from the wind, seas and ice flows. In this season, boilermakers were the prominent players who now came onto the stage out at Stannard's Rock. Their task was to form and apply all of the wrought iron works and do the needed riveting that would be required in the construction. Quarters for housing these workers were this season's priority and by mid-June that task was complete. Now the iron casting of the permanent pier was formed and fitted to the structure and placed around the base of the foundation. Oakum-filled canvas pipe was placed at the bottom of the casting and when complete, the structure made up a cofferdam. The water was then pumped out of the coffer-dam exposing the reef's bottom. Any loose rocks were cleared and any leaks were plugged so that concrete could be poured and the base of the lighthouse created. Like everything else in 1879, the mixing and pouring of concrete was not the same as it is today. On the Stannard's Rock project, the "Col. J. C. Duane's Concrete Mixer" was used. This was a four-foot-square steel box suspended by two corners on a pair of one-foot-square oak beams. The box had a two-foot-square wooden hatch through which the concrete mixture was loaded and removed. Workers would walk a plankway above the mixing box, dump the concrete mixings in through the hatch, and then once the hatch was secured, a steam pulley would move a series of gears that would cause the box to rotate and the contents to mix. Once the product was sufficiently mixed, the hatch would be pointed downward and opened so that the wet cement could be poured into a

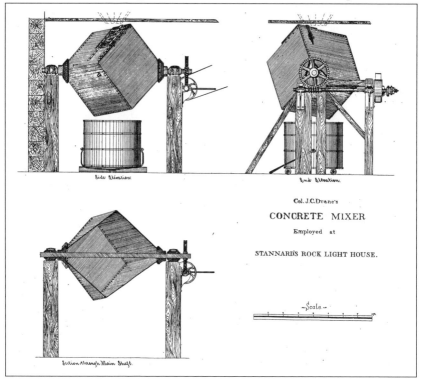

A fascinating three-view drawing of the Col. Duane's cement mixer which was operated by steam and pulley. Note that the scale indicates that the bucket in the two upper views is almost four feet wide! This mixer was later used on the construction of the Detroit River Lighthouse.

three-foot-deep by four-foot-diameter bucket which was equipped with wheels on the bottom. Once filled, this bucket was pulled by hand to the location where the cement needed to be placed. It was a labor of pure elbow grease, but in the late 1870s, it was "state of the art." By the time that the Stannard's Rock Lighthouse was finished, a remarkable total of 7,246 tons of concrete had been poured using this process. The work of pouring the concrete continued until October 6th when the cement structure was nine and one-half feet above the water line at the center and eight and one-half feet high at the outer edge. Work for the season was stopped on that date with 2,300 cubic yards of concrete having been laid—by hand.

In a clear demonstration of just how much the local weather hampered the construction effort, the records state: "From August 6 to October 3, 1878 and from May 28 to June 8, 1879, the reef working party were quartered on vessels afloat. During this time, embracing a period of 69 days, 42 were lost by the party being driven from the work, or unable to land on the pier on account of heavy weather, or 61 percent of time lost."

Twenty men went out to the site of the new lighthouse on May 15, 1880, and began the work of clearing the ice. So thick was the ice encasing the structure that it took the laborers until the 23rd of May just to clear it. Now the task was to complete the pier upon which the lighthouse tower would stand. On June 16th of that year another $50,000 appropriation was made for the construction project. By August 3rd the pier reached 35 feet above bedrock and measured 62 feet in diameter. Some damage had been inflicted by the previous winter's ice, so in an effort to protect the structure in the upcoming winter, six-by-12 inch timbers were used to sheath the pier and a skirt of one-quarter-inch iron plate that was three feet tall was set in place. When all of this was done, on August 19th, the pier was ready to have the tower stones placed upon it. The problem was that not enough cut stone had been produced and shipped at Marblehead, Ohio, to warrant the start of construction of the tower. So, for reasons of "economy of labor," the work was stopped for the season on August 22nd and the labor crews were paid off and sent home.

A final appropriation of $73,000 was made for the construction project on March 3, 1881. Now the total appropriation for the Stannard's Rock Lighthouse added up to $323,000. Stone cutting was continued until late June, when it was felt advanced enough to allow work to proceed out on the reef. Starting on July 4th, the first course of stone were placed upon the foundation. Logically, we may think that the longest time and greatest effort would be consumed by the building of the lighthouse's elegant tower. In fact it took only until August 31st for all 33 courses of cut stone to be placed and the tower to stand tall. From that date until October 14th, a small crew remained at the lighthouse finishing the interior brickwork, housing in the tower itself and completing the ironwork. There was a delay in this work due to the late arrival of some of the ironwork.

When the crews returned to the Stannard's Rock Lighthouse on May 24, 1882, they found that the ice extended a full 18 feet up the tower above the permanent pier! The tower, however, was undamaged. The crew on the light worked until late June to complete the construction and by July, all

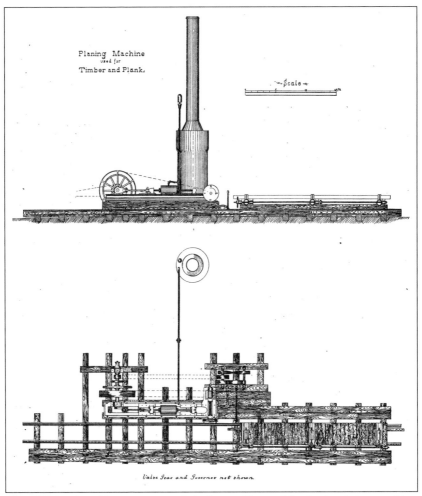

Detailed drawing of the steam powered planing machine used for shaping timbers used in the construction of the lighthouse.

was in readiness for the light's activation. On the 4th of July, 1882, the lamp was illuminated and for the first time Stannard's Rock was marked both day and night.

In the final accounting, some 126 tons of iron, 76 tons of brick, 1,270 tons of tower stone and 7,246 tons of concrete were used in the lighthouse's construction. This means that the estimated weight of the lighthouse is 8,718 tons, as stated in the official records. Interestingly, the total appropriation was $323,000, but of that only $284,777.38 was spent in the construction. This means that the Stannard's Rock Lighthouse project came in under budget by $38,222.62!

French immigrant John Pasque was selected to be the first keeper of the Stannard's Rock Light. His appointment as "acting" keeper was made on June 26, 1882, but he was only in the position for 11 months. On May 16, 1883, Pasque was transferred and his place was taken over by John Armbruster, a German immigrant who lasted less than a month before he "resigned". Armbruster was replaced on June 20, 1883 by a stalwart Englishman named James Prior. With Prior came some stability in the string of keepers as he remained in charge of the station for several seasons. Wages for all of these keepers was $800 annually. On August 3, 1883, an acting third assistant keeper by the name of George Prior was added to the lighthouse staff. George Prior was also an English immigrant, and was probably related to Keeper James Prior, although the records do not give this information. After starting out at acting third assistant keeper, George went from acting third assistant to second assistant keeper the following season to first assistant keeper on September 10, 1885. In all of that movement, his annual salary went up only $50. Wages for those who worked the Stannard's Rock Station as assistant keepers were $450 annually for third assistants and second assistants and $500 annually for first assistants. Apparently, the duty on Stannard's Rock was a rough as we can imagine, because in the listing of keepers and assistant keepers there are four resignations and three transfers in the first three seasons of the station's operation.

The name of the lighthouse remained in official records as "Stannard's" Rock until the *Annual Report of the Operations of the Lighthouse Board* for the fiscal year of 1892. In all areas of that particular report, for no given reason whatsoever, the possessive form of the name was dropped and it was published as "Stannard" Rock. From that point on, all of the government publications used that form of the lighthouse's name. In many local publications, the possessive form was retained for several years, and among mariners the light was called "Stannard's Rock" for more than a generation after the official change.

Most lighthouse buffs of today are far removed from the exact origins of the lights that charm them. Often the published material or on-site pamphlets give only the facts of an individual light's birth without giving the details, and too often those pamphlets contain incorrect information. Additionally, many of the records of the building of individual lights have simply "gone missing" with the passing of time. So, after reading this text, it is up to the reader to decide which name is correct, "Stannard Rock" or "Stannard's Rock." From a historian's perspective, it appears that some forgotten bureaucratic hand reached out in 1892 and decided that "Stannard" was more linguistically "proper" and thus forever edited the name on that whim. Such circumstance alone is enough for this author to always use the original name. The reader, however, may elect to use either form of the name, certainly, both are correct.

III
IN SEARCH OF JOHN HERMAN'S GHOST

For nearly nine decades, the Waugoshance Lighthouse has sat inactive and sadly sulking in northern Lake Michigan. Over the years, the lighthouse has been neglected, subject to aerial bombardment, vandalized and generally abused. With its lamproom reduced to nothing more than a skeleton, its foundation crumbling and its iron sheathing having fallen off into the lake, this lighthouse is one of the saddest places on the lakes. It is no wonder that it has been said to be haunted.

When someone first enters the circle of the Great Lakes lighthouse people, one of the first stories that you hear is that of the ghost which haunts the Waugoshance Lighthouse. For most folks this is a fascinating, and humorous yarn that rings of the romance of the old forgotten lighthouse and the people who dedicated their lives and perhaps their afterlives to their keeping. To a research historian, such as this author, such a story triggers the instinct to dig into the story and get to the documentation from which the yarn was born. Unfortunately, tracking down such a tale does not always lead in the direction that we would like to move. In researching such stories, the historian must put aside romance and folly and proceed to the facts. This means that even if the yarn is one of your all-time favorite stories, you still must evaluate the facts as they are. Tracking down a ghost can often be as elusive of the apparition itself.

Waugoshance is one of the oldest lights on the upper Great Lakes having been established as a lightship in 1832 and then later as a lighthouse in 1851. Located in the extreme north eastern end of Lake Michigan, the lighthouse is two miles from the nearest island and 18 miles due west of the southern ramp of the Mackinac Bridge. When the station was established, Mackinaw City, which is also 18 miles east of the lighthouse, was the closest civilization. Construction of this light was probably a project unlike anything that had ever been seen on the Great Lakes. It was well off shore and in an area of amazing isolation. Records as to the details of the construction are scarce, but knowing how hard it was to build the Stannard's Rock Station 20 years later, we just imagine how large the task was to establish Waugoshance.

Part of the quandary of the Waugoshance Lighthouse is that it is located in what has always been considered to be a remote area. Another part of the quandary is that the light has always seemed to be somewhat misunderstood. A good example of this is the description given of the facility in the 1852 *Annual Report of the Operations* of the Lighthouse Board. The report mentions the newly established lightstation as follows: "These principal lights on the lakes should be fitted with third order lenses of smaller or larger model, according to circumstances, similar to the one recently placed in the Wagooshance Light, built under the direction of the Topographical Bureau." Interestingly, the spelling of the lighthouse's name as "Wagooshance" did not stick, but the use of this spelling demonstrated that the site was pretty far removed from the bureaucrats, even after being an extensive building project.

When the lighthouse was completed and activated it was equipped with a fourth order fixed optic. This optic was white and varied with flashes at one minute and 30 seconds. The light was listed as being visible for 15 nautical miles. There was also a fog bell that was "struck by machinery" installed at the station. The site was fully staffed in October of 1853, but is listed as "built" in 1855. Since 1853 was the time when the lighthouse was actually fully staffed, we can assume that this was also the likely time when the lighthouse was placed into actual operation. The light list, however, indicates that it was "built" two years later. The discrepancy could be simply one of equipment logistics as it is possible that the station was staffed and activated in 1853, but its permanent optic was not available to be installed until 1855. Thus the light list may actually be indicating the building date of the optic and not the station's date of activation.

John Levake, the light's first keeper was designated to the Waugoshance on January 7, 1852 at a wage of $600 annually. His designation appears to have been nothing more that a paper-work formality, because on March 3, 1852 he was replaced by Lewis Lasley. Still, there was some apparent shaking-up of the ranks of assigned keepers because on July 7th of that same year, a name that appears to be "Nathl. Sohnson" appears as keeper and

Standing abandoned since 1913 the Waugoshance Lighthouse just looks like it should be haunted, so perhaps it is. (Mark Fowler photo)

Lasley's name is crossed out and denoted as "revoked." Then, on June 18, 1853, the Nathl. Sohnson name is crossed out and replaced with Lewis Lasley again. These records are all hand-written and in quill pen styled form, thus it is the strike through and penmanship that makes the Nathl Sohnson name nearly unreadable. On October 27, 1853 Keeper Lasley was assigned an assistant keeper, William H. Rice. He received an annual salary of $400, which was considered a good living by 1853, standards. The only problem was that there was no place to spend it! By 1855, the pay for the keeper had been increased to a whopping $800 annually, and by then the lighthouse was on its fifth keeper. The records are somewhat deceiving, because it is likely that Lavake and Sohnson were simply listed as keepers during the light's construction. It took several decades and many changes of lighthouse keepers before the name of John Herman appeared on register of keepers.

The basic story of Herman's ghost is where the research must begin. Published time and time again, told at one lighthouse event after another and passed on from Great Lakes lighthouse buff to another, the story has many different specific versions, but consists of one basic core tale. So that readers may begin in the proper place, the basic tale goes as follows:

Lightkeeper John Herman was a jovial tender if the lamp who is said to have liked a good practical joke as much as he liked his liquor. Such was not uncommon in the mid to late 1880s as it seemed that people were either hard drinkers, or teetotalers. Duty out on a lighthouse such as Waugoshance was a lonely and often isolated service that probably required both strong drink and a strong sense of humor. Although the rules of the Lighthouse Board absolutely forbade the use of any alcoholic beverage while on duty at any station, the odds that anyone would catch such an infraction at an isolated station like Waugoshance were astronomical. So long as the light was activated each night and the station was kept in proper order, no one would take particular notice. Besides, if anyone were likely to complain about such conduct, it would probably be one of the assistant keepers. In the case of John Herman, it is easy to conclude that a happy, drunk, practical joking keeper would be far easier for the assistant keepers to get along with than would be a teetotaling tyrant. If Herman were to be turned in and removed, the Lighthouse Board may well replace him with someone that would make life on the light miserable for the assistant keepers.

One day, so the basic yarn goes, Keeper Herman was feeling good as a result of the consumption of distilled spirits. Some where along the way to inebriation, the jovial lighthouse keeper entered into a round of practical joking with his assistant keepers, Josh Townshend and Louis Beloungea. In the process, Herman found the opportunity to lock one of his assistants in the lighthouse's lamproom and then he made off with the key. One version of the story says that the assistant keeper last saw Herman staggering happily along the station's narrow pier. The keeper was never seen again. The thoughts were that he had fallen off of the pier in a drunken stupor and drown in Lake Michigan.

Continuing, the legend says that shortly thereafter strange and mischievous things began to happen at the lighthouse. Consistently told are events such as the keepers who fell asleep while tending to the light having their chairs kicked out from under them. Another tale is that buckets of coal left empty were mysteriously filled, and boilers stoked by an unseen shovel. Doors were said to be locked by an unseen key and other ghostly happenings were routinely observed. Finally, the hauntings became so annoying that the Lighthouse Board could no longer get anyone to staff the Waugoshance Light. The story concludes by saying that rather than troubling with Waugoshance any further, the Lighthouse Board constructed the lighthouse at White Shoals and thus declared Waugoshance obsolete and redundant.

In hearing this tale, most folks are simply entertained by the thoughts of a jovial spirit who haunts a forlorn and abandoned lighthouse to this day. To the research historian, however, the tale triggers the instinct to get to the facts and see what really is going on with the abandoned light at Waugoshance. In that pursuit one may want to start with the modern published accounts of this story. A good place to do that would be author Fred Stonehouse's book *Haunted Lakes*. In that text, the author cites a number of sources including a piece written by Jack Edwards in *Great Lakes Cruiser* and the book *The Northern Lights* by Charles Hyde. Another published account is in Chuck and Jeri Feltner's terrific book, *Shipwrecks of the Straits of Mackinac*, which cites only Hyde's book as the source for the story. Other than that, you will be hard-pressed to find any other accounts of the John Herman story.

When all of the published accounts of a given story begin to point back to a single book that was published as late as 1986, any good researcher would tend to put up a red flag. The question is, where did the author of that text get the story? Hyde's book, which is a wonderful piece of work that includes facts, rare drawings, historic pictures and spectacular color photos of lighthouses, should be on the shelf of every lighthouse buff. But it is missing a complete bibliography. The author, however, is a dedicated historian and would not have published the story without at least one written

Completed in 1912, the White Shoals Light made the Waugoshance Light redundant. This light, and not a ghost, was why Waugoshance was abandoned and not the other way around. (Mark Fowler photo)

source. Through another historian it was discovered that the source was a newspaper story published in a Petoskey paper back in the 1930s.

Taking a closer look at the records, we find that the Lighthouse Board's *Register of Lighthouse Keepers*, which is in repose at the National Archives in Washington, D.C., does list John Herman as a keeper at the Waugoshance Lighthouse. Herman, in fact, began at the station on April 21, 1887 as an acting second assistant under Lighthouse Keeper George W. Marshall, who was another member of the vast Marshall clan of Straits lightkeepers. Herman replaced acting second assistant keeper J. H. Messler, who had been "removed" six days earlier. Over the next year, Herman would be made permanent, then, on July 6, 1888 promoted to first assistant keeper after the transfer of Charles Marshall. First assistant keeper John Herman remained at that position for only two years before being appointed as acting lighthouse keeper on August 21, 1890. This was a command that he would hold for more than a decade. Although the records contain a gap of nearly 11 years, it appears that Herman's tenure on the light was, up to that time, second in length only to Keeper J. McHany who served as keeper at Waugoshance from August 21, 1865 to January 30, 1877. Records show that the pay for Herman was terminated 14 days into the second quarter of 1901, and from that we can speculate that his death occurred on or about that date. By looking at the official register, it becomes clear that the keepers and their assistants at the Waugoshance Lighthouse seem to come and go every two or three or four years as a matter of normal movement. Some of the assistant keepers are shown to only stay a matter of weeks before moving on. Even the members of the lightkeeping Marshall family regularly move on and off of the station records. After Herman is taken off of the records, the pace at which keepers and assistant keepers move on and off of the Waugoshance light remains about the same as before his time.

Considering that the movement of the keepers remains consistent both before and after John Herman's time at the station, it is clear that there was not problem getting people to man the Waugoshance Station because of the supposed hauntings. The simple fact is that there is always a high movement among keepers at all of the off-shore reef lights on the upper lakes. Both Spectacle Reef and Stannard's Rock show similar movement among crews. These lights were hard places to be assigned to, and there was always a lot of movement in the ranks of lighthouse crews in general on the Great Lakes.

Why then was the Waugoshance Light replaced by the White Shoals Lighthouse? The answer to that is quite simple, Waugoshance was indeed outdated. Recall, that the Waugoshance Lighthouse was constructed in the early 1850s to replace a lightship. Likewise, the White Shoals Lighthouse was erected to replace a lightship. The lightships in the Straits of Mackinac were always forced off of their stations by roving packs of ice in both the late fall and early spring, the exact times when they were most needed by the mariners attempting to navigate those waters. The lamps on these old lightships could be seen for about 15 miles or less in good conditions. On the other hand, the lamp from the White Shoals Lighthouse was visible for 20 miles. Additionally, by 1912 when the White Shoals Station was operational, the Waugoshance Lighthouse was pushing 60 years of age. All of its equipment was antiquated, and the station itself had been made of substandard stone and mortar which was always in need of repair. Having been one of the earliest off-shore shoal lights, Waugoshance was literally built the best they could with what they had.

Evidence of the Waugoshance Lighthouse's poor construction can be seen as early as 1867. That season it was decided that the light's foundation was in need of repair and re-enforcing. A caisson was sunk around the lights foundation and stone work was built up from the lake bottom to 15 feet above the water's surface. By 1882 the tower was in bad need of reinforcement as the winter ice was eroding the masonry to the point where large pieces were falling off. Bids were taken and the Buhl Iron Works of Detroit were awarded the contract. For a cost of $23,000 the contractors would take a working gang of 39 men out to the Waugoshance Light and sheath the tower in 136,000 pounds of boiler iron plating. Additionally, a new fog signal building, also sheathed in boiler iron would be constructed by the Buhl Iron Works team to replace the original fog bell. The new foghorn would be steam powered by twin boilers and would make two blasts of four seconds duration every minute. A scaffold standing 60 feet tall was erected around the light tower and over the 1883 season the boiler iron sheathing was attached with 24,000 rivets and connecting bolts. The *Detroit Free Press* expressed the confidence in the work stating, "It would seem that the lighthouse on this more exposed situation was now finished for generations, as nothing but an earthquake or tornado can effect it, and it would be safe to give the lighthouse the odds against the average tornado."

Still, Waugoshance continued to crumble from within. A century after the sheathing was applied, the masonry let go and the whole 136,000 pound jacket unwrapped and fell into the lake. Although the survival of a century of Lake Michigan's wear plus the bombardment of naval aircraft isn't bad, it is interesting to point out that the fog signal building, which was constructed at the same time that the sheathing was applied, still retains its iron skin.

This is pretty good evidence that the masonry was substandard. The bolts that were cast into the tower to hold the boiler iron to it simply crumbled loose. Waugoshance was not quite as strong as her later companion lighthouses.

White Shoals was proof that the technology of constructing offshore lights had reached an apogee. The station's pier was placed in much the same manner as those of Spectacle Reef and Stannard's Rock. Atop that was constructed a 105-foot-tall conical tower that has a steel support structure backed with brick and faced with terra cotta. The upper fixtures are of cast iron, but the gallery deck, watch room and lantern all are made of aluminum, which in 1912 was an advanced material for construction. In describing the lamp, the illuminating apparatus itself was described in the 1912 Annual Report as:

> Consist of a second-order flashing lens of two panels each made up of 7 refracting and 15 reflecting prisms, rotating on a mercury float, driven by clockwork, and giving a white flash every 8 seconds. The intensity of the light is estimated at 1,200,000 candles, and the focal plane is 125 feet above mean lake level, and the light is visible 20 miles in clear weather. The light is furnished by a 55-millimeter double-tank, incandescent oil vapor lamp.

Quarters for the crews manning the light were within the nine-story-tall tower. The first floor of the tower contained the fog signal, heating equipment, storage closets and a powerboat. On the second floor was a toolroom, bathroom and the storage for the light's kitchen. The kitchen itself was located on the third floor along with a living room and a bedroom. On the fourth floor were built two more bedrooms and a toilet. Located on the fifth floor was the last bedroom and a general sitting room while the sixth and seventh floors contained what is simply described as, "one large room each." The service room was placed on the eighth floor and the ninth floor was the watchroom. This entire lighthouse was built at a cost of $224,563.83. That is $60,213.55 less than the cost of Stannard's Rock which was built using labor and materials that were 30 years cheaper! How on earth could the old Waugoshance lighthouse compete with that?

During the fiscal year of 1913, there were 234 lights discontinued in the United States by the Lighthouse Board. Among those listed on that roster is the 12th District's light at Waugoshance, Michigan, and its fourth order optic. There is no official reason given for the discontinuation in any of the reports. Additionally, it is worth reporting that a search of the National

Archives Washington D.C., National Archives Chicago Branch, Coast Guard Archives, Coast Guard Historian's collection, Museum of Science and Industry, Western Reserve Historical Society, Library of Michigan, Great Lakes Historical Society and assorted private collections yielded no log-books from the Waugoshance lighthouse which would verify the story of John Herman's ghost. Also, if the story was some sort of malformation of actual events that was picked up and retold by a small-town newspaper look-ing to fill space, there is the possibility that they got the wrong lighthouse keeper. The fact is that John Herman is not listed in the records as having drowned at the lighthouse. This is due to a change in the style of the ledgers that were being kept. Between 1898 and 1901 the ledgers, although still handwritten were changed so that far less information was contained. Dates

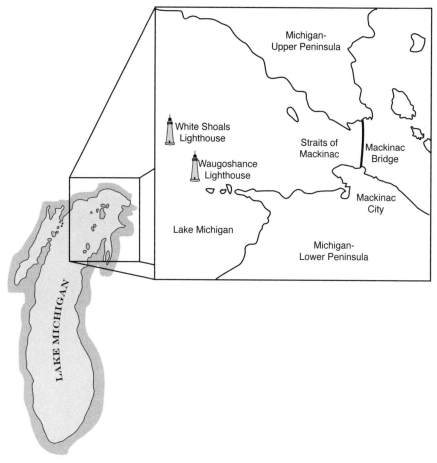

of service were changed are shown as simple checkmarks in boxes for each quarter, and the reason for vacating of a station by a keeper was eliminated from the record completely. Thus, John Herman's checkmarks simply stop after the first quarter of 1901 and a "14" is penned into the upper left corner of the second quarter to show that he was paid for 14 days of that quarter. Oddly too, his rate is listed as $700 annually, when in previous records it is clearly shown as $800. For all that the records show, he could have simply retired from the lighthouse service, and not drown at all. The only keeper actually listed in the official records as "drowned" is Thomas Marshall who did so on May 28, 1886.

Is there a ghost of a long-lost keeper that haunt's the abandoned lighthouse at Waugoshance? The answer to that is within what you, the reader, wish to believe. Perhaps every lighthouse has wondering around it the spirits of those who dedicated their careers to that service. As with the search of every ghost story, the possibilities are unlimited. Perhaps there is a logbook out there that this author has yet to locate, or maybe there are news clippings that remain undiscovered which will go far to prove this story. Perhaps the people who are working to restore the Waugoshance Light will come face-to-face with the apparition and debunk this entire account. Or maybe, this is just a tale that is so fun to ponder and tell that the lighthouse romantics will continue to retell it in spite of the facts. It is this author's recommendation that those who hear and tell such stories not look too deeply into the documented facts, because it is just no fun at all. And what is this author's opinion about the whole matter? Well, I hope that the ghost does exist, whether it be John Herman or Thomas Marshall. Yet it is my honest opinion that the ghost of John Herman was on the grassy knoll when JFK's motorcade went by, and then was taken to area 51 and frozen next to Bruce Lee and will get thawed out when society is ready to know the truth. It is a lot more fun that way.

IV

ANDREW SHAW'S CONCERN

Drawing near the beach neighboring the Shaw farm the lifesavers from the Pointe aux Barques Station viewed a scene from Hades itself. The barn, house, fences, trees, wagons, windmill—everything was aflame. Worse yet, apparently, no one alive was anywhere to be seen. As the keeper tillered the lifeboat from Lake Huron toward the beach and its low bluff, he was sure that everyone at the farm ahead had lost their fight with the wildfire. Dashing ashore and scrambling up the bluff, the lifesavers found Lighthouse Keeper Andrew Shaw, Mr. Pethers, Mrs. Pethers and the five Pethers children laying scattered around the farmyard like so many fallen toy soldiers. All around, the once green and thick forest was a wall of fire and the wind was sweeping across the scene as the air was drawn from the lake and consumed in the firestorm. It was Monday afternoon, September 5, 1881, and as the shocked lifesavers cautiously came up from the beach, the earth seemed to radiate from the heat while all around every blade of grass smoldered in preparation of combustion. The lifesaving crew had always trained to do battle with a storm-tossed Lake Huron, but they had never imagined that disaster would come from the forest.

On Sunday, September 4, 1881, just a day before the lifesavers found themselves cast into that hell on earth, Lighthouse Keeper Andrew Shaw stood on the parapet walkway of the Pointe aux Barques light-tower, gazing with great concern into the distance. Keeper Shaw's eye of worry was not directed toward the lake, but rather was turned directly inland, down the thumb of Michigan. Through the haze, billows of smoke were visible, but what concerned Keeper Shaw the most was the fact that the smudge appeared to stretch from horizon to horizon. Making matters worse, the conflagration also seemed to be getting closer. As dusk began to fall, an orange glow took the place of the smoke. Halfway through the night, the sea breeze did its normal shift to a land breeze and that brought the smoke which now began to hang heavily across Pointe aux Barques. The lamp of the lighthouse reflected a glow into the smoke and it seemed as if a heavy fog had set in. So thick was the smoke that it permeated every corner and crack in every structure. There was no escape from the cloud. In the lightkeeper's quarters, every room was blurred with the haze and even if you opened the cupboards there seemed to be smoke inside. It was impossible to sleep, and the eyes of those who remained awake burned from the smokes irritation. For hours on end Shaw kept his eyes toward the south as the winds began to grow in strength bringing more smoke and concern. With visibility cut down to just a few hundred yards, there was no telling how close the fire was, but

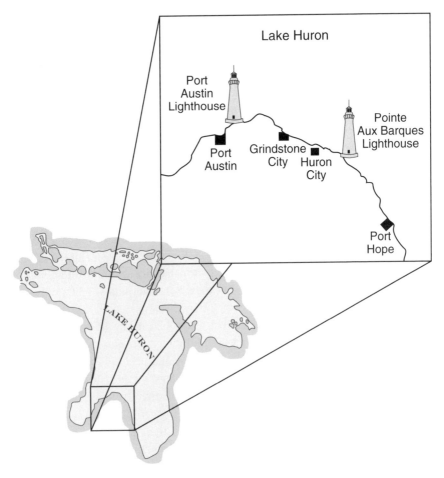

the telltale smoke hinted that an inferno was closing in. As the pungent haze grew more dense, the concern of the local residents grew with it. This was a time and a place when there were no newscasts, or televised warning spots, or emergency management system, or patrolling police cars to warn and advise the residents how and when to evacuate. All that any individual had to assist in survival was their own personal concern and instinct. Although Keeper Shaw had his suspicions and concerns, what he had no way of knowing was the fact that hellfire, the likes of which he had never seen before, was fast approaching and nothing on earth could stop it.

Located on the tip of Michigan's thumb, Pointe aux Barques is about nine miles north of its namesake lighthouse. A light was established on the site in 1847, but was replaced a decade later by the light which stands today. The whitewashed brick tower is 89 feet tall, and in Keeper Shaw's day he tended to a third order optic. In the early days of the light's existence, this was a lonesome spot. Thick woods grew right up to the light and the blue expanse of Lake Huron was the keeper's only company. Keeper Shaw was given charge of the lighthouse by appointment on February 24, 1863 and soon discovered the job to be far beyond simple tending to a lamp. At this isolated location he was touched by everything from shipwrecks to good old-fashioned politics. In fact, on June 16, 1884, a Mr. L. Hubbard, who was apparently a local resident, transmitted a letter to the Lighthouse Board insisting that Shaw be removed from his position as lighthouse keeper for "political reasons." That effort did not succeed because Shaw is in the records as being the lighthouse keeper until the last day of August, 1895 when he finally resigned after more than 30 years in charge of the light. Still, the station was always a secluded spot, and when the weather turned foul, the possibility of shipwreck was always feared. In 1876, however, the United States Lifesaving Service established stations on the Great Lakes for the first time. "Station Number 1" was located about 100 yards southeast the Pointe aux Barques Lighthouse. Now, at least the lighthouse keeper and his family would have some company during the navigation season.

In the mid 1800s, at about the same time as the Point aux Barques Lighthouse was being constructed, the lumber industry was beginning to boom on the Great Lakes. At that time the state of Michigan was completely covered by a dense forest, and by the middle of that century the growing nation was demanding lumber. Harvest of the lumber products soon turned into a major industry, and countless trips were made by lumber vessels across the lakes. Lumbering in these boom times had little mind for the regrowth of the forests or for the preservation of the lands from which the timber was cut. The woods and the supply of lumber were perceived as endless and only the best trees were to be cut. Men known as timber "cruisers" or "landlookers" went out into the deep woods and marked the areas where the best growths of desired timber could be found. Then lumber camps were established where lumberjacks would spend the winter months cutting as many of the prime trees as possible. Any poor quality trees were simply left behind as was all of the waste and excess cuttings. This was a form of clear-cutting that would cause any modern environmentalist, naturalist, or conservationist to faint dead away. No one really gave too much concern to the forest being cut. Lumbering was done by hand with an ax and the logs were dragged to the sawmills and cut one at a time. There appeared to be so much forest that no one could imagine that the timber could ever run out. As time went on, however, mankind got much more efficient at logging and the great wilderness began to feel the weight of the industry. Providence, however, has not set up nature's game in a static form. When you cause an action, you also cause a reaction, and the removal of the trees to build the civilization would now have its reaction.

In the wake of the lumber industry were left massive areas of stumps, dead trees, discarded cuttings and assorted "junk trees." This all was a mixture for disaster, and it was certain that those who had cut the trees would soon have to pay nature's price. All that was needed to set the elements in motion was a good drought. One of the first payments that nature charged against the lumber industry came on October 8, 1871, the same day that the Great Chicago Fire erupted. On that fiery night, a forest fire, unlike any ever seen in the region before, started on the Lake Michigan shore and swept across the state of Michigan to the shores of Lake Huron. Lumbering towns and camps across the whole state were turned to ashes. Yet, if Providence was sending some kind of a message to the lumber industry, no one was listening. The need for timber was too great, everything from housing to transportation depended on wood products, and the most handy supply was in Michigan. Ironically, one of the reasons why the Great Chicago Fire was so extensive in its damage was because the city was made mostly of wood. Now, its rebuilding would only increase the demand for more Michigan timber. Across the Michigan thumb and deep into the Saginaw valley the axes swung and the steam-saws spun as the lumber industry went into high gear. Just one decade after the big 1871 fire, the conditions were again right for another hellfire.

The year 1881 had been one of the driest in memory on the Great Lakes, and the summer had brought with it high temperatures and very little rain.

All of the cuttings and remains of the timber industry in Michigan's thumb had dried and were ready to ignite. The element of ignition came in the from of a common practice used by farmers in that era. In an effort to clear land left over from logging into that useful for farming, the sodbusters would simply burn the dense underbrush and discarded log piles left from the lumber camps. There were no permits required or controls of any sort, if you were a farmer, and you wished to clear some land you simply went out and torched what you needed. The practice was so common that no one really paid any attention to such burning. On Monday, September 5, 1881, a number of farmers were burning some land clear when things apparently got out of control. There is no record as to how the whole event got started, but soon a massive forest fire erupted, fanned by a southwest wind. Soon a few of these fires linked up with one another and formed a line of wildfire. Towering into the sky the fire began to march up Michigan's thumb and in the 1880s, there was no way to fight such a blaze. Forest fire fighting

The Pointe aux Barques Light stands with its original buildings, thanks to the people who fought the wild fire more than a century ago. Note: the light tower appears to lean due to the wide-angle camera lens used in the photo. (Author's photo)

technology was nearly three-quarters of a century into the future. So, when the wildfire started its march up the thumb, all that anyone could do was let it burn and try to get out of the way. It was the smoke and glow from these fires that caught the attention of Keeper Shaw at the Pointe aux Barques Station. As it turned out, the lightkeeper's concern was quite valid. As he pondered the distant glow and the smoke that now thickened the air, a line of holocaust two counties wide was heading directly toward him!

Shaw's concern was not only for his lighthouse, but also for his family farm located about a mile north of the lighthouse. Unlike the brick lighthouse, the wood framed buildings of the farm were far more vulnerable to fire. As soon as the sun came up on Monday morning, keeper Shaw left the light and headed for his farm. By now the smoke was so thick that the light was nearly useless as a navigational aid. To make the matter worse, the smoke also made it impossible to tell how close the line of fire actually was. Surely, thought Shaw, the family farm must be threatened. Later in the morning, the Pethers family passed the station on the trail headed toward the Shaw farm. They stated that they intended to help the Shaw family defend their farm against the fire. The lifesaving crew at the Pointe aux Barques Station wished them luck, and then prepared to make their own stand against the flames.

Getting out of the way of a wildfire is an effective tactic, that is until the licking flames back you up against the lake. Then there is no place left to run to, and you can either lose all and take a swim, or stand and fight. So it was on that smoke-strangled Monday afternoon, when the flames came suddenly bursting from the woods. At the Pointe aux Barques Lifesaving Station, the crew was prepared. The station's surfboat had been launched and was anchored out in the lake. Any of the equipment that would burn was placed in the lake, and safely covered by the water. Ropes, oars, the beach cart and all of the station's removable apparatus was taken down and either placed in the water or left on the beach. The station's supply of gunpowder was also "...moved to a place of safety." This place was likely on the end of the long pier that extended from the station out into the lake. The station's new lifeboat was carted out onto the pier and made ready for launching. Next, any container that could hold water was filled, and made ready to fight the fire. One advantage to fighting a fire at the lakeside was that you have an endless supply of water. The contents of two big pork barrels were dumped out, and the barrels were hauled atop the station, filled with water, and prepared to fight the flames.

This is the actual lifesaving station from Pointe aux Barques. It is now a museum at Huron City, Michigan. (Author's photo)

Just as the crew were fully prepared to fight the fire, they saw that the lighthouse appeared to be in greater danger. Without hesitation the crew turned their attention toward fighting the fire around the lighthouse. Somehow, they managed to defend the beacon, tower, and adjacent quarters. As soon as it was clear that the lighthouse was safe, the lifesaving station keeper grew concerned over the well-being of the people up at the Shaw farm. The shift of the wind seemed to be carrying the flames over in that direction. Soon his instincts as a lifesaver were eating at him, and he ordered the station's lifeboat to be launched. The woods had always grown right up to the water's edge, and now that tree line was a mass of flame. The only way to get to the farm was to row, and that was something at which the lifesaving crew was well practiced. Blinding billows of smoke were spread across the surface of the lake and the lifesavers had to navigate by instinct alone. Visibility was cut to just a few feet amid the brown haze, and the heat could be felt on the face of each man in the lifeboat as they pulled along the shore.

When the lifesaving crew reached those apparently dead people scattered around the Shaw farmyard, they found that every person was still alive! Overcome by the heat and smoke they were unconscious, but alive. Each lifesaver grabbed a body and headed back toward the lake. Loading the victims into the boat, the storm warriors took to their oars and pulled back to the station. Once at the station's pier, the now semiconscious people were unloaded and soon began to recover. This was fortunate, because the fight with the wildfire was far from being concluded. As soon as the fire had consumed the entire area around the Shaw farm, including the farm itself, the blaze went looking for more fuel. As if to help, the winds shifted and now sent the flames back, directly toward the wood-framed lifesaving station. If the lifesavers were going to save their station, they would soon need every person that they could muster to fight the fire.

At eight o'clock that evening, the firestorm had reappeared through the scorched treeline and on its way toward the lifesaving station. Using the porkbarrels that they had prepositioned atop the roof of the station, some of the lifesavers and their confederates kept the wooden station well soaked while the rest of the used buckets and shovels to beat back the fire. Through the entire night the station crew along with Lighthouse Keeper Shaw and the Pethers family fought with a wall of fire. Illuminated only by the fire itself they hauled water from lake Huron and doused every flair-up. By sunrise, the surrounding tree line was so blackened that it could no longer support combustion. Then, like a reprieve from nature, the winds shifted to blowing from the north, off of Lake Huron. In the locality of the lighthouse and lifestation, the fires were now blown back upon the area that they had already burned and rapidly died. Still, all along the entire horizon, other fires continued to burn for days.

Once finished with their rampage, the wildfires had blackened nearly every square foot of land on the thumb of Michigan. What only a few years earlier had been dense forest was now a scorched moonscape. Reporters of the popular culture of modern times would have called this, "...the worst environmental catastrophe ever...," but the land and the lakes have a tendency to make right all human blunders. The fires had the effect of clearing the land and allowing for the development of easy farming and the development of a farm industry that is productive to this day. Today, the entire area is almost devoid of forest, yet is the home of countless acres of rich farmland. For generations following the great firestorm, families have earned income and fed millions of people through the use of this land.

Any time of the year seems a good season to go to Michigan's thumb and visit the Pointe aux Barques Lighthouse. This is one of the most easily accessed lighthouses on the Great Lakes. No matter if you begin at Port Huron or Bay City, driving northward on M-25 will always take you to the lighthouse. Just eight miles above Port Hope, or six miles outside of Port Austin, the tourist will come upon Lighthouse Road, which is a turn off of M-25. A very short distance up that road will lead you directly to the light-house and its rustic campground. The attached keeper's quarters are today a fine maritime museum, but the lifesaving station is missing. However, the original station which Keeper Shaw, the Pethers family and the lifesavers fought so hard to save still exists. The actual structure that was placed on the point in 1876 has been moved just up the road to a collection of historic buildings called the Huron City Museum. The site is open for visiting from the first day of July until Labor Day. It is the last of the original 1876 life-saving stations on the Great Lakes to remain preserved in its original condi-tion, and is a must-see.

Visiting the Pointe aux Barques Lighthouse, you can hardly believe that it was once covered in dense forest. The neighborhood is farmland and the immediate area around the light is a treeless campground. The buildings, tower and lamproom remain intact, thanks to the efforts of those who appre-ciate their maritime heritage and those who fought and won the fight with the 1881 wildfire.

Standing on its lonely point of land the Pointe aux Barques Lighthouse shows its beacon.
(Author's photo)

V

DISASTER ON THE DOORSTEP

Tending to the Outer Island Lighthouse, 60-year-old Lightkeeper John Irvine had expected Lake Superior to make trouble today, and that was exactly what happened. It was the first Saturday of September, 1905 and through the morning the mighty lake had been throwing a particularly violent tantrum. In this, his eighth season on the light, Irvine knew that whatever evil that the lake had in mind, it would likely involve a stinging cold and soaking wet disaster. He really did not know if misfortune would occur in the vicinity of his lighthouse, but he had to remain vigilant just in case. In a gale this heavy, Lake Superior was certain to deliver a disaster on someone's doorstep, and Outer Island was just as likely as any place to be the recipient. As the storm's spume obscured the lake beyond, Keeper Irvine did all that he could do from his island-bound station. He kept the light fueled and working and also kept a lookout into the gloom beyond. The normal steamer track to and from the port cities of Duluth and Superior was just nine miles off of the light, but by the time that the storm grew to its worst, the lightkeeper could see less than a few thousand yards onto Lake Superior. Pacing along the parapet rail, he strained his eyes and ears in the search for trouble. If he was lucky, the expected disaster would come elsewhere and would only be his to read about in the next newspaper that the lighthouse tender delivered.

Outer Island is one of 20 islands that make up a group called "The Apostle Islands." This chain of wooded specks are located at the western most end of Lake Superior and are an ice age detachment from DeTour Point which wedges into the lake between Ashland and Duluth-Superior. As the hunger for iron ore grew with the industrial revolution, the shipment of that product grew and so did the sizes and numbers of vessels needed to haul it.

Outer Island Light, Apostle Islands, Lake Superior. (Wayne Sapulski photo)

From the opening of the locks at the Soo in 1855, the ore trade steadily boomed. With the demand for iron ore, the ore shipping ports on Lake Superior boomed as well. Soon the hazard of the islands that stood between the two main ore shipping ports became apparent. Aptly named, Outer Island was the rock that was located the greatest distance out into the Lake Superior from the mainland, and by 1874 a lighthouse was in service on the island's northern tip. This is a cold, stormy and isolated place—and that is what it is like in the summer. In autumn, even the sea gulls get too depressed and tend to stop hanging around Outer Island. By 1905, the traffic of lake-boats passing the island was in the form of a steady parade as they hauled coal and package products upbound and ore and grain downbound. Throw in the lumber fleets and what you have is nearly a constant passage of vessels. The demand for ore was so great that often it was worth the risk of losing a boat just to haul the "red gold." Autumn gales, or spring season ice and the damage that they could cause were simply the cost of doing business, the cost of keeping the blast furnaces of the lower lakes fed.

Activated in 1874, the Outer Island Lighthouse consists of a brick keeper's quarters, fog signal building, privy and a classic Poe-style light tower. The Poe-style light tower was a design that was the trademark of General Orlando M. Poe, a marine engineer of the Great Lakes region. In the service of the Army Corps of Engineers, Poe set the pace in a number of areas of lakes marine architecture. His influence is most widely seen in the elegant conical brick light towers at sites such as Presque Isle, Tawas Point, Sturgeon Point, South Manitou Island, Seul Choix Point, Little Sable Point, Wind Point, Iroquois Point and Au Sable Point. All of these towers have ornate stone knees supporting their parapet walkways and most sport elegant stone arches over the four windows below the walkway. It is an eye-pleasing design to say the least, and whether Poe influenced them, or they had an early influence on him is unclear. In that weekend storm of 1905, the

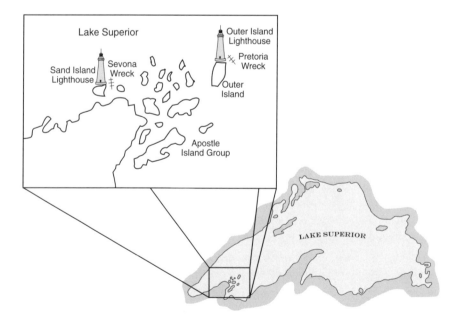

mariners could have cared less what the lighthouses looked like, they only prayed that the keepers were performing their duties and keeping the lights bright and the foghorns blowing.

By four o'clock in the afternoon on that rude second day of September, 1905, the lake was screaming in a classic Lake Superior northeast gale. What Lightkeeper Irvine could not know as he squinted against the whipping rain and wind was that 22 miles to the east at another of the Apostle Islands, a giant steel oreboat had already suffered a fatal wreck. She was the 372-footer *Savona* which had loaded at the port of Superior on Friday. By the first hours of Saturday morning, Captain Sutherland McDonald had the *Savona* off of Outer Island and was taking such a beating that he elected to turn her and run for shelter among the Apostles. Running before the storm and blinded by the driving rain, the *Savona* hit Sand Island Reef and immediately began to break up. Pounded by the surf, and resting right on the doorstep of the Sand Island Lighthouse, the steel boat split in half like tinfoil. The gap between the bow section and the stern isolated the captain and forward crew from the rest of the boat's people on the stern. Using his megaphone, Captain McDonald ordered the after crew to drop the lifeboats, but keep them at the boat's side until it would be safe to board them. Tossing the two yawls like toys, Lake Superior would surely throw anyone attempting to go aboard them into its icy grip. Six hours later, at 11:00 Saturday morning, the after cabins began to shatter and the people on the *Savona's* stern took to those lifeboats. The force of the waves and churning wreckage barely allowed them to escape the steamer, there was no chance at all that they could maneuver back and pick up the seven souls on the bow section. The storm forced them to abandon their shipmates to their fate as dictated by Lake Superior.

From the Sand Island Lighthouse, Lightkeeper Emanuel Lueck had witnessed the whole event, and later claimed to have seen the big steamer hit the reef while looking through his binoculars. As the lightkeeper watched, the two lifeboats departed the after section of the wreck and were grabbed by the wind. The castaways attempted to row, but the wind was just too strong—the boats were completely under the control of the storm. One boat was blown away from Sand Island, but made the mainland six hours later, while the other was blown onto the island and then smashed by the surf. Its occupants dragged themselves ashore and survived. As Lueck continued to watch, the bow of the *Savona* began to founder, and the seven men aboard it made a desperate attempt to escape using a handmade raft. Struggling for their lives, the mariners made a losing swim for the island. One by one they

Sand Island Light, Apostle Islands, Lake Superior. (Wayne Sapulski photo)

were overwhelmed by the lake and perished. Soon the last remaining men on the raft went down as it broke apart. Lightkeeper Lueck remained on his light tower and simply watched while the *Savona* and seven of its mariners died on his doorstep.

At half past two o'clock on that same afternoon, Outer Island Lighthouse keeper John Irvine was scanning the storm with his binoculars when he spotted what he thought to be "a schooner," hove to and snag her anchor two miles northeast of his light. Behind the curtain of rain, the boat was nothing more than a shadow in the distance. It was impossible to tell if it was a vessel in distress or simply riding out the storm. It was also impossible to see that what the lightkeeper was looking at was actually one of the largest schooner-barges in the world, the *Pretoria*.

Between half past four and the hour of five, Lightkeeper Irvine was still keeping his eye toward that schooner from atop his 80-foot-high lighthouse tower. It was then that he saw it coming through the rain and spume. It was a sight that chilled him beyond the winds of Lake Superior and startled him more than anything ever had in all six decades of his life. Tossing like a cork, and raked by every wave, there, on that raging gray lake appeared a single struggling lifeboat. Within the yawl, a crowd of 10 men were pulling at the oars and bailing for their lives. As the lighthouse keeper watched the lifeboat, in the background their schooner-barge, the *Pretoria*, suddenly sank like a tub to the bottom of the lake.

Irvine knew too well that between the lifeboat and the island a barrier of breaking surf waited to chew the yawl and its occupants. People would soon be floundering in the ice cold surf, of that there was no doubt. Irvine was certain that he could not simply stand upon his light and watch, he had to do something, and he had to do it quickly. Dashing down from his light tower, Irvine descended the circular stairs and headed for the place on the shoreline where he figured that the yawl would make its landing. Pitching among the towering waves, the lifeboat drew closer and closer—and then it happened. As the *Pretoria*'s yawl got to within 500 feet of Outer Island, the breakers took hold and flipped the boat. In near shock, the lightkeeper saw some of the occupants tossed nearly 10 feet into the air like rag dolls while some of the others were simply consumed by the lake on the spot. A heartbeat later some of the mariners surfaced and began to thrash in the surf in an effort to claw their way to land. Waves peppered with life and death were now rolling directly at Outer Island, and the only human on the beach was 60-year-old Keeper John Irvine. There was no station filled with trained lifesavers, no town with helpful residents running to help, there was not even another lightkeeper, there was only one man on a rocky island. Lake Superior had brought the *Pretoria's* disaster to his doorstep, but the next move was his.

There have been many savvy and imaginative vesselmen in Great Lakes maritime history, but by far the most wily and creative lakeboat man was Captain James Davidson, the creator owner of the barge *Pretoria*. Born and raised in Buffalo, New York, Davidson spent some time sailing the Atlantic before returning to the Great Lakes and throwing his hat into the ring of shipbuilding. By the early 1870s, Davidson was putting down roots in Bay City, Michigan which was then fast becoming a center of lumbering, and shipping. In 1874, he constructed his first steamer at his developing West Bay City facility. Appropriately, this vessel was named after Davidson himself, and was of the most advanced design. Following in the wake of the *R. J. Hackett,* the boat had her pilothouse forward, engine aft, and a clear cargo deck between. This was just the beginning for Davidson, who had in mind the construction of the biggest wooden vessels ever to haul a cargo. It was also in his character to innovate and do things that the mainstream vessel builders would never have imagined. As the decade of the 1890s rolled in, and other shipyards were turning to constructing boats of steel plate, Davidson was building the largest oak-hulled boats in the world. Each time a Davidson oak monster splashed into the Saginaw River, the vessel-men would shake their collective heads and say that wooden boats could get no bigger. In short order, the next hull would be launched and would be even larger. James Davidson never paid much attention to the "main-stream" of vesselmen.

Along with his tendency for building the largest boats on the lakes, Davidson also used other tactics that lead to success. He located his shipyard in West Bay City, smack in the heart of the richest supply of white oak, pine, tamarack and other woods that were to be used in the construction of his boats. Stockpiling the best lumber products from the nearby mills and forests, Davidson insured his raw material needs for the decades to come. Constructing giant steamers and massive schooner-barges as their consorts, a Davidson team of oak boats had more than the capacity of any single steel steamer of the day and cost less to construct. When a ready buyer for a Davidson-built boat was not available, he simply added the new boat to his own fleet and began construction on the next boat. Financing was also kept locally as Davidson money recirculated into more Davidson money. So strong was the influence of this financial circle that in the Great Depression of the 1930s the Davidson-supported and managed bank remained sound while others folded. It has also been said that Davidson did not insure his boats to cut costs. This is untrue because the savvy vesselman "self-insured" his boats, and by the turn of the century was able to claim a million dollars in savings by not having to pay insurance premiums to some outside compa-ny. The Bay City boats of the Davidson fleet were always locally built with local materials by local labor who were paid in local dollars that were more plentiful because the fleet was locally insured.

On July 26, 1900, Davidson stunned the maritime mainstream once again when he launched the *Pretoria*. Not only was this the biggest wooden schooner-barge in the world, but she slid down the launching ways a day early! In spite of the surprise announcement of the early launching, a crowd of just over 1,000 people had gathered at the Davidson Shipyard to see the *Pretoria* born. Much in keeping with his innovative mind-set, Davidson had completely finished the *Pretoria* and had her rigged "ready for sea" while she was on the building ways. This was highly unusual, as most vessels were launched as soon as their hull would float and their superstructure was in place. Then the builders would "finish" or "fit-out" the rest of the vessel's workings while she floated in the shipyard, thus freeing the building ways

This rare photo shows the Pretoria loading and dwarfing the huge dock. (From the collection of the Milwaukee Public Library)

for the next hull. The *Pretoria*, however, was constructed to the point where her workings were finished and even her sails were fully rigged. Davidson would be able to tow her from the yard within days of her christening and she would begin making money straightaway. The boat's cavernous hold could swallow 300,000 bushels of oats, or 5,000 tons of iron ore. The reasoning for the surprise launching, however, was caused by tradition and superstition rather than Davidson innovation. Great Lakes tradition has always dictated that no vessel of good fortune will be launched on a Friday. On Wednesday, July 25, 1900, Davidson surveyed *Pretoria* and deemed her within two days of launch. But then the Friday launching hoodoo was pointed out to him, and he knew too well the superstitious nature of lake mariners.

"Well then," the master vesselman must have huffed decidedly, "she'll launch tomorrow."

With that the shipyard management went into a frenzy. Newspapers were alerted, labor was mustered and a bottle of champaign was procured in preparation of the launch. At 4:20 on Thursday afternoon, July 26, 1900, the *Pretoria* slid majestically down the ways and the largest schooner-barge on the planet was born.

Details of the construction of Davidson's wonders are scarce. Nearly every drawing, log book, shipyard record, photo, ledger and associated document are just plain missing. The reason for this is said to be intentional burning of everything relating to Davidson's shipping activity by a member of the family after the death of Davidson's heir, James E. Davidson. No record of such a burning exists, but Bay City maritime historians tell the story. As one local historian put it, "The orders were to take it all out and burn it. So they piled up everything, threw kerosene on it and burned it all." The reasoning behind this destruction is unknown. Perhaps some obscure order was left in the younger Davidson's will dictating this action to protect the secrets of the building of these unique vessels. Or, maybe this was just the wasteful spite of a family member. Some historians believe that Davidson did not keep the usual records that other shipbuilders retained. To protect his many tricks of the trade, Davidson may have directed construction face to face and depended on the know-how of his shipwrights rather than engineer's drawings. For that reason many of the drawings would never have been made in the first place. No matter what story a person subscribes to, the fact is that the vast majority of the Davidson records are missing. Drawings of his vessels have to be gotten from the technical journals of the day, and descriptions of equipment from local newspapers of the era. As a result many of the details of the Davidson boats remain unknown.

Measuring 337 feet long, and 44 feet in beam, the *Pretoria* was a wooden boat dimensioned beyond the imaginations of all of the "mainstream" vesselmen. In marine circles it was widely held that wooden ships could be no longer than about 250 to 300 feet. Davidson, however, had broken the 300 foot mark long before the *Pretoria* hit the water. Officially called a three-masted "schooner" this boat was never intended to grab the wind and sail happily across the lakes. The mass of this vessel with a bellyful of ore would have required giant sails to move her, and the girth of the hull would have rendered her rudder nearly useless. A necessary wind needed to propel her by sail would have to have been near gale force.

It was 23-foot drop from *Pretoria's* open hatch to the bottom of her cargo hold, taller than a two-story house. The vessel's hold itself stretched nearly as long a football field. Her keelson alone was a mighty oak beam that measured 20 inches wide and 17 inches tall. The outer planking of the boat was made up of timbers that ranged from eight and one-half inches to 10 and one-half inches by four and one-half inches. These hull timbers were supported by 5-inch-wide iron straps that were one-half of an inch thick! Steel cords were used in some mysterious manner to aid in the hull reinforcement. A special hydraulic steering mechanism was an important part of the big schooner-barge. One of the best kept secrets of the giant barges was the fact that their mass was difficult to control in a seaway or in any heavy weather, so assisted steering equipment was essential. In all, the *Pretoria* was a close sister to the *Matanzas* which had been launched in 1899 measuring 324 feet long. By the year 1900, and the *Pretoria's* launching, the mainstream vesselmen were still amazed at the Davidson boats—but no longer surprised. These oak behemoths just seemed to get bigger and earn the Bay City vessel magnate more profits.

Like his other giant barges, the sly Davidson may have enrolled the *Pretoria* as a schooner to forever grab a record or two for wooden hulled vessels built on the Great Lakes. Yet, no matter how you looked at it she was not about to unfurl canvas and carry cargoes across the lakes. This was a big oak box with a yawning hold hungry for ore, grain or coal as well as the profits attached to those products. She was not, by any stretch of the imagination, an elegant sailing vessel. That all mattered little when you consider that an ore load aboard the *Pretoria* could be worth more than $30,000 on a single trip depending on that day's market. Indeed it was well worth Davidson attaching one of his big wooden steamers to the barge's towing post and pulling her across the lake.

In its October, 1900 issue, *Marine Engineering* magazine ended its discussion of the new *Pretoria* with the following paragraph:

Crew space is located forward under decks. The cabins are located on the upper deck, and all of the cabins are in hard wood, cabinet finish. The Master's quarters as well as the officers' are located in the cabin aft. The *Pretoria* is now engaged in the general carrying trade on the Lakes, which consists of coal, ore and grain. While she was built to tow as a consort after large steamships, yet she is equipped with masts, and these masts all have sails, and she has a sail area of 1,800 yards. These sails are utilized when the winds are fair, or in the case of storms.

Then in what was a most prophetic, but disastrously incorrect conclusions the paragraph ended by saying, "...Should she break away from the towing steamer, she will be able to take care of herself all right until the weather moderates."

Seen here where she was abandoned to rot, the last of the Giant Davidson schooner-barges, and also the Pretoria's *sister ship,* Chiefton, *is moored off of 38th Street in Bay City. Later she was set afire by vandals. (Author's collection)*

This statement would prove to be as misplaced as the commonly mis-quoted one in *The Shipbuilder*, a British trade journal which actually called the *Titanic* "practically unsinkable."

Iron ore was the *Pretoria's* primary burden, and by the end of the summer of 1905, the $60,000 barge had paid for herself many times over. As the hefty *Pretoria* hunched below the ore loading dock at Superior, Wisconsin, she remained the biggest capacity wooden schooner-barge on the Great Lakes and perhaps in the world. Two of the *Pretoria's* sister ships had now outsized her by a small margin in length, but the big barge still held the tonnage title. Launched in 1902, the *Chieftan* was a near twin to the *Pretoria*, but was five feet longer. The following season, Davidson's last work of the shipbuilding trade, the *Montezuma*, was launched and although four feet longer than the *Pretoria*, she was a foot shorter than the *Chieftan*. Both the *Montezuma* and *Chieftan*, however, were enrolled with significantly less tonnage than *Pretoria*. Listed as having a 2,790 gross ton capacity, or 1 gross ton for every 100 cubic feet of "space available," the *Pretoria* had notably more space within her hull than the *Montezuma* and *Chieftan* which were listed at 2,704 and 2,722 gross tons respectively. Apparently, in his last two giants, Davidson had gone for length, but not capacity. The exact reason why this was done died with Davidson, but we can take a good guess at the cause. The true end of the construction of these massive boats came because the supply of "lakeboat quality" white oak needed in their construction was getting extremely scarce. As a matter of fact, the *Montezuma's* construction used up the last of Davidson's supply of quality boatbuilding oak. Perhaps he had to cut down the depth of the last two boats to better use his timbers. Also it is possible that the *Pretoria* immediately showed some tendencies in her girth that Davidson later designed out of the next two barges. So, without regard to the reasoning behind these differences, the *Pretoria* was, in terms of tonnage, the biggest wooden schooner-barge on the lakes.

Early in the morning of Friday, September 1, 1905, the big wooden Davidson steamer *Venezuela* maneuvered into Duluth harbor. Loaded with iron ore that she had taken aboard at Two Harbors, Minnesota, the *Venezuela* was ordered to sail back 28 miles to the west to pick up her consort, the *Pretoria*, which had taken aboard her own cargo of ore at Duluth. Once the giant oak schooner-barge was securely tied to the towpost of the *Venezuela*, the two lakeboats huffed out onto Lake Superior. They picked up a course of 068 degrees and would run that for 90 miles, then when 14 miles off of the Outer Island Light, they would turn to a course of 079 degrees and haul 123 miles until off of Copper Harbor. From that point the two Davidson boats would steer a 111-degree heading in a 148-mile slog to Whitefish Point, and thereafter the Soo. It was a trip that both boats had made countless times before, but Lake Superior had another plan in mind. Superior's trip involved much shorter distances as well as a meeting with the keeper of the Outer Island Lighthouse.

Aboard the *Pretoria* were a crew of 10 mariners. In command was Captain Charles Smart of West Bay City, Michigan, and in his charge were First Mate Charles Fierman, Seaman William Smart and Donkey Engineer Henry Schwartz, all from West Bay City. Seaman Axel Lendlis was from Marinette, Wisconsin; Seamen Isaac Myers and Oscar Orling were from Milwaukee, Wisconsin; Ned Blank was from Buffalo, New York, and Alfred Pebsal was from Sweden. There was a cook aboard, but his name was not recorded. In all, this was a small number of bodies to run an oreboat that was as long as a football field whether it was a barge or not. But, the rules for the operation of barges are far different than those for running powered lake-boats. fewer bodies were required, so fewer were carried. The result was that in good weather, the labor costs were low and the profits were high, but when things got bad, the costs could get very high. The lesson here is signif-icant, considering that in modern times more and more giant steel lakeboats' crews are being cut down, and barges operated under the same reasoning. The lesson modern vessel operators would do well to learn is the lesson that Davidson learned in 1905 with the *Pretoria.*

As the two wooden oreboats pressed onto Lake Superior, a strong autumn gale was fast developing. Winds waves and rain appeared to be the order of the day and every indication was that the situation was going to get worse. For just over a half of a day the *Venezuela* and *Pretoria* had beaten their way across the lake as the weather fell apart. By the time that the two lakeboats were passing Outer Island, Lake Superior was blowing a classic nor'easter. Giant waves, the likes of which only Superior can muster, came to assault the boats. About 30 miles northeast of Outer Island, the Big Lake found the *Pretoria's* single weakness, her newfangled hydraulic steering equipment. Suddenly, the massive wooden barge began to fall off of her course in the grip of the wind. A quick examination by the boat's crew showed her steering equipment in shambles and there was no other way to move her huge two-story-tall oak rudder. The *Pretoria's* big hull, having no power of its own, caught the wind and strained at the towing hawser. Signaling that her steering gear had failed, the *Pretoria* got the point across to the *Venezuela.* The steamer attempted to make a turn back toward the shelter of Outer Island. In this maneuver, the towline snapped and the

Pretoria went adrift. The *Venezuela* made a run toward recapturing the wayward barge, but in the gale it was pointless. At best, the *Venezuela* could only hope to save herself.

On deck the *Pretoria's* crew scrambled in an effort to get her sails up, but there was just too much boat and far too little manpower to compete with Lake Superior. As soon as the forward sail was being raised, the wind blew it to rags. In the trough of the seas the barge rolled insanely, and Captain Smart ordered the boat's anchor dropped. He knew too well that the Apostle Islands were waiting to leeward and soon his boat would likely be smashed into one of their rocky coasts. His only hope to survive was to have the anchor grab the bottom and then hope that the chain held. The *Pretoria* was designed to haul big cargoes of ore at low cost, and despite the news releases at her launch, she was never intended to fight a Lake Superior nor'easter on her own. Now Smart found himself in command of too much boat with too much cargo in too much weather with far too few crew—and no propulsion at all.

No sooner had the flashes of the Outer Island Light been sighted than the anchor of the *Pretoria* took a hold on the bottom. By this time the big barge's hull timbers had sprung and she was taking water into her hold. The boat's steam pumps had been started, and were holding the lake back, but then another of the boat's design characteristics was found by the lake and quickly exploited. Most lakeboats have a tall "bulwark," which is an extension of the boat's side that rises above the deck and helps keep the seas from washing over her deck. In pursuit of greater cargo capacity, Captain Davidson had built his oak monster with no bulwarks! Her deck was nearly flush with the meet of her beam and now this trait was going to spell the end for the *Pretoria*. Able to wash freely over the barge's spardeck, the seas made quick work of her hatch covers. Soon the water entering the hold was far more than the pumps could handle, and they gave out. Shortly after the pumps went out, the hatches were smashed in by the seas and Lake Superior cascaded into the cargo hold. Even in the tossing seas, the crew could feel the boat rapidly settle toward the bottom. Next the decks actually began to come off and it was clear that the *Pretoria* was sinking.

Taking to the lifeboat the crew of the *Pretoria* pulled away from the oak-hulled giant, and with not a moment to spare. As they rowed from their place of work the barge simply sank like a brick. With some men rowing and others bailing, the castaways made progress toward the Outer Island Lighthouse. As they got within 500 feet of dry land, however, the lake reached out with a wave and tossed the lifeboat end over end. All 10 crewmen were dumped into the cold depths of Lake Superior, and only five returned to the surface. Left clinging to their overturned lifeboat and weakened by the cold and shock of the lake were Captain Smart, Mate Fierman, and Seamen Smart, Orling and Blank. The others were all taken by Lake Superior.

Drifting toward the rocks of the island, every one of the survivors of the *Pretoria* knew that they would not have the strength to make the fight through the surf to the beach. As the breakers neared, they were sure that death neared as well. It was then that the 60-year-old Lighthouse Keeper John Irvine waded into the frigid breakers. In a deadly swirl the icy water stung his legs. Like a hundred invisible hands of frozen death, the vicious undertow that came with the surf grabbed at his boots and tried to pull him out into the hungry lake. As the first wave broke nearly as high as his head, and then slapped him in the chest, the unimaginable cold shocked his breath away. The ice water now soaked his entire uniform and Lake Superior began sapping away his body's heat. Still he fought on without a thought for his own life as wave after wave marched toward him. For reasons known only to himself, he was not about to let the lake claim those mariners whom he had spent a career sworn to protect. John Irvine would save those lives, or die trying.

For the record, on that storm-raked day, Irvine fought off the undertow, the icy waves and the elements in general and dragged all five of the survivors from the death grip of Lake Superior—one by one. After this astonishing effort, Irvine helped the five castaways to the lightkeeper's quarters and along with the help of his wife, made them at home until they were all well recovered. The following day, the steamer *Venezuela* hove into sight in search of her lost barge. All that she found was the tops of the masts showing above the waves, and Irvine's signal to come to the light. Once near Outer Island, the *Venezuela* lowered her lifeboat and a party of her crew went to fetch the castaways. Once the *Venezuela* had the five survivors aboard she headed for the port of Ashland, Wisconsin to report the *Pretoria's* loss. At that same time, Keeper Irvine returned to his work of tending to his lighthouse.

As you read this the remains of the *Pretoria* rest on the bottom in a mass of flattened oak wreckage submerged in a little more than 50 feet of water. Her sisters *Montezuma* and *Chieftan* were left to rot in the Saginaw River at the onset of the Great Depression of the 1930s. Those two boats were laid up at the remains of the abandoned Davidson shipyard along with several others of the Davidson fleet. *Montezuma* just went to the worms and sunk to the river's bottom, but the *Chieftan* was raised in the mid-1950s and towed up the river to 38th street. It was hoped that she could be reactivated as a barge, but the plans never materialized and she ended up set afire by vandals. She burned to the waterline and was soon forgotten.

Today, at Outer Island, the lighthouse remains an active aid to navigation. Her lamp is a 190-millimeter plastic lens that is automated and solar powered. As with nearly every lighthouse on the lakes, a heroic keeper is no longer needed. The whole site, like all of the lights in the Apostle Island chain, is part of the Apostle Islands National Lakeshore preserve. These lights are under the care of the National Park Service and are opened to tourists during the summer months.

One trend from the *Pretoria's* era has returned to the lakes, however. That trend is the employ of giant barges. Outdated lakeboats are being converted into big self-unloading barges. With their cabins cut down and their sterns notched to accommodate a tug, the boats no longer fall into the category of a self-propelled vessel, but are considered as tug-barge combinations. Thus their crew requirements are cut by more than two-thirds, and so are their labor costs. Additionally, barges do not fall under the same Coast Guard five-year inspection requirement that their self-propelled counterparts must comply with. Again costs are cut. Simply by purchasing a laker out of the scrapyard and replacing the boat's engine with a tug, the owner can beat the regulations and earn a greater profit. In an additional throwback to the past, these tug-barge abominations are run by small one- and two-vessel companies. Thus when a bad storm blows up and the big carriers can afford to order their fleets into shelter and absorb the losses of waiting out the weather, these small tug-barge companies are motivated to keep hauling. It is a formula that has spelled shipwreck over and over again in this author's research.

Time will tell if those who are beating the costs of labor and are beating the Coast Guard regulations can also beat the vengeful and unforgiving lakes. Those who do not learn from history are doomed to repeat it, and those of us who live daily with their shipwrecks can do little more than write the stories. It is this author's bet that one day, one of the big lakes will show, once again, that small crews, big capacity, and big profits are no match for the power of the Great Lakes. This was a lesson learned by James Davidson, one of the most innovative and savvy men on the lakes. The odds are that this lesson will soon be learned again on some violent spring or autumn day in the future. This time, however, there will be no heroic lightkeeper to spot the disaster on the doorstep and to pull weakened crewmen from the lake. There will be only solar panels and neatly stacked picnic tables and perhaps—no survivors.

VI
FREEMAN'S DUNKING

Not a lot is known about Lighthouse Keeper Samuel Freeman, other than the fact that he was the keeper of the Oswego West Pier Lighthouse. One thing that we can say for certain is that Keeper Freeman was as dedicated to the tending of his station as was any other keeper, in fact from the telling of this tale it may appear that he was a bit more dedicated to his assignment than most of us would be able to imagine. Although this chapter in the career of this individual light keeper may be short, it speaks volumes as to just how much sacrifice these lighthouse tenders were willing to give to their everyday duties on any chosen occasion. The fact is that this glimpse into Freeman's life is just a look at an average day in the life of an average lighthouse keeper at an average light-station in the year 1851—and nothing more.

Although in modern times the port city of Oswego, New York, rarely sees any traffic from the Great Lakes merchant fleets, such was not the case in the mid-1800s. Located on the far eastern end of Lake Ontario, Oswego was a strategic point on the Great Lakes navigation charts practically since the start of navigation on the freshwater seas. This port of cliffs and bluffs had been active in lakes trading and commerce in the early 1700s and by the time that the War of 1812 drew to a close, the maritime industry at Oswego was beginning to boom. One of the characteristics that made Oswego an advantageous port was the fact that the local waters are normally clear of winter's ice at an early date in the spring. Often when shippers in Buffalo were waiting for the ice flows to clear, the Oswego shippers had usually been running for several weeks. Traditionally, Oswego was also the eastern-most located U.S. Great Lakes port with access to the eastern seaboard. All of these elements made the port significant in the eyes of the maritime industry, but in the eyes of the military powers, early Oswego was also viewed as critical. The French, British, and United States forces all used this site to stop, hold and kick one another.

Considering all of its importance it was only logical that such a place as Oswego should be given one of the first navigation lights on the lakes. In the 1822 expansion of lighthouses on the Great Lakes, Oswego was selected as the site for establishing one of the new lights. This light is said to have been a simple stone tower and modest keeper's quarters. The site of the light is supposed to have been on the east side of the Oswego River on the shore of Lake Ontario. By 1836, another expansion of Great Lakes lighthouses was in the making, and the federal lighthouse people elected to plant a better light at the port of Oswego. The new light would be located on the end of the west breakwall and would be topped with a Third Order optic that would show a steady white light. Sources say that this light was visible for 15 miles out onto the lake. The tower itself was of stone, had an octagonal shape and was gray. It was this lighthouse that was in the charge of Keeper Freeman as the 1851 season began to draw to a close.

Until the establishment of the Coast Guard in 1915, the official dates for the closing of navigation on the Great Lakes had far more to do with insurance companies and contracts than navigation regulations. Such was very true in 1851, and although most of the vessels had already been tied up for the winter for nearly a full month by Saturday, December 20, there were still a number of vessels and owners willing to challenge Lake Ontario. The desire to squeeze every last dollar out of their boats caused many an owner and many a master to wink at the late date and go after another cargo. Still, traffic in and out of Oswego was quite sporadic, and for that reason, and the fact that navigation was supposed to be officially closed, Keeper Freeman did not light his lamp every night. Normally, he knew in advance who was due in and about when, so on those nights he would go out and activate his lighthouse. This simple-sounding act was actually quite a chore in late December. Since the lighthouse was located on the end of an extended breakwall, the best way to get out to it was to row across the open mouth of the river. In any hint of weather, the low breakwater was normally swamped and nearly unpassable on foot. The trip out, however, was one that Freeman had made countless times in all kinds of weather, so he probably thought nothing of the dangers involved. Still, Freeman was described at this point in his life as being "aged," and no doubt the task of rowing out to the light was hard on him.

As that December Saturday passed, a winter gale blew across Lake Ontario. The ice that had already formed behind the breakwater was now broken into large cakes that were shoved against the piers and shore, grinding together in the waves. Across the mouth of the river, whitecapped seas grew and soon the entire distance between the lighthouse and Freeman was a heaving churn of ice water. Duty was what was most on the mind of the aged lighthouse keeper and not the current state of the local weather. There were several lakeboats due in and they may have to run into the river during the hours of darkness. Many lives would depend on that steady white light that was Freeman's responsibility. As dusk approached, Freeman engaged the assistance of two strong oarsmen who once bundled up in layers of clothing to fend off the cold, boarded a rowboat and headed for the light.

Rowing against a strong wind from off any of the Great Lakes can be a chilling exercise in mid-summer, so doing the same task in late December is beyond freezing. Waves came slopping into the tiny boat and sloshed among the feet of the three occupants. There were no high-tech or chemically treated fabrics to fight off the cold and wet and lock in the heat of the body. This was the year 1851 and the best that anyone could wear were layers of hand woven wool and cotton augmented by buckskin and fur overclothing or oilskins. Footwear was of leather and waterproofed with saddle or mink oil, if anything. To say that the trip out to the lighthouse was wet and cold would certainly be an understatement. Through the entire trip a near blizzard of snow was spit from the deep gray skies and the wind came at the three men with a chilling bite the likes of which none of them could remember from— even the most bitter of winter nights. If it were not for the exercise of pulling at the oars, surely each of them would have been stricken by the cold. It was the thought of those mariners out on that open, angry lake that kept the heat in their souls and drove them on. Perhaps by that strength alone they reached the breakwater and the lighthouse.

Freeman fetched the whale oil fuel, climbed the steps within the tower, and succeeded in lighting the beacon. The work inside did absolutely nothing to warm the three men. Inside the tower there was only the shelter from the wind and snow, but the bitter December cold saturated the structure like a frozen tomb. It seemed as if every structure, every fixture and every drop of water was waiting for the opportunity to sap the warmth from any of the three men who should be luckless enough to come into contact with it. As soon as the light was fully functioning, Freeman and his two oarsmen returned to their little craft and began the row back to Oswego, and hopefully something—anything—warm! This part of the trip should be easy because they were pulling the boat *with* the wind, or so they thought. The reality is that a rowboat is best controlled while heading into the wind and seas, and so they found that the boat was nearly impossible to keep on any sort of course. Soon they found themselves firmly in the grip of the wind and being shoved directly toward the teeth of the cakes of ice that the storm had blown ashore. Now, there was no stopping the rowboat's appointment with the tossing cakes of ice. Soon the men were no longer concerned with their cold feet, but with a battle for their lives between the ice and the gale. Oars did double-duty pushing at the ice cakes and gouging pointlessly at the frigid water. In this struggle the men became their own worst enemies, and soon their thrashing let the wind, waves and ice have its way with the rowboat. In a bitter cold instant the boat was rolled over and all three men were deposited into the icy water.

No one who has not been previously immersed in the frigid winter water of the Great Lakes can fully expect the shock of the cold. The sting is like

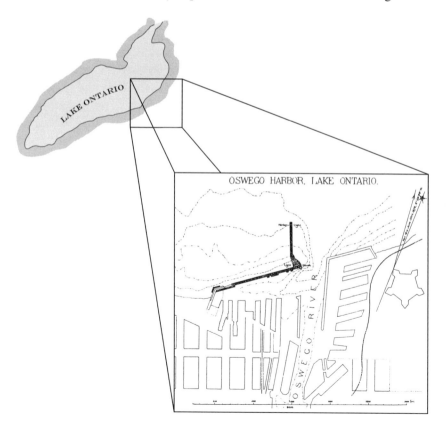

OSWEGO HARBOR, LAKE ONTARIO.

being stabbed by shards of broken glass on every inch of skin all at once. Every ounce of life seems to instantly drain from the depths of the body as the numbing sensation of impending death grows instantly near. Teeth instantly chatter without control as the body tries in vain to regenerate the heat that is rapidly being lost. The joints of the body instantly cramp and limbs refuse to function as the lake comes to take you into its cold depths forever. The bundled layers of clothing now worked against them. The bitter water saturated the garments and held the cold against the skin. To make matters worse the saturated clothing now weighed the men down and threatened to pull them under. Each struggled to regain the overturned boat and somehow keep their heads above the water. Their instantly benumbed hands worked at what they hoped would be a grip on the capsized boat as the waves slapped rudely at their faces and the snow spit at what remained of their lives. The winds and waves began to do their best at shoving the castaways and their boat beneath the cakes of ice and to their doom.

This would probably be the end of our story had it not been for Captain Malcom Bronson. Watching from west side lower dock, Captain Bronson had witnessed the struggle of the tiny rowboat and its three occupants as they ventured from the lighthouse. The moment that the little boat turned turtle, the captain wasted not a heartbeat before springing into action. In moments he obtained the help of three other men and they all set out in a small boat to rescue Keeper Freeman and his oarsmen. The storm, however, was not about to be beaten so easily. Now the winds gave up on pushing them under the ice and began to push the overturned rowboat toward the legs of a pier where they would surely be dashed against the thicket of wooden piles and drowned. The scene turned into a desperate race as Captain Bronson's boat attempted to reach the castaways before they were thrust into the piles. It probably took no small degree of skill to reach the three frozen men. Then, pulling them into the second boat without capsizing it, too, was likely a major undertaking. Freeman was unconscious and had to be dragged from the water, but all three were eventually brought aboard the rescue boat and later placed on dry land. It was a cold and frozen rescue, but it was certain that the four men in the rescue boat felt a special sense of pride following the event. On many occasions, Freeman and his lighthouse had saved the lives of Bronson and every other master who worked Oswego, and now the score was somewhat closer to being even.

For some time after his dunking in the frigid lake, Freeman languished in a state of insensibility. There were grave concerns for the aged keeper, but he later recovered fully. This one event speaks volumes of the lighthouse keepers and their sense of duty. It is likely that Freeman never gave a thought to his own safety until after his lighthouse was illuminated. Up until that point his motivation and concern was for the mariners and vessels that may be depending on his lighthouse.

The hazard of moving keepers out to a lighthouse has always existed, and even in modern times there have been losses of keepers on their way to and from lighthouses. A case in point being a 1942 boat accident that killed a crew of Coast Guardsmen on their way out to change crews at the Oswego Light. This was not the same light that was tended by Samuel Freeman. That light was replaced by the current light in 1934, which is located nearly a half-mile farther out into the lake and the lost Coast Guardsmen had a greater distance to travel, but the duty was the same. It is doubtful that in the despair of the loss of that crew, anyone gave a thought to the number of other close calls and losses that had occurred under similar circumstances.

Today the port of Oswego is a quiet place indeed. The big lakers do not find much business in the tiny town and its port these days. Even the small private recreational vessels navigate by way of the Global Positioning System's network of orbiting satellites, and there is very little use for navigation aids as outmoded as lighthouses. The 1934 lighthouse is fully automated and no keeper is needed any longer—the 1942 accident is said to have hastened the automation. Keeper Freeman's light was deactivated when the 1934 light was constructed and later was torn down. The 1822 land-light was also removed, but the original keeper's quarters still remain today. Located just outside old Fort Ontario, the keeper's quarters of the 1822 light are now the quarters for the director of the historic fort. The port, its lights and its keepers have all been largely forgotten by the majority of the Great Lakes community. The sense of duty that was seen in the story of Keeper Freeman's dunking, however, should never be forgotten.

VII
YARN OF DISASTER

It was the 11th day of December, 1909 when Captain Frank J. Hackett guided the lightship *Kewanee* into Cleveland harbor. Coated with a thick layer of ice the wooden lightship seemed to give a sigh of relief as her beam passed safely through the breakwater and into the protected confines of the river. The 1909 season of navigation was over for the *Kewanee* and she could now leave her station at Southeast Shoal and tie up for a well-earned winter rest. Likewise, Captain Hackett and his crew had earned their return to dry land. Sub-zero temperatures made the lines stiffen as the lightship's crew secured their boat to the dock. In less time than it takes to cook lunch the *Kewanee* was buttoned up and idled for the winter.

Much like a floating lighthouse, lightships were used to mark hazardous areas of navigation. To all of the mariners who worked the Great Lakes, the spot marked by the *Kewanee* was considered to be one of the most treacherous areas to navigate. Due south of Point Pelee and north of Pelee Island, Ontario, the Southeast Shoal is part of the narrow corridor that makes up the zigzag of "Pelee Passage." Westbound traffic that departs from any port east of Cleveland must run the gauntlet of shoals and islands that makes up the passage, in order to enter the Detroit River and proceed to the upper lakes. The bones of many a proud laker are resting in the shallow waters near the Pelee Passage bottleneck. Thus, the service of assorted beacons, horns and buoys have been used over the years to warn the mariners of the impending dangers. Yet for some reason, the lakers continued to find woe in and around Pelee Passage and Southeast Shoal.

As the 1800s turned into the 1900s and the industrial boom on the lakes was in full swing, it became clear that something had to be done about the hazard of Pelee Passage—and Southeast Shoal in particular. The problem

The lighthouse tender Kewaunee served as a compromise lightship on Southeast Shoal from 1901 until 1910.

was that the shoal itself was in Canadian waters, and the Dominion was largely reluctant to place a light there. A solution came from the Lake Carriers Association which entered into a contract with the United States Lighthouse Board for the maintaining of a lightship on Southeast Shoal. It was calculated that the lightship would cost $4,000 to operate each season, an expense that was covered through a special appropriation from the United States Government. Constructed in 1900, the *Kewanee* first appears in the annual reports of the Lighthouse Board as being in service in the 1902 season. Interestingly, since the board did not maintain the lightship, unlike every other lightvessel on the lakes at that time, she was not assigned a number. Her contracted operation with the Lake Carriers Association did, however, keep her free of the political baggage that would be expected to come with the placing of a U.S. Government vessel in Canadian waters. Her beacon not only signaled the location of Southeast Shoal, but a compromise to a difficult political situation.

This lightship was actually a conversion from a steam-powered lighthouse tender. Measuring 106.8 feet in length, 24 feet in beam and 8.4 feet in

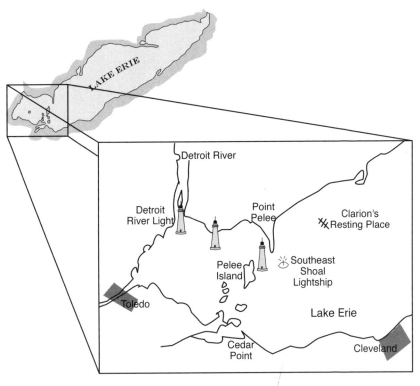

depth, the little lightship displaced 143 gross tons and was assigned an official number of 161165. Since she was actually not under the control of the Lighthouse Board, there is no record as to exactly what type of illumination equipment was installed aboard her. What is on record is that her original owner was James Smith of her namesake port. Later she was purchased by George P. McKay of Cleveland who probably was the person running her as a lightship for the Lake Carriers Association.

For Captain Hackett, this end of the 1909 season could not have come quickly enough. In fact, for all of the mariners on Lake Erie, the close of this terrible season of navigation was a welcomed event. By the time that the *Kewanee* closed her season the death toll on the lakes had reached nearly four times that of 1908. Lake Superior had taken 40 mariners to their doom and Lake Michigan had swallowed six souls while Lake Huron had reportedly not taken a single life. That report, however, was incorrect as one crewman from the steamer *Caledonia* had fallen overboard on Saginaw Bay and in another incident the cook from the schooner *Rose Simmons* had gone insane and jumped overboard, making Lake Huron's death toll two persons. In a disastrous year this was a record low death count for the lake that normally had claimed more than its share of mariners. Astonishingly, Lake Erie had more than made up for Lake Huron's shortcoming as 75 mariners had found their doom there—two-thirds of them being killed in less than two days in December. Those were among the days leading up to the end of the *Kewanee's* season. Nursing a frostbitten foot, Hackett limped along the lightship's deck as the last of her winter lay-up lines were made secure. Still fresh in his heart was the feeling of utter helplessness in witnessing the horror in Lake Erie's most recent tantrum. There was the vision of a vessel aflame, another run aground, and a lifeboat filled with a doomed crew that replayed over and over in the back of his mind. Indeed, December of 1909 would not be soon forgotten by Hackett, but the eighth and ninth of that month would stand out as the most ghastly days. In that 24-hour period, $100,000 in losses would be incurred with the loss of three lakers and 52 souls.

Notice of the appalling death toll on Lake Erie during that disturbing week was taken by many others, among them being Harry Coulby, the president of the Pittsburg Steamship Company, and William Livingston, the president of the Lake Carriers Association. Coulby elected to take drastic steps with his fleet of tin-stackers announcing: "As long as I am connected with the Pittsburg Steamship Company, navigation, so far as this company is concerned, will close officially on November 30. We will not load the vessels of our fleet nor will we charter outside tonnage to load after that date."

Livingston was of a like mind stating, " I think that it would be better for all interests concerned if the season of navigation would close every year on December 1. On an average of years the carriers would be men and money ahead."

Such declarations were prudent, but were far too late for the mariners lost that week. It was also too late to wipe the images of disaster from the minds of Captain Hackett and the crew of his lightship.

Wednesday, December 8, started out with the continuation of Tuesday's wild gale. Winds in the previous 24 hours had reached hurricane force in some areas of Lake Erie and a blinding snow had blanketed the whole lake. Aboard the *Kewanee*, Hackett was keeping a close watch on the lightship's oil illuminated beacon. Its light would be needed, not only to warn of the shoal, but also to keep storm-tossed lakers from ramming the lightship. Dawn revealed the south, southwest gale thrashing large cakes of ice all around the vessel, and the waves towered toward 18 feet in height as the clouds reached down toward whitecapped seas. The crew of the *Kewanee* knew all too well that those mariners navigating this treacherous passage of Lake Erie were relying on the lightship for their very lives. What Hackett and his crew of three could not know was that the lake had already claimed the big carferry *Marquette & Bessemer No. 2* somewhere to the east of the lightship's position. Modern accounts vary in the carferry's death toll as being 31 to 36 souls, but the bodies and wreckage from the boat would wash up for the next year from Long Point to Buffalo. Lake Erie, however, was not satisfied with that vessel, and continued to rage all day Wednesday in search of its next casualty.

Held in place by her moorings the lightship *Kewanee* had been showered by the spray from the breaking seas all day Tuesday, and now resembled an iceberg with a beacon atop. Shadowed in the snowy distance only an occasional lakeboat passed on either the upbound or downbound track in spite of the gale. The temperature on the open lake had dropped to 10 degrees below zero and only the thrashing waves kept the lake from freezing solid. In all, it was a long Wednesday aboard the lightship, and it was about to get longer. As nightfall set in the snow began to let up a bit, but the wind continued to wail from the southwest. Shortly before nine o'clock on that ugly evening, Hackett caught sight of a flickering orange glow out in the snowy darkness. The continuing snow squalls obscured the lake, but it was obvious that some stricken vessel was afire out there. What soon became more alarming was that the floating blaze was upwind of the wooden-hulled *Kewanee* and drifting in Captain Hackett's direction.

For what seemed like several hours, but was actually minutes, Hackett watched the glowing vessel as it neared his position. By this time the crew of the lightship had joined him and everyone was speculating, not only as to what vessel it was, but on how close it would come to the *Kewanee's* position. It would take a great deal of time to raise the mooring anchors and move the lightship, and even at that the storm was likely to beat her down if she were to let go of her firm anchorage. Certainly the *Kewanee's* meager power plant was no match for such a storm and Hackett was left with one option—hold tight and let the cards of disaster play out. Soon the burning vessel was close enough that the actual flames were visible and it was becoming possible to distinguish the outline of the superstructure. Apparently, she was drifting directly at the *Kewanee* and she was no small boat at that. From what he could already see, Hackett concluded that she was one of the big package steamers. But even as the guessing as to the vessel's name continued, Lake Erie upped the stakes of terror.

"Look!" one of the *Kewanee's* crew shouted, pointing toward the burning monster, "There's men still aboard her!"

Indeed, a close look at the mass of flames revealed the images of crew scrambling about the deck. As the ill-fated laker drifted closer the shouts of distress from the poor souls could be heard over the storm winds. So close did the burning vessel come to the *Kewanee* that she was easily recognizable —it was the *Clarion*.

Closer and closer the burning hulk was blown toward the *Kewanee*, but happenstance saved the day for the lightship. It was apparent that the flaming package vessel would not collide with the defenseless lightship, but would pass within 100 feet of her, close enough to feel the heat. For Hackett and his crew, however, there would be a price for this spectacle that was nearly as horrible as a collision. It appeared that they would be forced to witness helplessly as the lake played its death game with the *Clarion* and her crew. Silhouetted by the mass of flames that once were the vessel's cabins were the images of frantic mariners moving along the deck in a stage show of disaster. At the *Kewanee's* rail her four crewmember's stood glued to the inferno as it passed. As the *Clarion* neared its closest point to the lightship, some of the crew of the burning steamer mustered around one of her lifeboats. A gaggle of crew boarded the yawl and, illuminated by their burning vessel, successfully lowered it to the thrashing seas in a desperate effort to reach the *Kewanee*. A moment later the bobbing lifeboat was swallowed whole by Lake Erie and all aboard went to their icy doom. Now there appeared to remain about a half dozen souls aboard the *Clarion* and to the men of the *Kewanee* the options for these men appeared to be either jump into raging lake, or burn alive aboard the steamer. Captain Hackett ordered one of the crew to the *Kewanee's* 8-inch Modoc whistle to begin blowing a distress signal. The echoes of the whistle probably reached less than a half-mile into the screaming gale, but it was better than simply standing there and doing nothing. From the incinerating steamer, the cries for help could still be heard as the silhouettes beckoned to the crew of the *Kewanee*, in the background the Modoc whistle bellowed, Lake Erie continued to rage and the lightship's crew watched helplessly.

Reportedly, the *Clarion* "departed" Detroit at noon on that same awful Wednesday in the company of the steamer *H. P. Bope*. The package freighter had started her voyage at the port of Chicago and made it as far as Detroit under routine conditions. Accounts of the day are unclear as to if the *Clarion* had stopped in Detroit to load or unload additional cargo, or was simply waiting for Tuesday's wild weather to blow itself out. For whatever reason, Captain Bell had elected to leave the relative safety of the Detroit River and take the *Clarion* out onto Lake Erie. In good weather the *Clarion* slugged along at about 10 miles per hour, but when entering Lake Erie into the teeth of a southern gale the package freighter's "over the bottom" speed was cut to about six miles per hour at full steam. Those closely-spaced, sharp waves for which Lake Erie is so infamous attacked her long before the Detroit River Light had been reached. Even the modern day lake mariners find the channel leading into Lake Erie from the Detroit River to be shallow and narrow and no place to be caught off guard. In the face of this December gale, it was all that Captain Bell could do to keep his boat in the channel.

The pressures that drive a vessel master to depart into appalling weather conditions are hard to appreciate when we are far removed from the pilot-house at that particular time and place. Vessel managers who were more concerned with the safety of their boats than with the bottom line in profits, such as Harry Colby, were few around the turn of the century. A master who was considered "timid" could easily find himself serving the next season as a mate, or worse. Even in modern times when lake shipping companies are spring-loaded to the caution position and prone to order their bottoms into shelter from an approaching gale, being "too timid" can be considered a poor quality in a skipper. In 1909, the captains who were the "heavy weather" masters were those most wanted by vessel managers. Completing a trip or two in weather that caused other boats to anchor in shelter could mean that margin of profit that would keep the vessel barons competitive. And that desk where the accounting ledgers are balanced at the end of the season is a

After serving three decades on the Lakes the Clarion ended her career as the crew of the Southeast Shoal Lightship watched in horror.

great distance from that pilothouse where the wind is screaming and sleet is pelting on the windows. Reasons for sheltering seem to ring hollow in the ears of the accountants as the profit line is drawn months after the weather decisions have been made. For Captain Bell, other factors entered into the equation. This was the last trip of what had been a very hard season, other vessels were heading out onto the lake and the gale may have appeared to be letting up a bit. Also, this was an era when men such as Bell routinely ignored storm signals and pushed right ahead into all kinds of weather with the general attitude that no wind could blow that could beat down their vessel. So, for motivations that were completely his own, Bell directed the *Clarion* into the maelstrom that was Lake Erie. Oddly, the gale would not be the source of Bell's undoing.

Working faithfully since her launch at the Detroit Dry Dock Company in 1881, the *Clarion* would close out her 28th season with this run to Erie, Pennsylvania. After more than two dozen seasons of doing battle with the worst that the Great Lakes could throw at her, the rugged steamer showed few signs of age. Such resistance was due mainly to the boat's "composite" construction. Composite vessels normally had framing and some upper works made of iron and then were sheathed with oak planking. This method allowed the boat to take advantage of the strength of iron and the flexibility of wood. In the era when icebreakers were nearly unknown and harbors were studded with boulders, the iron and wood combination suited many a vesselman and their insurance underwriters as well. In fact in the era of the *Clarion's* birth, a substantially lower rate could be gotten for a iron-hulled boat by simply lining her bottom with oak planks. As time passed, hulls of all-iron construction were found to be some of the strongest ever constructed. In fact, when the time came to send an old iron hull to the scrap yard the ship-breakers often had great difficulty taking them apart. However, the forces of economics spelled the end of the composite hulls and the iron hulls, and not the forces of the Great Lakes. Steel hull plating soon became cheaper and more abundant than either iron or oak thus bringing an end to the days of iron construction.

Specifically designed to haul package cargo, vessels such as the *Clarion* were meant to bridge the gap that the railroads could not. Along the upper lakes shoreline in 1881, when the *Clarion* was built, most of the towns were accessible only by boat. Supplies for every aspect of living in these areas needed to be transported by lakeboats such as the *Clarion*. Everything from sewing machines to baking powder could be loaded through side-ports in the boat's hull and stacked in the form of a floating warehouse. The wares were then transported to waiting communities that were not accessible by rail. By 1909, the job had changed a bit. Now, rather than supplementing the rail service, the *Clarion* was bypassing the rail service and was the direct competition to the iron horses.

Beating her way south, through the lower Detroit River, the *Clarion* was soon clear of the protection of the Michigan and Ontario shorelines. The blizzard which had swept around the boat on the Detroit River seemed much more intense as Lake Erie welcomed Captain Bell into its grasp. A nasty roll began as the vessel battled her way though the storm-tossed channel. From her pilothouse, the *Clarion's* master had to strain to spot the buoys and lights that marked the channel. Each of the pilothouse windows had become obscured with a translucent coating of ice and frozen snow and even with the windows opened the path ahead was sackcloth-black. Atop the boat's pilothouse on the open-air bridge, the wheelsman was nearly blinded by the sleet. Fortunately, Bell knew the zigs and zags of Lake Erie well enough to make the run blindfolded, and he easily reckoned the turns that headed him toward Pelee Passage. Beneath the captain's feet the *Clarion's* hold was packed with sacks, crates and barrels containing flour, lard, and cattle feed. All of this seemed a harmless cargo when the stevedores brought it through the side-ports and shoved it aboard. What none of the *Clarion's* people gave consideration to, however, was that when exposed to an open flame the air-borne powder of flour is as explosive as gunpowder, the lard and oil-cakes would burn like kerosene and the cattle feed would do its best to nourish a blaze.

Fire was the last thing on Bell's mind as he squinted through the pilothouse window in the hope of sighting the Southeast Shoal lightship. The darkness of night had smothered in around the *Clarion* long before she reached Pelee Island and now the snow squalls came leaping out of the blackness without warning. After what seemed like a full night's steaming time, but it was in reality just past seven o'clock in the evening, the dim glow of the lightship was spotted. Beyond the Southeast Shoal lightship there was just over 50 miles of open lake between the *Clarion* and the port of Erie. Although no records exist documenting the vessel's exact movements that night, circumstance seems to indicate that, considering the winds, Bell planned to clear the northern tip of Pelee Island and then run south, southeast hugging the lee of the island as near as he dared. If he could keep her in deep enough water the *Clarion* would not be blown near the shallows around the lightship. Once well below the shoal he could haul due east and make for Erie with the gale near to his heels. The whole distance was with the quartering wind and Bell knew that his boat was more than a match for the miles ahead. When the seas moderated, the pilothouse crew knew that they were coming into the lee of Pelee Island and the time to outfox the storm was at hand. Sighting on the Pelee Island and Pelee Passage lights, Bell ordered his wheelsman to head her south and the obedient package freighter skidded through the narrow gap. Now it would be about a seven-mile run until the Middle Island Light came into sight. At about the same time as the vessel cleared the island's lee and the seas returned, the haul toward Erie would be made. By dawn the *Clarion* should be steaming safely into the harbor. As the *Clarion's* captain was considering his success against the lake, the doom of his vessel was beginning to spark three decks below.

Keeping a watch on the *Clarion's* engine works was Chief Engineer A. E. Welch, and joining him in the engineroom was Second Engineer John Graham. Dinner was just finished and Second Cook Michael Toomey was left to clean up as the engine crew changed shifts. Shoveling the coal that gave the *Clarion* the power to plow through the storm was now in the hands of Harry Murray who took turns with Theodore Larson and Joseph Baker in rotating shifts. Unlike some boats, the crew of Chief Welch's engineroom were a close-knit group and loyal to the boat as well as the chief. When it came time to change shifts in the engineroom, there was no complaint. In fact, the atmosphere was indeed lighthearted, in spite of the storm. This was the last trip of the season and all aboard the *Clarion* were looking forward to soon being home for the winter. Lit only by the dim glow of a few lamps augmented perhaps with a single incandescent light bulb, and garnished with black coal dust, the fire-hold's normal gloom was overwhelmed tonight by the fever of the season's end.

Shortly before seven o'clock in the evening, Chief Welch's nose detected a smell that did not normally hang in the overheated atmosphere of his engineroom. Casually he strolled over to his second engineer.

"Smell that?" he asked Graham.

Wrinkling his nose Graham dutifully sniffed a series of samples of the surrounding air.

"Yeah," the puzzled second engineer retorted, smells like wood burnin'."

"Go see if you can find it." Welch assigned.

Graham put aside what he was doing and headed up the companionway to investigate the smell, which seemed now to be getting fairly strong. In what seemed like a heartbeat the second engineer came scrambling back down the stairs in a near panic.

"There's a fire amidships!" he cried at the top of his lungs.

In that same instant billows of smoke came rolling aft through every crack in the engineroom.

No one knows exactly where or how the fire began. Perhaps one of the oil lamps used to illuminate the odd areas of the cargo hold was tossed from its peg with the rolling of the boat, or a careless crewmember discarded smoking material in just the wrong place or some other type of spark sprang up to cause the flame. It mattered not—in a matter of moments the fire was burning readily. As the *Clarion* wallowed past Pelee Island on that fitful December night, she was already burning deep in her hold and nobody knew it. By the time that Graham discovered the flames, it was far too late to stop the inferno. Again, there is no record as to exactly when or who came crashing into the pilothouse to report that the *Clarion* was now carrying an inferno where the cargo should be, but what is recorded is that when the event was discovered the whole crew manned the fire extinguishers. It is important not to think of this event in terms of modern vessels with Halon flood systems, fire resistant suits and powerful fire extinguishers. This was 1909 and the term "fire extinguisher" was more apt to describe a hand-pumped can or water bucket. First Mate James Thompson dutifully rushed into the cargo with his extinguisher at the ready, he never returned. In just minutes the situation had escalated to become terrifyingly hopeless. The wooden conduits that held the fragile wiring which powered the *Clarion's* meager lighting soon burned through and the boat went black with only the flaming cabins left to illuminate the scene. Now the engineroom crew were driven from their stations and the deck crew were driven from their rooms by the thick billows of smoke that were rapidly followed by flames. The *Clarion* was about to swiftly incinerate herself and those aboard her were now faced with an awful choice, burn or drown.

It was at this moment that the crew of the *Kewanee* were watching the horrible exhibition. Drifting close by the blazing *Clarion* illuminated the night so that those on the lightship could not miss the images of the desperate men attempting to launch one of the lifeboats. Rolling insanely, the *Clarion* dipped the dangling lifeboat in the seas and then ripped it back into the air. Ice-cold lake water flung across the freighter's hull and hissed against the superheated iron workings as the cabins crackled and popped in their fiery delight. Choking billows of thick smoke poured from every opening as the *Clarion's* hull moaned and squealed in a frightening melody. From the lightship, it appeared as if a dozen men were in the lifeboat as it continued to be lowered on the leeward side of the burning vessel. No sooner had the yawl been released from the *Clarion* than the angry lake reached up and engulfed it and its occupants forever. The waves were so large and the sea churned to the point where a tiny lifeboat stuffed with castaways was easily overturned, and in lake water whose temperature was right at freezing, human life was snuffed out in an instant. This left only seven men on the stern of the burning boat as it drifted away from the Southeast Shoal light-ship. They scrambled up and down the deck like bugs that suddenly discover themselves at the edge of a campfire and their cries for help were so shrill that they could be heard above the gale. Never had any of those aboard the *Kewanee* experienced such a hollow felling of helplessness, surely the entire crew of the *Clarion* would perish before their eyes.

Remaining on the *Clarion's* stern were Chief Welch, Second Engineer Graham, Crewmen "Mac" McCauley, Coal Shovers Larson, Murray and Baker and Second Cook Toomey. The situation could not have looked more hopeless as the flames made rapid progress in their direction. Soon they would have no choice other than jumping into the frigid lake. The launching of the leeward lifeboat and its instant swallowing by Lake Erie showed the folly of attempting to escape by use of the lifeboats. Still McCauley was unconvinced that the *Clarion* would send him to his doom that easily. Making his way over to the windward side of the boat, McCauley began to struggle with the other lifeboat. The smashing of the seas on the windward beam would make the launching of the boat on that side impossible, but McCauley was determined to drag the yawl to the leeward side and launch it. As an ant would grapple with a twig that is a dozen times its own weight, so did Mac with the lifeboat. By this time the seas were boarding the *Clarion* and washing over the deck. Between the cascades of bitter water the benumbed crewman wrestled at dragging his lifeboat to the other side of the deck. Suddenly, Lake Erie reached out and ended McCauley's toil. A single massive sea swept the deck and washed both Mac and his lifeboat forever away into the annals of Great Lakes tragedy. Seeing this, the remaining crew knew that their own end was soon to come—it was just a matter of waiting.

Just when the scene appeared hopeless, a pair of the mightiest lakeboats afloat shoved through the blizzard to the rescue. The lights of the 552-footer *Josiah G. Munro*, and the 524 footer *Leonard C. Hanna* hove onto the scene like two massive saviors. Keeping the valor that terrible night were Captain C. E. Sayre, aboard the *Munro* and Captain Matthew Anderson, aboard the *Hanna*. Both men focused steely eyes on the six mariners who were stranded aboard the *Clarion*. Their goal was to run in close to the flaming vessel and save those crewmen, no matter what. Circumstances of this effort went far

In an effort to save the Clarion's crew, Captain Sayre ran the Munro solidly aground on Southeast Shoal. (From the collection of the Milwaukee Public Library)

beyond running vessels in proximity. The *Clarion* had drifted past the lightship which, after all, was there to mark the shallows and treacherous reefs in the area. One of the worst gales in Lake Erie's history, a storm that had already consumed the giant carferry *Marquette & Bessemer No. 2* and its entire crew, was at its high point. Any damage that should be inflicted on the vessels, regardless of the circumstances or humane intent, would be blamed directly on the captains. Dollar losses are the master's responsibility and the office-bound bean-counters would have no mercy on a captain who causes such a loss. A venture such as this could cost either skipper his command come spring. Vessel managers like masters who take chances, but only if it is to bring a paying cargo into port. Both Captains Sayre and Anderson knew this lesson as well as they knew their vessels and the waterways on which they sailed. They steamed ahead anyway.

As if to provide a clear view of the drama to come, the snow squalls parted and allowed the crew of the lightship *Kewanee* a front-row seat. Captain Sayre drove the *Munro* in toward the *Clarion* in his effort at rescuing the stranded crew. No sooner had the *Munro* hauled toward the flaming package vessel than the oreboat gave a lurch and shuddered to a sudden halt. Having run hard aground, the *Munro* was now out of the rescue effort, and Sayre and his crew could do nothing more than watch as the *Clarion* drifted out of reach. Seeing the *Munro* snag the shallows, Anderson quickly calculated a different plan for the *Hanna*. Using little more than his mariner's instinct he ordered his big oreboat on a seven-mile arc around the shallows to a point where the winds would bring the *Hanna* and *Clarion* together. Like a racing snail the *Hanna* drew a distance from the other boats. Slowly her dim amber lights grew faint and then changed direction back toward the *Clarion*. Once his boat was back within the reach of the *Clarion*, it took a bit of maneuvering to line up with the drifting wreck. Nearly four hours had passed since Graham discovered the fire, and now the prospect of rescue was apparently at hand. From the *Kewanee* the view was now little more than that of lights coming into the path of distant flames and little detail could be seen. As the two vessels came together the light of the flaming package freighter illuminated a portion of the rescue boat for a moment, then the lights of the *Hanna* moved rapidly off into the storm. Soon the snow squalls returned and all that was visible in the distance was the dim orange glow of the *Clarion* as she continued to incinerate herself. The show was now over and the crews of the *Kewanee* and *Munro* could only hope that the *Hanna* had succeeded. Returning to the warmth of the lightship *Kewanee's* cabin, Captain Frank J.

Captain Anderson took it upon himself to put the Leonard C. Hanna between doom and the crew of the Clarion. (From the collection of the Milwaukee Public Library)

Hackett discovered that amidst the drama and sub-zero temperatures his foot had frozen. In all of the trepidation he had not noticed that the cold had gotten him.

At seven o'clock Thursday evening, exactly 24 hours after John Graham had discovered the fire aboard the *Clarion*, the Lake Shore Limited came to a stop in Buffalo and the six survivors of the wreck stepped onto the platform. Clad in his warmest winter overcoat and bowler hat, a reporter from the *Buffalo Express* craned his neck and dashed his glance up and down the platform attempting to spot the half-dozen castaways among the disembarking passengers. It was so cold that the reporter was certain that his mustache would shatter like glass if he should sneeze. It was that fact alone that gave away the identities of the *Clarion* survivors. They had escaped with only the clothes on their backs, and were thus the only passengers getting off of the train who were apparently underdressed. With the reporter in tow, the six survivors made their way into the warmth of the station.

"Oh, but it's good to be back in Buffalo," Chief Welch commented as the reporter scribbled the words onto his notepad. "We never thought that we'd make it out there in that black storm with a burning boat under us and no rescue for four hours. I didn't think we had a ghost of a show." The chief's words soon began to weave a firsthand yarn of disaster as the reporter scribbled more rapidly. "Captain Bell and the forward crew had lowered the metallic lifeboat and made off, 13 in all. They headed toward the lightship, but we never saw them again."

Using a most nonchalant manner the mariners went on to describe their rescue by the *Hanna*. Once near the *Clarion*, Captain Anderson made a series of maneuvers to allow the wind to shove the *Clarion* stern-first into his beam. Rising and falling on seas that the survivors described as being "20 feet high," the flaming wreck pounded her stern against the *Hanna*. With the groan of unhappy steel plate meeting iron plate and wooden fenders the two boats ground together in a dance of desperation. One by one the *Clarion's* crew waited until the decks of the rocking vessels were about even and then they jumped for their lives. Lake Erie would only allow the two boats to rub together for a few moments before she reached out and attempted to pull them apart. Chief Welch was the last man off and his was a leap of remarkable distance that only a person who is jumping for their life can make. And make it he did, leaving the *Clarion* to her own ends on the lake. Welch would be back at his home at 308 Plymouth Street and Graham would be at his residence at 20 Heath Street before the portrayal that they had given would appear in the paper, or fully sink in the reporter's thoughts.

A total of 15 brave mariners had perished right before the eyes of the men that he had interviewed and then they had been forced to leap for their very existence from one giant lakeboat to another. It seemed such a bitter cold fate to meet and a terrible choice to be forced to make, the reporter's thoughts pondered the experience of the *Clarion's* crew. Then it suddenly occurred to him, surely, he had a front-page story on his hands!

On the Saturday following the loss of the *Clarion*, Captain Hackett had gotten the *Kewanee* ready for her long winter's lay-up. It was not until the *Kewanee* had reached Cleveland that the lightship's crew got the news that the six men on the *Clarion* had successfully been removed from the wreck and taken to Cleveland where they boarded the Lake Shore Limited train for Buffalo. Still limping from his frostbitten foot, the lightship's keeper would thrill guest and friend alike through out the dark winter nights with the tale of the *Clarion* as he told it time and again, embellishing here and there when needed.

By the time that winter released Lake Erie from its ice bondage, Hackett's yarn of disaster had lost most of its drama among the din of the lake fleet fitting out for the new season. In fact, most folks had little or no interest in his yarn of that horrible December night. Surely the 1910 season would bring new and more exciting events worthy of other yarnings. With the promise of this new season in mind, Hackett prepared his lightship once again. By April 10, 1910, the *Kewanee* was back on station and her light was warning the lakeboats of the dangers of Southeast Shoal. In less than two months, however, the ways of politics and nations would finally take effect and Hackett's charge would be relieved from Pelee Passage for the last time. On June 5, 1910 the Canadian government would establish their own lightship on Southeast Shoal and in doing so made the *Kewanee's* use pointless. On that date Hackett removed the lightship from Pelee Passage for the last time.

No one saw the *Clarion* actually sink, but she ended up in 70 feet of water to the northeast of the Southeast Shoal Light. In fact the vessel drifted about 16 miles beyond Hackett's station before her burning hull went to the bottom. For a few days there was speculation that the 13 men in the metallic yawl that Captain Bell had used to escape his burning vessel, may be found alive. In the following days it was rumored that they may soon be found frozen stiff. In fact they were never found and remain to this day listed as "missing" on Lake Erie.

Captain Sayre managed to get the *Munro* off of the reef with little more than a few scratches and that vessel went on to sail productive seasons until it was scrapped in 1967 as the *Lebanon*. The *Hanna* worked until 1965 when she too went to the ship-breakers. Interestingly, both of the rescue boats ended their days in the same fleet, that of the Bethlehem Steel Corporation. With them went the last physical players in the yarn of the *Clarion's* disaster. It is interesting to wonder if through her career, the *Hanna* carried a dent or two in her steel hull plates where the ill-fated *Clarion* had banged against her on that terrible night in 1909. The odds are good that season after season, crewmen painted right over the nondescript dents, never knowing that they were the marks of the boat's forgotten but greatest moment of valor in an otherwise uneventful career. The *Kewanee* only served as a lightship one more time, and that was to mark the wreck of the *Joliet* in the Detroit River in 1912. She did other backwater duties around the lakes until she was abandoned like so many other wooden hulls amidst the Great Depression. Records indicate that she was abandoned in April of 1935, but there is no record as to where.

Lightships no longer work the Great Lakes, having been replaced by automated lights which are cheaper and far easier to maintain. Today, despite Harry Coulby's concerns in 1909, the modern giants of the Pittsburgh Steel ancestry, although no longer under the ownership of lakemen, sail well into the month of January as do most of the lakeboat fleet. Use of oak and iron to build lakers stopped long ago and the last iron-hulled boat left afloat is, as of this writing, only a barge resting in the backwaters of the Saginaw River. Since Captain Hackett and the *Kewanee* were taken off station the commerce of the lakes has seen world wars, depressions, recessions, disasters and countless gales. Through it all the shattered hulk of the iron-hulled *Clarion* has slept in a heap on the dark bottom of Lake Erie. Well north and east of the shipping lanes her wreck is almost totally forgotten and routinely ignored. Today she is falling prey to the infestation of the dreaded zebra mussel and is nothing more than side trip for occasional dive charters. Soon the elements will cause her to fade away as completely as the interest in Captain Hackett's yarn of her loss.

VIII
SPIRITS OF THE POINT

Author's Notes

In researching and creating this chapter, the author found it necessary to travel to Point aux Barques and obtain additional photographs of the keeper's quarters to illustrate the text. The day was overcast with thin gray clouds and the view across the lake was limited by a thick haze on that unusually warm November day as I dashed around the property and snapped photos of the assorted buildings. All of the structures had been locked up tightly for the winter since early October and I was the only person on the grounds. As any photographer would do, I snapped about two rolls of film and captured the buildings from assorted angles. In photographing the keeper's house where Pamela Kennedy had encountered the apparition that is featured in this chapter, I found a clear shot of the front that captured the whole house, then stepped about 50 feet to my left and shot again. About a week later, the film was sent out for processing and returned a day later as finished. Bringing the packages containing the photographs home I spread them out on the coffee table and gave each a quick inspection before returning them to their respective envelopes. Two weeks later, I was carefully sorting out the art work that was to be used in this book and when I got to this chapter I took a good look at the photos of the keeper's house. Of the two best, one was of good contrast and background and could certainly be used, the other appeared to be discardable, because the nose of my car was in the background—it was while making that decision that I saw it. There in the upper front bedroom window, there appeared to be the image of someone pulling aside the sheer curtains and looking out of the window, but in the

This photo was taken first. Notice the closed curtains in all windows—then I stepped 50 feet to my left and...

photo that was taken just 90 seconds earlier and from 50 feet to the left, those same curtains appear to be tightly closed!

Being a skeptic, a researcher and born cynic I could not allow myself to believe my eyes. Certainly I had been pre-disposed to wanting to "see" something there in that window. Perhaps it was a reflection of a branch from some tree in front of the house, or perhaps a defect in the print. I looked at the other photos and saw that there are no trees of the size needed to make such a reflection located in front of that window. Moreover, any such reflection would continue on a line into the adjacent window—this image did not. Next I grabbed my camera and removed the 50 mm lens. Using it like a jeweler's loop I magnified the image for my eye- there was someone there, looking out toward the park area behind the lighthouse. There appeared to be a translucent face and the image appeared to be wearing a high collared white dress. Still convinced that I was talking myself into see-ing things, I took the photo upstairs where my wife and sister-in-law were baking Christmas cookies. My sister-in-law Karen had absolutely no knowl-edge of any aspect of this story so, handing her the photo I asked simply, "Look at those windows and tell me what you see?"

Without an instants hesitation she said, "You mean that one there with someone lookin' out of it?"

Her comment knocked me three steps backward, and a wave of chilled shock came across me the likes of which I have never before experienced. I

*...took this one. Note that someone is peeking from the window. This is **not** a reflection.*

am a professional aviator, a trained observer with a college degree in the sciences, my training causes me to think in terms of physics, facts, limitations, rules and data, but I was holding in my hand a photo of a ghost, and there was no way for me to discount the photographer, because I had taken it myself. In the hours that followed I obtained the negative, and the specter in the window showed up there as well. I scanned the photo into my computer, and enlarged it, enhanced it, reversed it, adjusted it—still the image in the window was there and without explanation. I knew now how Pamela Kennedy must have felt after her encounter with the strange lady that haunts the Pointe aux Barques lighthouse. With that in mind I quickly called Pamela. I asked her to recall everyone who had scoffed at her sighting of the ghost and then told her to call them up and set them straight. They all needed to be told that Pamela Kennedy was not seeing things, because I had the proof, I had the Pointe aux Barques lighthouse ghost on film!

The author attempts to not repeat a location for the setting of stories contained within a given book. However, in the case of the Pointe aux Barques Lighthouse, and the story of the mysterious lady who inhabits the site, the following firsthand account is just too compelling to resist placing within these pages. For that reason, the author must return the readers to the tip of Michigan's thumb and the classic lighthouse which resides there.

When the United States Coast Guard elected to turn the property containing the lighthouse over to the private sector in 1958, the local county was farsighted enough to jump on the opportunity and take charge of the site. Since that point, the light itself has been in the hands of the Coast Guard, but everything surrounding the tower became Huron County property. The original keeper's residence attached to the tower was converted into a maritime museum, and the grounds made into a camping area. To maintain the site, the county has taken to hiring a series of grounds keepers to reside in the newer keeper's dwelling and watch over the facility in general. Enter Ray and Martha Janderwski who in 1992 became the latest of the groundskeepers. For both Ray and Martha the job must have been a unique opportunity, after all they were actually being paid to reside in one of the most beautiful

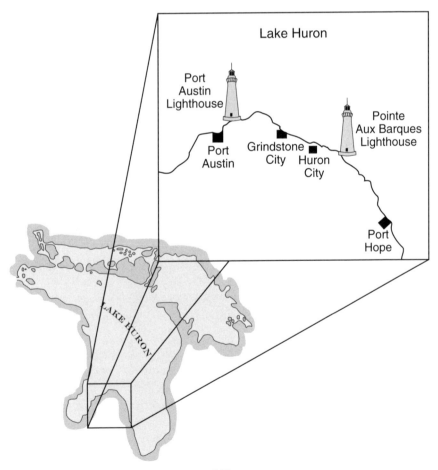

locations on the Great Lakes and to look after one of the most beautiful lighthouses on the lakes as well. What neither of them could know was that there was a lady already watching over the lighthouse, and hers was a vigil that was unpaid and would never, ever, end.

A light was established on Pointe aux Braques in 1847, but the current standing tower was not constructed until 1857. It was originally listed as having a fixed white light with a Third Order optic that was visible for seven miles. Later listings, however show the light as being a flashing white light that osculated at 10-second intervals and was visible for 16 and one-half miles. Listings between 1857 and 1880 also vary in the height of the light, with the 1857 listing showing it as being 65 feet tall, and the 1880 listing showing it as being 79 feet tall. This is easily explained by the fact that the 1857 records used the height from the base of the tower to the center of the beacon. The 1880 listing, on the other hand, used focal plain which is the distance from the average water level to the center of the beacon. Since the lighthouse is constructed on a small bluff, the difference in the two listings is the height of the bluff above Lake Huron. The difference in the distance from which the light can be viewed is likely due to an 1873 refit of the lamp. It is probable that the new flashing characteristic was installed at that time as well.

Soon after Martha and Ray took charge of the lighthouse grounds, they began asking their adult daughter, Pamela, to spend the night in the historic keeper's quarters that was now in their charge. Pamela had been to the lighthouse a number of times, but really had no desire to stay there. For some reason that she could not explain, the place just gave her the creeps, in fact, she plain did not like being there. Now, Pamela is just as average a person as you would ever want to meet in mid-Michigan. She had never had any types of excursions into the supernatural, other than reading her horoscope in the newspaper and then watching the predictions not come true. Still, there was something about that lighthouse, and particularly that keeper's residence, that gave her a bad feeling that she could not explain.

As it is with all children who have grown to become adults, the pressure to satisfy one's parents can grow far larger than any unexplained bad feelings such as those that Pamela felt about the lighthouse. So it was that one day during the first summer that Ray and Martha were tending the property, Pamela simply gave in and agreed to spend the night at Pointe aux Barques with her folks. After all, what could happen? She was to be residing so far from any of the woes of the big cities that any evildoers of the metropolitan areas would likely get lost before finding her. The most fearful noise that

Although closed for the season, the light at Point aux Barques stands tall against Lake Huron. Note the date "1857" above the walkway door.

would occur would be the gentle lapping of Lake Huron's waves upon the nearby beach, and about the only excitement that one may expect would be if one of the local cows got loose. Certainly, that bad feeling that she had was simply nonsense. Besides, there was also "Shadow," the family dog, keeping a watch on her and the house. She would be as safe as she could ever imagine. At least, that is what she kept telling herself as she settled into the upstairs west bedroom. Indeed, she was absolutely correct in that assumption, because she was being watched over constantly, but during that night, Shadow the dog had help watching over Pamela.

After some fitful tossing and turning, Pamela finally slipped into a state of quiet slumber. Late into the night, for reasons that she could not fathom, Pamela suddenly awakened. It was the kind of unexplained, middle-of-the-night awakening that we have all experienced, where your eyes suddenly pop open and you lay there completely alert for no reason whatsoever. The room was quiet and the house was peaceful, and there was no apparent commotion, yet something had drawn Pamela from her sleep. Looking around she noticed that Shadow, the lovable mutt, was laying just outside her door intently gazing down the stairway. Pamela muttered the series of rhetorical verbal commands that most people would speak toward a pet doing something strange. The dog ignored her and remained fixated on the stairway. Finally, Pamela decided that she would find out what was the matter with the dog, and got out of bed. Making her way toward the door she noticed that Shadow did not look toward her as she approached, but continued to gaze down the stairs. As she approached the dog and again asked what was the matter, Pamela glanced in the direction in which Shadow was peering. To her shock, she saw that there was a woman standing at the bottom of the stairs.

Garbed in a long, cottony dress, the lady at the bottom of the stairway appeared to be aged about in her mid-30s and was very slim. Her dress was long-sleeved, of a light color, had a printed pattern and a high collar. Around her waist was tied a long kitchen apron whose upper portion had been folded down, as if she were in the middle of cooking or cleaning. The lady wore her hair tied back in a very old-fashioned manner and simply stood at the bottom of the steps with one hand placed upon the banister all the while looking directly up at Pamela.

It was an event that most of us would consider terrifying. Yet, standing in a darkened old house in the middle of the night looking directly into the face of a ghost, Pamela Kennedy was neither terrified nor shocked. Oddly, she felt greatly at ease, as if being welcomed in some way. For a long moment the two stood and gazed at one another and Pamela almost expected the spectral lady to speak. Suddenly, the apparition simply turned and walked away through the door and toward the lighthouse. A sense of relief cascaded over Pamela, and she returned to bed feeling as if she now was welcome at both the lighthouse and the keeper's quarters.

At breakfast the following morning, Pamela sat down with Martha and Ray and the family engaged in the normal early morning small talk. Somewhere within the conversation Pamela casually mentioned that her parents should not worry about the lady in the house with them, because she was not there to hurt anyone, she was simply hanging out. The room went silent as her parents froze with shock.

"What lady?" they both asked.

"The lady, you know," Pamela responded in a matter of fact tone, "the ghost, the ghost that lives at the lighthouse."

Neither Martha nor Ray had ever had a hint of any ghost residing on the property.

So, just who is this spectral lady of the lakes? There are several possibilities, but first we must look closely at Pamela's description of the lady. Although, upon personal interview, it was found that Pamela had scant knowledge of the garb and appearance of ladies of pre-Depression era, and little knowledge about the fact that ladies worked the lakes aboard vessels long ago, her description has some interesting details. Although when talking about a ghost sighting, you are always dealing with pure hearsay and speculation we can draw some interesting conclusions. First, it is commonly held among those who deal with apparitions and their appearances, that the ghosts often appear dressed in clothing that they were the most often clad in, and thus most comfortable being seen in. Also, it is common for apparitions to be dressed in the clothing that they were wearing at the time of their death. It is thought that the ghost of a person will remain at a given location because of some sort of connection to that location in life or at the time of death. The dress worn by the individual sounds very much as if it befits a woman of the period 1870-1920. Also, the light colored fabric would indicate summer garb. The apron worn tied around the waist with the upper portion folded down indicates someone who performs household type work, but not currently engaged in such work.

In looking closely at the records of the events that took place at Pointe aux Barques, there is only one consistent official source and that is the *Annual Reports* of the United States Life Saving Service which, in 1876, established a station just 500 feet away from the lighthouse keeper's quarters where Pamela saw her ghost. In the hope that tragic events occurring at the lighthouse may be reflected in these reports, the volumes from 1876 to 1913 were completely searched, but yielded nothing. The complete holdings of the National Archives concerning the Pointe aux Barques Lighthouse were searched and, sparse as these holdings are, they also yielded no clues. According to the National Archives, no logbooks from the Pointe aux

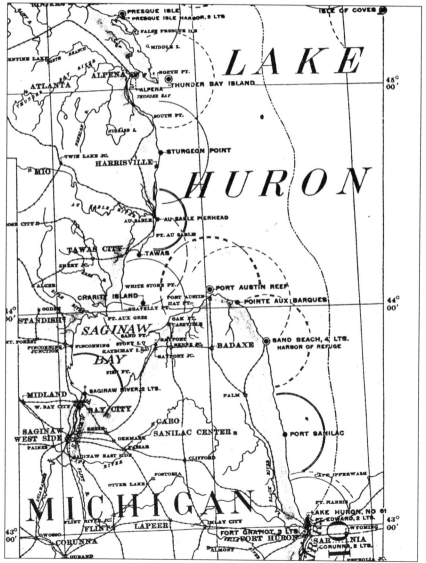

General map from 1892 showing the lighthouses of Michigan's thumb.

Barques Lighthouse are known to exist. Speculation may also lead us to the possibility that this lady of the light is someone who was lost in a nearby shipwreck. There are more than 30 shipwrecks which may have involved the loss of life that are known to have taken place in the general vicinity of the lighthouse, 14 of which are documented as fatals. Some of these shipwrecks may have involved female cooks among their victims, but a complete research of all of these wrecks is not yet finished. We do know that, in at least two cases, ladies of the lakes who fit the description of the Pointe aux Barques Lighthouse ghost are documented to having been lost in the area.

On August 20, 1899, the schooner *Hunter Savidge* was capsized by a summer squall and five of her crew were lost. This fatality included the captain's wife, Rosa Sharpsteen, the vessel owner's wife, Mary Muellerweiss, and her six-year-old daughter. Accounts indicate that Rosa was far to old to fit the description of the ghost, but Mary does fit the profile. The *Hunter Savidge* was lost on a repressively hot summer day, and the lost lady would have been garbed in light-colored summer clothing as described by Pamela. On May 23, 1910, the 436-foot oreboat *Frank H. Goodyear* collided with the oreboat *James B. Wood* in the general area of Pointe aux Barques. The *Goodyear* went to Lake Huron's bottom in minutes and just as quickly left her people in the water, struggling for survival. Among those who managed to surface after the sinking was Lillian Bassett, the wife of the ship's cook. She had been in the galley helping her spouse clean up after breakfast when the collision occurred. Moments after she surfaced, one of the *Goodyear's* massive and heavy wooden hatch-planks shot up end-wise from under the water and then slammed down upon her as she bobbed in the lake with her infant son in her arms. She, too, was likely wearing the garb described by Pamela and would likely fit the description of the lady who haunts the lighthouse. The complete story of the *Goodyear* wreck can be found in this author's second book, *Sounds of Disaster.* Oddly, both Mary and Lillian were lost with children in arms. Lastly, there is a lady listed as having been washed overboard from a vessel on November of 1901. This event is still being researched, and may lend some insight to this story.

There is also the cynic's reasoning that Pamela may just be making the whole thing up, or may have simply dreamed the whole event. This conclusion can be discounted for two reasons. First, being a person who upon interview demonstrated limited knowledge of the period garb and manner of the ladies of the lakes, her description of the specter seems too accurate to have come from anyone but a historian or eyewitness. Second, there are plenty of ghost stories to go around on Pointe aux Barques, and it is an area that even the most hardened research historian, such as this author, has to admit seems to be haunted.

One haunting story begins at dawn on the stormy morning of April 23, 1879 when the Pointe aux Barques Station wasunder the command of Keeper Jerome Kiha. Before daylight Lake Huron took hold of the scow-schooner *J. H. Magruder*, and proceeded to maul her in an evil manner. But the lake did not want the *Magruder* as her prize. The Pointe aux Barques Lifesaving Station's crew had robbed Lake Huron of nearly 100 victims since 1876 and now the lake would have its revenge on the daring mortals, and the *Magruder* would be the bait.

Just before nine o'clock on that ugly spring morning Samuel McFarland was tending to his small farm a short distance from the lifesaving station when the sound of screeching seagulls drew his attention down toward the lake. After a short distraction, McFarland elected to ignore the cries of the birds and get back to his chores, but a moment later his dogs bolted toward the beach, and the annoyed farmer decided to follow and find out just what was going on down there. As he looked out across the breaking surf McFarland saw an overturned surfboat bobbing about 200 feet from shore. At that point the beach is nothing more than a protracted stretch of rounded boulders that lead up to a bluff shore that can be higher than 15 feet. Figuring that some mariner may be in distress, McFarland made a dash toward the lifesaving station with the intention of alerting the crew. When the breathless farmer reached the station, however, he found it vacant with the doors to the boathouse propped open. For a long moment the puzzled plowman pondered the situation until a shocking realization snapped him back to reality. What he had spotted from the beach was the surfboat belonging to the station! In a second mad dash McFarland found the door of the lightkeeper's residence and pounded frantically upon it. A heartbeat later Lightkeeper Andrew Shaw flung open the door to be confronted by the flustered farmer who made his point clear in very few words.

As fast as their feet would carry them the lightkeeper and farmer set off in the direction of the capsized surfboat. If it was indeed the station's boat that meant only one thing, that the occupants were out thrashing in the frigid seas, and in the month of April the lake is as cold as it can get without being a sheet of ice. Arriving at the scene both men saw the station boat already washed ashore and 30 feet away a horrid figure stood wobbling on the slick boulders. With one hand clutching the root of a fallen tree and the other using a lath stick as a pitiful cane. The man's face was a horrid purplish color and swollen like that of a corpse. His eyes glared straight ahead as if McFarland and Shaw were not there at all and an eerie foam flowed from his nose and mouth as he attempted to walk but moved not an inch. Looking upon the monstrous image the farmer and lightkeeper at first thought that they were in the presence of the ghost of a ghastly drowning, then they realized that this was not an apparition at all, but a survivor.

Stepping closer to the stricken man, McFarland and Shaw reached out to lend support to the trembling refugee. At that moment they discovered that the walking deadman was station keeper Jerome Kiah. Taking Kiah between them the farmer and lighthouse keeper attempted to walk him back to the station. Each step was a painful ordeal for all three men and as they moved along Keeper Kiah began to mumble.

"Poor boys," he whispered through swollen lips, "they're all gone."

One agonizing step after another lead the three men toward the lifesaving station. Suddenly Kiah stiffened out both legs, threw his head back and convulsed violently. McFarland and Shaw were certain at that instant that they were holding onto a dead man, but a moment later the benumbed keeper recovered from his fit and again began to make an effort at walking. As they arrived at the station, the keeper's wet clothing was removed and he was wrapped in dry blankets and put to bed. While Kiah drifted unconscious in his bed, Lake Huron proceeded to deposit the fruits of her vengeance at the very doorstep of the Pointe aux Barques Lighthouse and Lifesaving Station. The bodies of all of the lifesaving crew were spit from the lake and put upon the rocks within a quarter of a mile of the station but, the only man on earth who knew what had happened to the surfmen lay inside the station nearly dead.

So what did happen to the crew of the Pointe aux Barques Station? The answer is amazingly simple, they were just doing their duty. Shortly before sunrise surfman James Nantau was standing his watch in the lookout tower when he spied a vessel southeast of the station flying her flag at half-mast upside down and having a red lamp in her main rigging in a signal of distress. Nantau sounded the alarm and alerted the rest of the crew who then prepared the surfboat for launch. As the crew manned the boat, Surfman Dennis Deegan came running from his beach patrol. He, too, had spotted the distressed vessel from McGuier's point a mile and a half north of the station, and had run all of the way back to the station to report it. When he reached the station, Deegan was given a cup of the hot coffee that was being passed among the crew in preparation for their pull across the angry lake. Also taking the hot beverage were Robert Morison, James Pottenger and William Sayres. Surfman Walter Petherbridge, like James Nantau, was beginning his first season at the station. Once all of the crew had gulped their coffee, they launched the surfboat down the ramp and took to the oars with Kiah at the steering oar. It was just before eight o'clock in the morning and no one ashore witnessed the crew's departure. The wind blew from due east and the waves were running northeast. Calculating the nearby reefs and shallows, Kiah directed his boat so as to most effectively clear the breaking surf. His zigzag course worked perfectly and the surfboat transcended the whitecaps with grace. The spirits of the surfmen soared and they began congratulating one another on the fine job as their arms pulled at the oars with renewed energy. Kiah then headed the surfboat directly for the imperiled schooner. It was then that Lake Huron chose to extract its revenge on the Pointe aux Barques lifesavers.

Running nearly due east, the surfboat was taking the seas from the northeast on her port quarter and Kiah would head his bow in that direction each time a big wave came calling in order to take it on the bow. The seas were bigger than he had expected, but no larger than others that he had been in before. Soon the surfboat had pulled to within a quarter of a mile of the stricken schooner, and just about a mile out into the lake, when a giant breaking wave came roaring toward them. There was no time for Kiah or his crew to turn the surfboat as the sea seemed to simply rise up and crash

Hull planking from an old wooden shipwreck, cast up onto the point by a recent storm, is stored behind the lighthouse.

toward them. In an inkling a cascade of cold water swallowed them and then left them floundering. Immediately the keeper gave the order to the crew to begin bailing, but it was pointless because the surfboat was filled to her rails. A moment later the bantam surfboat rolled over and spilled the lifesavers into the stinging cold bath of Lake Huron. As they had been trained, the surfmen took hold of their boat and righted her, but the trough of the seas had her now and was not willing to let go. Again the surfboat was rolled by the lake, and again the surfmen righted her. This was a chore that took nearly superhuman strength and coordination. The crew would take hold of the righting lines strung along the sides of the boat and using their weight and feet, turn the surfboat right-side up. All of this was done while bobbing chest-deep in the frigid lake supported only by a cork life belt. It was a drill that the crews all practiced weekly, but now they were in a heaving sea and dunked in water that had been ice a dozen days earlier. Putting their training to work the crew righted their craft again, but no sooner did they turn her over than the seas capsized them again. Once more the crew pulled their surfboat onto an upright keel, just in time to have it rolled upside down for a third time. What had happened was that the surfboat had been lodged in the sea trough at exactly the proper angle to the wind to make her an easy victim for capsizing. No matter how many times the surfmen righted the boat, as long as it was filled with water, the very next wave would roll it back over. After a few of these dunkings in the ice water of Lake Huron, the strength of the lifesavers was quickly sapped. After three-quarters of an hour the lake had won the fight. Now all of the crew were left holding onto the lifelines of the overturned surfboat and drifting in the waves, too benumbed to do anything more.

Lake Huron had beaten the lifesavers, but that was not enough. Now the lake started to take the surfmen one at a time. Pottenger went first, the strength being drained from his body he bowed his head into the water and simply let go, drifting away. From the distressed schooner *J. H. Magruder*, which was now riding at anchor, her crew stood helplessly by and watched the lake take the surfmen. Keeper Kiah did his best to keep his crew alive. They tried time and again to crawl atop the overturned hull and escape the bitter water, but the waves would wash them off each time. The keeper urged his men to think of their families and hold on until they washed ashore, but it was no use. One by one the lake plucked them away. Surfman Deegan was the last to let go, leaving Kiah alone with Lake Huron. Eventually the surfboat drifted back across the reef and into calmer waters where the lone survivor managed to drag himself onto the rolling hull. As he floated atop the capsized surfboat Kiah passed in and out of consciousness. In the times when he was conscious, the benumbed keeper pounded his limbs against the boat in an attempt to regain his circulation. Being too frozen to move he also screamed with what little strength he had remaining. At the top of his frozen lungs he shouted toward the gray sky above in the hope that he might attract some kind of attention of those ashore. His cries went unheard and the lake finally dumped both him and the surfboat on the rocks near the McFarland farm. By noon that same day Kiah was recovered to the point where he was back on his feet and the lake was giving up the bodies of his crew one at a time just as she had taken them. One after another the lifeless surfmen found the beach and were properly collected by the local residents. The schooner *Magruder* that the surfmen had given their lives attempting to get to, managed to free herself later that tragic day and escaped to shelter at Harbor Beach (then known as Sand Beach). Lake Huron would allow her to survive until September 18, 1895 when it would wreck on Sturgeon Point. Keeper Kiah went on to become the district superintendent of for the United States Life-Saving Service. He retired at age 72 in 1915 after the Lifesaving Service had been merged with the Revenue Cutter Service and thus became the United States Coast Guard.

It was later reported that in the mid-1960s, a befuddled yacht skipper, who was groping his vessel through the fog off of Pointe aux Barques, was startled by a wooden surfboat that suddenly came from the fog and cut across his path. In reaction to the surfboat's sudden appearance, the yacht was forced to alter course and in doing so accidentally missed running aground on Pointe aux Barques Reef. The surfboat was reported to have been occupied by eight surfmen and one keeper who stood aft with a steering oar. Has the late Keeper Kiah joined his lost "boys" in the afterlife, and now all are bound to Point aux Barques by their dedication to duty, and so are protecting mariners even to this day?

In one final twist to this story, a modern mariner found himself in the same painful dilemma as Jerome Kiah in nearly the exact same location, but 87 years later. On the gale-ripped night of November 29, 1966 the 600-foot oreboat *Daniel J. Morrell* broke in half just over two dozen miles north of Pointe aux Barques. When the boat went down it left behind its life raft with four crewmen aboard, 36 hours later only one of them, Dennis Hale, remained alive. While several other authors have taken stabs at the tale, the best account of Hale's ordeal can be found in Dwight Boyer's outstanding book *Ships and Men of the Great Lakes*. Just before his rescue by a Coast Guard helicopter, Hale's raft ran aground in the shallows within a mile of the spot where Keeper Kiah's overturned surfboat had found the shore. Hale knew he was close to land, but was so frozen that he was unable to move. Shouting in hope of attracting attention, his voice emptied into the distance just as Kiah's had in 1879. Having been without food and water since his boat went down, Hale had previously been dipping the lanyard on the handle of a broken flare gun into the lake and drinking from the runoff, now his body was absolutely paralyzed with frostbitten pain and he took to nibbling at the ice on his pea-coat, which had been his only cover while on the raft. (It is important to note that accounts of Hale's ordeal universally state that he sheltered himself beneath the bodies of his dead shipmates. This author has spoken often to Hale and he has stated that such claims, although good for storytelling, are absolutely untrue.) As soon as he began to nibble on his icy garment the ghostly figure of a man appeared on the raft. With deep set eyes and long white mustache, the stranger was a commanding figure and told Hale not to eat the ice, then he vanished. A little later the castaway again began to nibble at the ice and once more the imposing ghost appeared and he warned Hale, shaking his finger with a cragged hand that the tormented crewman remembers to this day, "Do not eat the ice..." he told the castaway, because it would lower the body temperature and he would die. A short time thereafter the Coast Guard helicopter hovered down and pulled Dennis Hale from the grip of Lake Huron. Oddly, Hale's description of the ghostly man who warned him away from eating the ice is very close to the image of Keeper J.W. Plough who was in charge of the Sand Beach lifesaving Station, which was located just over a dozen miles south of Pointe aux Barques. Keeper Plough and his surfmen rescued hundreds of souls from the frigid lake, and he probably knew more about hypothermia than any man living on Lake Huron in his day.

By the time of that awful event in 1966, most of the lifesaving stations had been abandoned and the service as it had been known prior to 1915 was long forgotten. The Pointe aux Barques station was deemed "inactive" in the 1937 fiscal year and that ended 60 years of operation. It is interesting, however, to ponder that if the station at Pointe aux Barques had been in operation in 1966 in the same manner as it was in 1879, the lookout would have surely spotted Hale's raft and the surfmen would have launched their boat and rushed out onto the lake to save his life. Then again perhaps one of them did exactly that, in the form of a white apparition who knew a great deal more about hypothermia than Hale did.

Today anyone can make the pilgrimage to Huron City where the structure of the Pointe aux Barques Station has been relocated as part of a preserve of historic buildings of the Huron City Museum. As state road M-25 cuts across the very tip of the thumb between Port Austin and Grindstone City, the large white signs lead the way to the contemporary home of the original Pointe aux Barques Station. Visitors can see first hand the building from where the crew departed to rescue a distressed *J. H. Magruder*, but never returned. July 1 to the Labor Day holiday the buildings are opened for tours until about half past four in the afternoon. All of the apparatus used by the service is on display within the boathouse portion of the building

The Beacon of the Pointe aux Barques Light still flashes its warning, even if no one is watching anymore.

including two of the station's Lyle Guns, projectiles and faking boxes. A large picture of Keeper Kiah hangs in the living quarters as if still supervising the station. Standing outside the boathouse doors it is easy to imagine them about to swing open as the surfmen dash to the rescue of another vessel in distress. Then, driving less than a mile to the southeast on M-25 and turning off on Huron City Road, you will find the gleaming white Pointe aux Barques Lighthouse. At the base of the light in the quarters once occupied by Keeper Shaw a museum is now located with shipwreck artifacts of all kinds on display. Leaving the building you find Lake Huron spread out in front of you in all of her indigo glory. Visitors need only to walk about 100 yards to the east where the public access ramp to the lake has been constructed. This is the exact spot where the Pointe aux Barques Lifesaving Station once stood, and the jut of land that supported the launching ways for the station's boats still exists.

Discovering exactly who the people are who haunt Point aux Barques is a difficult and perhaps impossible task. Everyone who has encountered one of these specters swears that what they have seen is absolutely real, and most have been changed in some way by the encounter. A yachtsman was spared the damage to his vessel by a surfboat filled with lifesavers, the likes of which have not been seen on the lakes for nearly half a century, and went away certain that someone watches over Pointe aux Barques. Dennis Hale is sure that his life was saved by a mysterious ghost that knew how to survive the clutches of the lake. Pamela Kennedy never feels uncomfortable visiting or staying at the lighthouse anymore. She is sure that the lady of the light watches over the place and considers Pamela to be a welcome guest. In all, the spirits that haunt the point apparently do so with good intent and so it should not matter exactly who they are. Yet, every mystery begs to be solved and so you can be assured that this author's work at identifying the spirits of Point aux Barques will continue—perhaps into the next book.

IX

A KEEPER'S NIGHTMARE COMES TRUE

As Lake Superior fought not to let winter turn into spring, the winds of her tantrum screamed as she spit the last of her snow at the city of Marquette. It was the last day of April, 1909 and the bitter goddess of frozen winter was watching her blanket of snow and sheet of ice breaking their grip on her favored lake. In one last outburst, winter exploded in a mighty spring gale as if in an attempt to frighten away the inevitable change of the seasons. On the vast surface of Superior the men had already started their attempt to sail the lakes using their relatively frail steamships and barges. Such a pity that they should be caught in winter's temper tantrum—such a pity indeed!

Moored snugly to a Marquette dock the lighthouse tender *Marigold* strained at her lines as the blustering winds lashed at her hull. The boat's rigging made a musical tone as the winds gusted past, but her boilers pumped enough steam through her radiators to fend off the cold. In one of the *Marigold's* staterooms, Doctors Harkin and Lunna were attending to a very special patient, and were thankful that the boat was well-heated. Resting in the stateroom's bed was Lighthouse Keeper Frank Wittie, and the two Marquette physicians were aboard to see to the keeper's dislocated shoulder. The cure for such an injury in 1909 was much the same as it is today—pop it back into place, immobilize the limb and see to the patient's pain. Although the splint was the same as it would be in modern times, the painkiller was likely poured from a brown bottle with "XXX" on the label. Before long, Keeper Wittie was resting quietly, and the gale outside appeared to be subsiding. Both doctors prepared to leave the *Marigold* knowing that they had just treated a very brave fellow. His injuries were not caused by a careless accident, in fact the courageous lighthouse keeper had put himself between Lake Superior and mariners in distress. While in the jaws of the mighty lake

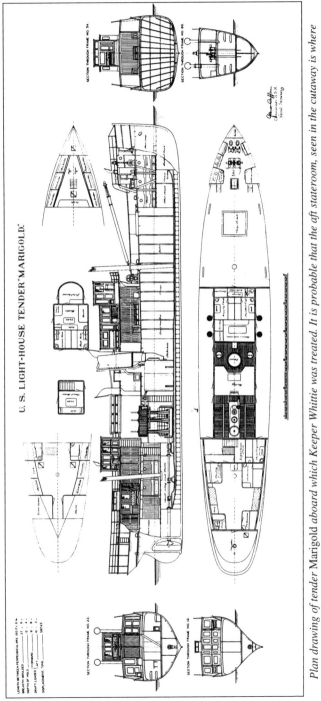

U. S. LIGHT-HOUSE TENDER "MARIGOLD."

Plan drawing of tender Marigold aboard which Keeper Whittie was treated. It is probable that the aft stateroom, seen in the cutaway is where he was treated.

he had actually been hit by a shipwreck! As Captain Cummins, the *Marigold's* master, escorted the doctors from the stateroom, he told them the incredible story.

Three days prior, while on her way to place the keepers of the Stannard's Rock Lighthouse at their station, the *Marigold* was caught in a sudden spring gale. The winds first came booming from the northwest, then suddenly shifted to coming out of the southeast and blew a pure gale. Cummins was within range of Huron Island and knew all too well that a spring gale on Lake Superior could be as deadly as its autumn counterpart. With that in mind he selected the better part of valor and ducked the *Marigold* behind the lee of the nearby island. The lighthouse at Stannard's Rock would have to wait to receive its keepers for a few days.

On the same Wednesday morning, April 28, 1909 that the *Marigold* was seeking shelter, the wooden steamer *Schoolcraft* hissed from the upper canal at the Soo locks and into the storm-tossed waters of the upper Saint Marys River. Attached to the stern of the 190-foot steamer by a length of thick hemp towing hawser, the schooner-barge *George Nester* came faithfully following. Schooner-barges, as a breed, were almost exclusively found on the Great Lakes. Leftovers from the heydays of sail-powered vessels, these once elegant wind-grabbers had their masts cut short and most of their sails removed. Left with only a forward "storm sail" for emergencies, the schooners turned barges were routinely overworked and overloaded until they had every ounce of useful life squeezed from them by their owners. Often these schooner-barges were towed by equally antiquated steamers using equally overworked equipment. These were the days long before the safety inspections Coast Guard, or any other type of true safety regulation. Owners and operators of these tired vessels spend as little money as possible on their boats, and there was little that anyone would or could say about it. Such was the case with the *Schoolcraft* and *Nester*. The steamer was in her 25th year of hard labor, and the schooner-barge was in her 22nd season of toil. Although the schooner-barge was owned by the man whose name was painted on her nameboard, Detroit marine mogul *George Nester*, it is doubtful that the "Nester Estate" saw fit to invest any large sum of cash in the boat's upkeep. The boat was simply expected to spend another season hauling whatever the owners saw fit to deposit in her hold. She was also expected to do so with as few complications as possible.

In command of the *Nester* that Wednesday morning was Captain George Dubeau of Algonac, Michigan, and the odds are that he was not exactly pleased at being pulled out into a Lake Superior spring gale. The *Nester* was upbound "light," or without a cargo in her hold. These old, wooden lake-boats were not equipped with ballast tanks of any sort and when running light would be subject to a maximum of pounding by the wind and waves. Still, the boat and her crew were being paid to make trips, and not to hunker in the shelter of the river. If Captain Bourassa of the *Schoolcraft* saw fit to sail, the *Nester* had little choice other than to follow.

Aboard the *Nester*, a crew of seven tended to the vessel's needs. As with most lakeboats of the *Nester's* ilk, the people who worked her were a transient breed. Often they would drift from one vessel to another through a season of sailing. Some of them would remain aboard just long enough to get a bellyful of either food or the ship's officers and would then "go up the street." When their pockets and stomachs were again empty and the felt that they could again put up with the next boat and her officers, they would return to sailing. Many of the mariners of this era often signed aboard under a false name, that is, if they "signed" aboard at all. The result of all of this muddle was that we often are left with scant records as to a given vessel's crew. Aside from the *Nester's* captain, only the names of four of her crew are recorded, and even those are unofficial. Said to be serving aboard the schooner-barge as she cleared the Soo were Fred Droillard, John Starr, Peter Prockett and Edward Peterson. The rest of the crew were simply faces in the crowd of history, and went out toward Lake Superior with their names never being recorded. They were simply regular folks doing a common job and the truth is that no one took much notice as the *Schoolcraft* and *Nester* left the Soo.

Conditions on the upper Saint Marys River were nothing short of a mess as the *Nester* and her steamer cleared the Soo. The ice in the upper river and on Whitefish Bay had just started to break up—and then came the gale! Massive packs of ice were shoved in assorted directions, and as many as 49 lakeboats were headed upbound. One giant steel laker, the steamer *Aurania*, was cut while trying to buck her way out of the ice and sank in the upper part of the river. Her crew escaped by hiking across the ice packs, but the boat was gone into the depths. There was no hazard to navigation caused by the *Aurania's* sinking, because the water in that part of the river is more than 400 feet deep. Other vessels found themselves trapped in the drifting ice, but somehow the *Schoolcraft* and *Nester* managed to get out onto the open lake. It would be a passage that they would soon regret.

Soon after clearing Whitefish Point, the two wooden lakeboats would have felt the full force of the gale. Howling from the northwest, the storm was raising Lake Superior's surface into an endless series of ice water waves

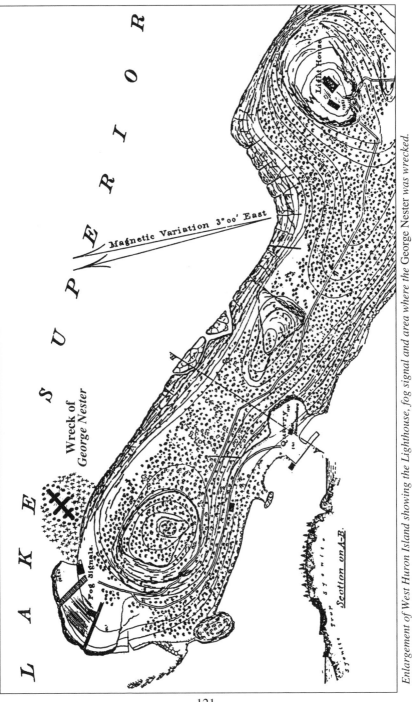

Enlargement of West Huron Island showing the Lighthouse, fog signal and area where the George Nester was wrecked.

that came combing across more than 200 miles of open water. Captain Bourassa probably quickly realized the folly of hauling out onto Superior in the current conditions, but it was too late to change his course. Any turning of the *Schoolcraft* would likely expose his tow to an extreme pounding and it was likely that the towing hawser would snap under the strain. Cast adrift, the *Nester* would likely be shoved into the ice packs on Whitefish Bay and then pounded between the seas and the ice. There was only one choice for Bourassa, and that was to put his bow into the wind and steam on into the storm.

Along with the towering waves, the storm brought a blizzard of snow and reduced the visibility to just a few feet. In 1909 the modern wonders of color radar and global navigation satellites were more than a half of a century into the future, and all that Bourassa had to his use as an aid to navigation was his compass and mariner's instinct. Wednesday evening Lake Superior and the reluctant winter decided to play a fateful trick on the lakeboats and suddenly shifted the storm winds to blowing out of the southeast. Blinded by the thick snow, Bourassa could do nothing more than fight his battle with Lake Superior, and Captain Dubeau and the people aboard the *Nester* could do nothing more than tag along.

When dawn began to illuminate Friday, the gale on Lake Superior was beginning its third day of rage. Now the winds were blowing from the northeast with all of winter's remaining power. At the Huron Island Lighthouse, located on the southeast tip of the island, Keeper Frank Wittie had spent the night insuring that the light over which he had charge remained lit through the stormy night. In fact, between Wittie, his assistant keeper, Casper Kuhn, and their second assistant keeper, they had kept the light shining through the past three stormy nights. The men at the lighthouse estimated that the winds were now blowing from the northeast at 60 miles per hour. A northeaster on Lake Superior has always been the strongest of gales. This was evidenced by the spectacle that Keeper Wittie witnessed as he left the lighthouse and headed out to check on the fog signals. The waves from the lake were smashing so hard into the cliffs below the lighthouse that spray was being flung completely over the light tower and landing in the lake on the other side of the island, a distance of more than 600 feet! Indeed, Lake Superior was in the midst of a stormy frolic that showed all of her power and dwarfed the humans and their machines.

Shielding his face from the spitting of the gale, Wittie began his trek to the fog signals on the northwest tip of the island. The second assistant keeper would remain on watch at the light, but considering that a blinding blizzard was accompanying the gale, the fog signals probably gave more aid to navigation that did the light. The foghorn was a large steam whistle that had its power provided by land-bound marine boilers. These boilers required coal fuel to be fed into their furnaces, and on a regular schedule the keepers had to go down and shovel the fuel. Unlike their waterborne counterparts, the fog signals used their steam only for the purpose of sounding the whistle. Vessel boilers, on the other hand used a great portion of their steam in propulsion of the boat, thus their steam pressure was greatly tapped and they needed constant stoking of coal. The fog signal needed only occasional stoking to keep up the required pressure and could be left to their own more often. Still, on a blizzard-bound day the fog signal was critical and Casper Kuhn had been on constant watch of their function and feeding. Wittie's duty was to insure that both the light and foghorn remained functional, and that meant making the half mile hike out to the fog signal buildings, no matter what the weather.

To get from the lighthouse to the fog signal, Wittie had to journey along a trail which, fortunately, ran along the western side of the island. Huron

Huron Island Light, Lake Superior. (Wayne Sapulski photo)

Island itself is a three-quarter-mile-long rock that suddenly juts from the depths of Lake Superior to a maximum elevation of 158 feet above the surface of the water. At that highest elevation sets the lighthouse, thus taking advantage of the terrain. The island is, at its most, just under 800 feet wide, but narrows to as little as 450 feet wide. Ages of the lake's seasonal rage have turned the northeast side of the island into a series of steep cliffs that stretch nearly 50 feet high. It is atop these cliffs that the fog signals have been constructed thus giving their sound every advantage in reaching out across the lake. As Wittie neared the end of the trail, however, the howling winds were overpowering the foghorn and it could hardly be heard. Squinting against the pelting snow, he kept his head down and followed the trail.

There are no records as to exactly what kind of work keepers Wittie and Kuhn were doing at the fog signal at 11:45 that Friday morning. All that is on record is that both men were in the vicinity of the fog signal when they heard the sound of a vessel's whistle blowing a signal of distress. Any whistle that could be heard above the gale must surely be very close to the island, and with that in mind, the two lighthouse keepers dashed out into the storm. They did not have to look far to see disaster headed their way from out of the blizzard. Heeled over and firmly gripped by the wind came a big wooden schooner-barge less than 200 feet from where the two lightkeepers stood. On her deck, the crew were working frantically in an attempt to raise the vessel's single storm sail, and drop her anchor before she hit the cliffs of Huron Island. With a 60-mile-per-hour gale at her beam, the vessel was moving so rapidly toward the rocks that even the fear of death could not move her crew fast enough to save her. She was doomed to smash upon the rocks—she was the schooner-barge *George Nester*!

Hidden within the nightmares of every keeper of every lighthouse was the image of a helpless vessel and crew crashing upon the rocks that the keeper's beacon was established to mark. There would be no greater feeling of helplessness as than when a giant hull of wood and steel slammed into the shoals and cracked like an egg. After endless hours and countless days of watchful care had been taken to warn the mariners of the hazard, suddenly all of the endeavor was erased. Somehow it was as if all of the efforts that any human could make were a failure, and the shipwreck found the rocks in spite of the lighthouse. Such was undoubtedly the secret dread of lightkeepers Wittie and Kuhn, and who knows how many times they woke from such a nightmare with heart pounding and cold sweat on the brow. On this stormy spring morning, however, there would be no awakening. The vision of the lakeboat and crew about to be tossed onto the rocks by the wild waves was real, perhaps too real.

Onward came the *George Nester* as her crew scrambled with her anchors and sail in a stormy puppet show. Then, before the startled eyes of the two lighthouse keepers, Lake Superior picked up the wooden vessel with a giant breaker and slammed her onto the rocks. At the base of the cliff where the two keepers stood, the hull of the *Nester* shattered like a china cup. A second foaming wave swept the wreck as she went swiftly to pieces. At the same moment her crew were thrown into the frigid water whose temperature was still hovering between ice and liquid. From the jumble of wreckage and the foam of the ice water waves, a single plea was heard—"For God's sake, throw us a line!"

Keeper Wittie had already grabbed a coil of heaving line which was stored near the fog signal. Stumbling as far down the cliff as he was able, he threw the coil with all of his strength toward the wreck. He was not aiming for any person or place, he was simply praying that the rope would drop in and save someone, somehow. With a terrific gust, Lake Superior simply blew the line back against the rocks at Wittie's feet. Gathering his rope as fast as he could he tried to work his way closer along the rocks, but each time he tried to throw the line it was cast back at his boots. Soon Wittie was right up where the surf was exploding over the rocks, but now it was too late. In moments, the seven mariners had simply vanished among the heaving wreckage and churning waves. It was then that the lake lashed out at Wittie himself. As if to punish the lightkeeper for attempting to rob the lake of its prize, Superior spit a timber from the shattered hull of the *Nester* from her waves and like a bolt of oak lightening and struck the keeper down. Slung like a javelin, the timber had slammed into Wittie's upper body and dislocated his shoulder. He crumpled onto the rocks in a helpless heap. Now the waves reached out and grabbed the stricken keeper's legs. Using the tangle of wreckage and undertow of the seas, Lake Superior turned its sights toward swallowing Frank Wittie as it had just swallowed the crew of the *George Nester*. Kicking with what strength he had remaining, Keeper Wittie thrashed on the rocks in an effort, not to save someone else from the lake— but to save himself.

When the helpless *Nester* was first spotted drifting toward the island, the second assistant keeper was reportedly dispatched to the southwest side of the island where the lighthouse tender *Marigold* was sheltering from the storm. It is reported that he alerted that boat as to the schooner-barge's wreck. Other accounts, however, report that it was the steamer *Schoolcraft* which rounded the island after losing the *Nester* and reported the schooner-barge as in distress. No matter which method was used to alert the *Marigold*, the fact is that as soon as Captain Cummins got the word, he ordered the lighthouse tender to get underway, and headed out to the east side of the island. The point was already moot, because any action that was taken by the *Marigold* was far too late to save the *Nester* or her crew. The eyewitnesses to the wreck stated that from the time the schooner-barge began drifting toward the rocks until she was shattered in the surf, no more than five minutes had passed. It would have taken the better part of a half hour, at best, to get the *Marigold* cast off, powered up and around the island to the scene of the wreck. Additionally, the time that it would have taken simply to get the word of the wreck to the *Marigold*, whether by way of lighthouse keeper or by way of the *Schoolcraft*, would have consumed at least another quarter of an hour. By that time, the *George Nester* was wrecked and her crew drowned.

Just what happened that sent the *Nester* and her crew to their destruction? As with most Great Lakes shipwrecks, the answer is in the storm. When the *Schoolcraft* departed the Saint Marys River with the *Nester* in tow, the gale was already blowing hard and it is likely that Captain Bourassa found that he had little choice other than putting the *Schoolcraft's* bow into

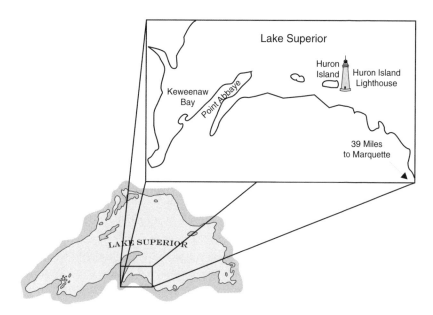

the wind and taking the seas as they came. All through the daylight hours of that Wednesday the winds blew a full gale from the northwest, and so Bourassa was forced to direct his course out into the middle of the lake. On Wednesday evening, the winds suddenly shifted to blowing from the southeast. Fortunately, the towing hawser that had been pulling the *Nester* was new, having just been put to work when the two boats departed Cleveland and was able to take a good deal of strain. When the *Schoolcraft* needed to turn and meet the newly southeast winds, the hawser held and brought the *Nester* along. Through all of Thursday the *Schoolcraft* and her consort pounded against the storm heading back toward the Soo. Now, however, the winds were far stronger than they had been when blowing from the northwest, and the pair of lakeboats made little over-the-bottom progress. By the time that Friday began to dawn, the winds again began to shift, this time they came howling from the northeast and brought with them a blinding blizzard. Once more, the *Schoolcraft* was forced to turn with the *Nester*, but this time Bourassa elected to turn and run with the wind at his heels. The tactic worked and both boats were making good weather of it, but Lake Superior had them right in her trap and was about to pull the string. What Bourassa could not have known was that Thursday's southeast wind had not carried the two boats as far out into the lake as he had guessed.

Using the only navigation tool available to him, Bourassa had estimated that his boat and its barge were on a good course for the mouth of Keweenaw Bay and their destination of Baraga, Michigan. In truth, he was not far off considering the two day gale that the boats had just sailed through. Another three miles to the north and Bourassa would have been right on course, but the gale had set him just that much too far to the south. Through the vale of the blizzard, he could see nothing until the sight of cliff of rock suddenly loomed in this pilothouse window. Confused, he thought he had directed his steamer and consort straight into the Michigan mainland and ordered a turn hard to port. It was his intention to bring the two boats in between the Huron Islands and end up in the relatively protected waters of their lee. Responding quickly to her helm, the *Schoolcraft* came about but, suspended at the end of the towing hawser, the *Nester* did not. Unable to see the *Schoolcraft's* turn through the snow, the *Nester* just kept coming, and her 791 tons of girth came too. In a deadly game of crack the whip, the *Nester* suddenly found herself at the end of a towing hawser that was leading in a new direction. This time the new towing line was stressed far beyond its strength, and it snapped like cheap thread.

What Bourassa had mistaken for the Michigan mainland was in fact Huron Island, and when the *Schoolcraft* made her turn, she was soon in open water again. Aboard the *Nester*, the shock of the towline parting in the sudden turn must have tossed the boat over on her beam ends and surely got the attention of everyone on board. Scrambling on deck, Captain Dubeau saw the same sight that had just scared the wits out of Bourassa—the cliffs of rock, and exploding surf that lay ahead. The fog signal was never heard, and the lighthouse was never seen In her act of vengeance, Lake Superior had negated all of their efforts at safe navigation. She would have the *Nester* and her people, and there was no tool of man that could make a difference in that decision. In just one-tenth of one hour it was all over and the lake had devoured another vessel and crew, leaving nothing but the wreckage to be cast up in the surf.

Keeper Wittie would not be the next victim of Lake Superior, however. Assistant Keeper Kuhn had rushed down and managed to get a hold on the wounded lighthouse keeper and dragged him safely. A few hours later, Wittie was snug and dry aboard the tender *Marigold* being transported to Marquette where doctors Harkin and Lunna would attend to his wounds. Later, and there is no record of exactly when, Wittie would return to the care of his lighthouse. With one arm in a sling, and his memory fresh with the images of the *George Nester's* wreck, he would walk the island and tend to his station. Much the same as Lightkeeper John Irvine at the Outer Island Light and the wreck of the *Pretoria* four years earlier, Keeper Wittie had put the lives of others ahead of his own and performed with great valor against Lake Superior. In Wittie's case, however, the lake had robbed him of the mariners that he had tried to save, and nearly taken his life as well. Now it was back to his prescribed duties and the tending of his station. The fog signal would have its steam, the lamp would burn its fuel and the station on Huron Island would stand its vigil over the nearby shipping lanes.

To this day there remains an active light on Huron Island to warn and guide the mariners as there has been since the establishment of the station in 1868. Gone, however, are the flocks of wooden steamers and schooner-barges, the lighthouse keepers, the tender *Marigold* and most of the reasons why the light was established on the island in the first place. Now the Huron Islands are a national wildlife refuge. Certainly, the waves of Lake Superior still pound the shore where the wreckage of the *Nester* once littered the rocks, but for the most part the whole event is forgotten. In visiting this lonely place, the modern historian will find that the only thing that remains is the power of the lake. Stronger and far more enduring than any of the machines created by human beings, Lake Superior will always be able to defeat any device, no matter how well- or ill-intended. The proof is in the ghostly calls from the shipwrecked mariners which can still be heard among the cries of the seagulls. The wreck of the *George Nester*, in spite of the complex of fog signals and lighthouse on Huron Island, was a graphic demonstration of the lake's power. How quickly we forget such lessons!

X

THE LAKEBOAT VS. THE LIGHTHOUSE

On Friday morning, December 12, 1997, there was a rather unusual collision at the lower mouth of the Detroit River. The weather was clear and the winds were reportedly near calm as the 634-foot motor vessel *Buffalo* snailed past Amherstburg, Ontario, downbound, and headed for Bar Point. One of the most modern vessels sailing the lakes, the *Buffalo* is equipped with every form of navigational technology from radar to a global positioning system. Her passage through the confines and swift currents of the Detroit River should be routine in fog and the dark of night, but on this trip the story would be slightly different.

As the *Buffalo* cleared Bar Point, the expanse of Lake Erie began to sprawl ahead. Still, the boat had to remain within the dredged channel, and the buoys ahead showed the way—or so it should have been. At approximately 5:20 a.m., just over three miles after passing Bar Point, the huge steel-hulled vessel suddenly lurched to a complete stop as her bow crashed solidly into an immovable obstruction. Oddly, this obstruction was not an old sunken hulk, or a forgotten submerged crib of some kind of un-marked and unlighted rock outcropping. In fact, this object was very well marked indeed, and had been that way since 1885. The obstruction that the *Buffalo* had run smack into was the Detroit River Lighthouse!

Vessels have struck lighthouses in the past and often the lighthouse comes out on the short end of the collision. This time it was different, the *Buffalo* had struck the lighthouse crib nearly head-on, and the collision could have not been any more direct if she had been trying to hit the light. Shortly after the ship had impacted the lighthouse, her befuddled crew had her backing off. The boat's barrel-bow was stove in like a pop can that had been jammed upon a brick with the exact outline of the lighthouse's crib

Seen here at Port Huron on June 26, 1984, the motor vessel Buffalo would have a head-on collision with the Detroit River Lighthouse in December of 1997. (Author's Photo)

forming a 20-foot gash in her nose. The collision resulted in the firing of the entire on-duty navigation crew of the vessel; a 1.2 million dollar repair bill for the boat's owners, and hardly a scratch to the lighthouse! Next came the question of just how all of this happened. Oddly, the answer may reside in the reason why the Detroit River Light and the other lighthouses have become obsolete.

Detroit River Light, Lake Erie. (Wayne Sapulski photo)

Shoals at the lower mouth of the Detroit River had always been a hazard and often costly damages to vessels had occurred at this rocky gateway to the upper lakes. In the early 1870s, maritime columns in local newspapers were already calling for a light to be established in the vicinity of Bar Point. As early as 1873, the annual reports to the Lighthouse Board by the district officers began urging the Board to consider the establishment of a lighthouse at the mouth of the Detroit River. Beginning in 1875, the Canadian Government had established a small lightship at the shoal three and one quarter miles south, southwest of Bar Point. Unfortunately, these Canadian lightships were normally contracted from private individuals and were often little more than worn-out schooners with a small lantern raised to the top of one of their masts. Often the owners of these light-vessels would simply remove them without notice, and in general their reliability was less than

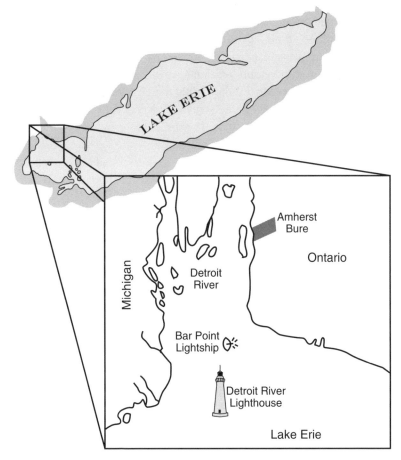

adequate. To make matters worse, a lamp raised to the top of an old schooner's mast as a lightship was nearly indistinguishable from a masthead light on any other vessel. In the case of the Bar Point lightship, her lamp was dim and had no distinct features, such as flashing or rotating, that would distinguish her from the lights of vessels that may be in the vicinity. The lights were simply two lanterns, one red and one white, one placed eight feet above the other, with the lowest light being raised 40 feet above the water-line. The lightship was painted red and sported white letters on each side saying "BAR POINT LIGHTSHIP," but its light was listed as only being visible for a scant 10 miles in clear weather. Additionally, the location of the light itself made it less than useful for navigation through the difficult shoals at the mouth of the river, because its location was about a mile too far east. Passing vessels were warned to not go within a half-mile of the lightship, and vessels of heavy draught should pass well to the southward. If the local visibility dropped below two miles, any vessel navigating off of the lightship would likely find itself aground by the time the light was spotted. Additionally, there was great concern that the lightship may be involved in a "mishap" with another vessel and damaged or perhaps even sunk. These concerns would all be negated if the United States Lighthouse Board were to establish a permanent facility in the area. Such a concept takes a long time to develop, however, and the mariners would have to contend with the Canadian light-vessel for nearly a full decade.

On August 7, 1882, the United States Congress finally approved action "For constructing a light-house and for the establishment of a steam fog-signal in connection therewith, at or near the mouth of the Detroit River, in Lake Erie, twenty thousand dollars."

That outlay of Federal cash was put to work beginning on September 14th of that year. On that date a portion of the United States Lake Survey chart was forwarded to the Lighthouse Board. This chart indicated the sites that the local inspectors considered the best for locating the new lighthouse. Sample 20-foot-deep "borings" of the lake bottom were then ordered by the board to select the best foundation location. These core samples were almost constant in their findings and showed that the first three or four feet of the bottom consisted of hard limestone, gravel and sand that was "very compact and difficult to penetrate." The next layer in each bore was of 12 feet of soft clay and fine sand. Lastly, a layer of very hard, blue clay took up the remaining five feet of the bores. Soundings of the lake bottom showed it to be quite level, and generally well able to support the building of a light-

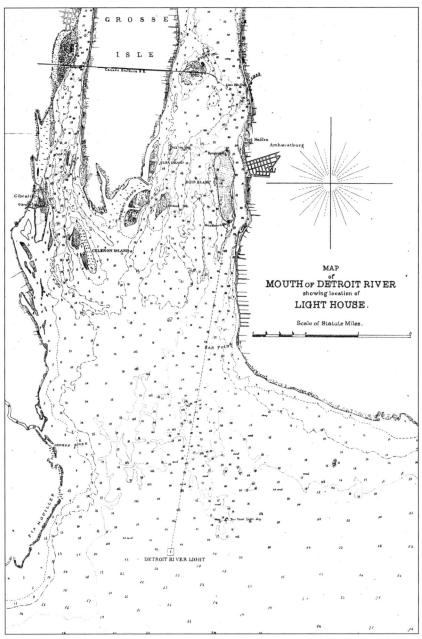

This enlarged map of the Detroit River Light's location clearly shows the mis location of the bar point lightship to the northeast of the lighthouse.

135

house. It was decided that a site one and one eighth miles southwest of the Bar Point lightship, with a water depth of 22 feet would be ideal for the location of the new lighthouse.

Before work on the lighthouse could proceed, more money would have to be extracted from Congress. Fortunately, this was the 1880s and not the 1980s, and projects of navigation on the Great Lakes were considered a necessary expenditure allocated without pork barrel strings attached. On February 3, 1883, Congress passed an allocation of an additional $40,000 for continuing the construction. Unfortunately, the project got hung up in the Michigan State Government. The Federal Government did not have "...title to and jurisdiction over..." the site where the lighthouse was to be built. It took until May 8, 1884 for the State of Michigan to convey title and jurisdiction.

Ice and the swift flow of the Detroit River were the primary concerns in the design of the crib onto which the new lighthouse would be placed. For that reason, a unique shape was decided upon, that being an elongated hexagon with the sharply pointed ends oriented to the upbound and downbound flows. The flat elongated sides would allow the water and ice to pass rather than build and obstruct, while the sharp ends worked as icebreakers. This crib was originally proposed to measure 52 feet wide and 140 feet long. The Lighthouse Board, however, amended the plans so that the upper part of the foundation was to measure 40 feet wide and 85 feet long while standing 10 feet above the mean high water line. Concrete faced with stone would be the

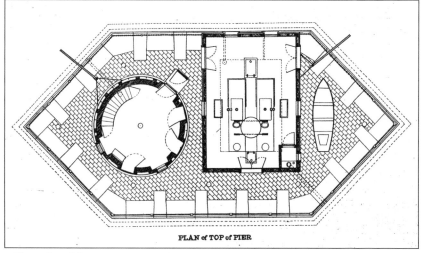

PLAN of TOP of PIER

Floor plan of the Detroit River Lighthouse showing fog signal boilers and most importantly, the flush toilet (lower right hand corner of square building). Note the "soil pipe" running from the toilet to the river through the foundation.

walls that the crib would be placed on, against the river and its ice. Small stone blocks, broken to shape and set in cement, like the lighthouse pier at Stannard's Rock, would be the paving that would cover the pier. Room for a boiler house and coal cellar would also be constructed into the crib, then the lighthouse and related structures would be placed atop those spaces.

Next, problems developed in the depths of water available and shoreside accommodations that were needed to facilitate the construction of the crib and the handling of the vessels in the project. The properties on the American side were simply not right for the needs of the project, but land, water and material at Amherstburg, on the Canadian side were well-suited to the task. For that reason, application was transmitted to the Canadian Governor-General to use the facilities of that nation in the project. On March 13, 1884, permission was granted and the project to construct the Detroit River Lighthouse went into high gear.

In advance of the gaining of permission to use Amherstburg as a base of operations, bids and contracts began to evolve for the construction of the lighthouse tower. The tower was to be made of cast iron and have a conical shape standing 32 feet tall. It was to have four stories surmounted by a main galley deck and a cylindrical watch-room that had to be eight feet high and 10 feet in diameter. The three lower stories of the tower were to be lined with brick with the lowest being 13 inches thick, the next higher being 9 inches thick and the upper most being 4 inches thick. Advertisements for the contractors to participate in the bidding were placed in local newspapers, and the bids came rolling in. On March 1, 1884, the bids were opened and it was found that the Russell Wheel and Foundry Company of Detroit had submitted the lowest bid at $7,450. Being a government project the contract was, of course, awarded to the lowest bidder.

A watertight box was constructed ashore at Amherstburg in the shape of the crib as the spring's warmth cleared the ice from the Detroit River. The construction of the crib was started on March 18, just four days after the Canadian authorities had given permission to use the Amherstburg site. This timber crib, reinforced with iron, had an empty weight of just over 300 tons and drew just over three feet of water. After seven feet of concrete was poured into its bottom to add stability and rigidity, it weighed slightly over 1,058 tons and drew 11.3 feet of water. By July 1, the crib was given its first load of stone and two days later was towed out to the chosen position for the new light and filled with water until it sat upon the river's bottom. A series of piles had been driven into this location previous to the crib's arrival and insured that the structure would be placed exactly where the engineers wanted it to be located. To keep vessels from hitting the crib, as the *Buffalo* would 113 years later, two red warning lanterns were placed upon it and would remain there until the close of navigation in the end of November. A temporary shack was erected on the crib and housed the two men who were charged with keeping the lanterns lighted. In effect, that shack was, technically, the first lighthouse on the site. Thus those two men were the first lightkeepers on the site—although it is a sure bet that they did not wear that position's snappy uniform. Once the crib was fully sunken onto the riverbed, it was decided that it would be filled with loose stone to hold it in

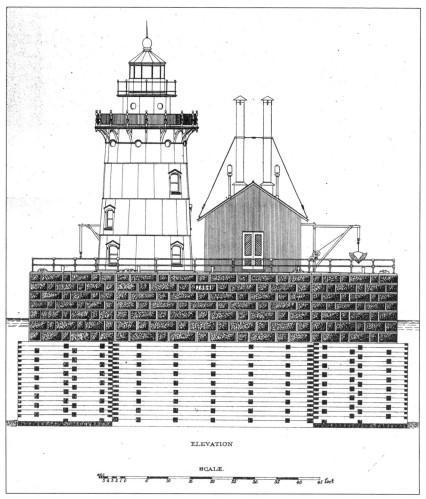

Drawing of the Detroit River Lighthouse as it was submitted to the United States Congress in 1885.

place. Next, it would be pumped free of water and the space between the stones would be filled with concrete. This was somewhat of a change from the plan that the Lighthouse Board had approved, which called for solid concrete to replace the loose stones which were to be removed. The engineers on the scene, however, felt that the technique would add uniformity of strength and thus presented the proposal to the board. Immediately upon receiving the idea, the board agreed and the concrete was poured into the pile of stone. By September, the stone facing was in place and the concrete pouring was finished.

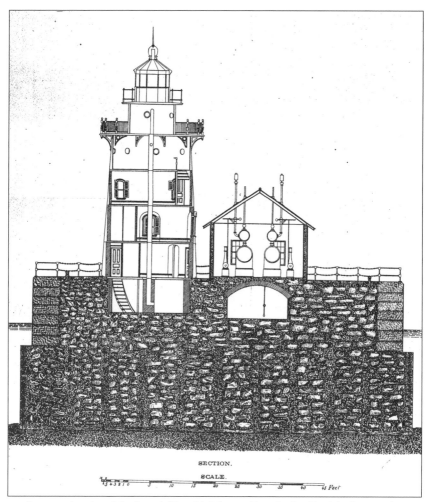

Cutaway drawing of the Detroit River Lighthouse. Note the details of the fog signal equipment.

In keeping with the Lighthouse Board's normal methods on the Great Lakes, some of the hardware from another site was reused in the Detroit River Lighthouse project. The steam plant and concrete mixer that were used in the Stannard's Rock Lighthouse project two years earlier were both used in the Detroit River project. Additionally, the Blake stone-crusher that had been used in the Stannard's Rock effort was transported and used at the Detroit River site.

During the initial placement of the crib, some settling of the structure was noted. For that reason, 85 cords of rubble stone which added up to 550 tons was distributed on the high side of the crib and left there over the winter. The following spring, on April 17, 1885 the engineers returned to the site and were delighted to find that the crib, although now 18 inches lower, had settled evenly. On the following day, the warning lanterns were relighted and their keepers restationed at the site. Unfortunately, the pile of ballast stone that had helped to evenly settle the crib now prevented the construction of a new shack for the lampkeepers. They were, instead, assigned to be quartered on the steamship that the Lighthouse Board had chartered to work the project. Odds are that those accommodations were far better than the shack of the previous season.

Spring was late that year as it followed a very severe winter, and the full construction effort could not be resumed until May. When the operations resumed, the first action was to clear the ballast stones. These were simply tossed over the side and into the river to add to the base of the structure. Some 288 additional cords of riprap stone were added to that base. Next, the construction of the tower and fog signal were started. The fog signal itself consisted of a steam operated 10-inch whistle. The boiler which provided the steam was a locomotive-style, return-flue type. For the purposes of lighthouse use, modifications were made in the system's whistle valve, pump-brackets and whistle gear. Twin signals were placed in the fog signal building. The building itself was constructed of heavy timber frames covered on the outside by two-inch planking and plain boards on the inside. Like a fortress, the space between the walls of the building were filled with a mortar that consisted of a mix of sawdust and lime. Lastly, the entire building was sheathed in number 18 corrugated iron on the outside and number 26 plain sheet iron on the inside. In one modern addition, a three-by-five-foot "water closet" was constructed in the northeast corner of the fog signal building. It came complete with a toilet that flushed from a water storage tank, and a "soil pipe" (for discharge) that was kept clean and clear of ice by the use of blow-off steam from the boiler. The term "blow-off" used in describing the toilet's function was the 1885 Lighthouse Board's, and not that of the author of this text, but appropriate snickers can be applied by the reader. The toilet's flushings emptied directly into the Detroit River. Including the toilet, the fog signal building cost just $2,594.

By mid-summer of 1885, the project was nearly complete and the tower was ready to be capped with its lamp room. A standard, 10-sided lamproom was planted atop the lighthouse. Inside the lamproom was placed a Fourth Order optic with a 56-foot focal plane. This optic covered the whole horizon for a full 360-degree span. It presented a fixed white light for one minute, followed by six flashes of white of 10 seconds each in the following minute, then the sequence repeated. In clear weather it could be seen for 14 miles which was only four miles greater than the old Bar Point lightship. The flashing capability of the new lighthouse, however, made it far easier to identify and tremendously more useful than the old lightship. On August 17, 1885 the work crews were removed from the site and on August 20 the light was displayed for the first time as the Detroit River Lighthouse was officially activated.

By the mid-1990s, the incredibly accurate Global Positioning System, or GPS, was making nearly every other form of navigation aid obsolete. With a series of satellites telling inexpensive ground units exactly where on the planet the user is located, things such as lighthouses are no longer needed— or so you would think. The odd characteristic about the computers and navigation systems that use GPS is that they are the world's most accurate idiots. These systems do exactly what they are told—and nothing more! Thus with the use of such systems comes the obligation of the users to consider the "human factors" involved in the utilization of such equipment and even then there is the uncanny capability of humans to simply screw up.

In defense of the *Buffalo's* owners, American Steamship Company (ASC), it is clear that they had gone to great lengths to try to assure that the human factors were under control in the operation of their vessels. The company is one of few that has a "Director of Safety and Navigation" to aid in assuring that their vessels are operated at the maximum level of safety. Additionally, ASC trains its crews in "Bridge Team Management" or BTM, a program similar to the "Crew Resource Management" (CRM) program used at every airline. This training is designed to teach crews to use all of the resources at their disposal to achieve the goal of a safe completion of a given journey. It also teaches the individual crew members to recognize and deal with the human factors element when it begins to show. There are safety audits, procedures training and a general atmosphere of a desire to achieve

Looking much like she did when she hit the Detroit River Lighthouse, the motor vessel Buffalo *rounds Mission Point in August of 1984 with the lights glowing. (Author's photo)*

the highest level of safe operations at ASC, yet, even the safest of companies can be caught in the web of human events. Thus it was that a simple human error garnished with just a hint of complacency lead to an embarrassing and expensive incident.

Although the modern operators of lake vessels and their crews make a maximum effort to avoid trouble, there is always that small human factor which can set in motion a chain of events that sometimes leads to an accident. Although we may train and manage our operations to the greatest extent possible, the oddest of coincidences are often impossible to avoid. In the case of the *Buffalo's* incident with the Detroit River Light, it appears possible that the same GPS system that has made the lighthouses obsolete, may have been the cause of the collision between the lakeboat and the lighthouse. We can only speculate that if the GPS had never been developed, the hands of a skilled mariner would have been on the wheel of the *Buffalo* as she slid safely past the flashing beacon of the Detroit River Lighthouse. Then again, if the lighthouse had never been constructed, the *Buffalo* would have missed the Bar Point lightship by one and one-eighth miles. Such speculation is worth only the time that it took to read this last paragraph. The lakeboats will continue to navigate by means of growing technology, the steamship companies will continue to fight to manage the human factors involved, the lighthouses will continue to become more obsolete, and accidents will always happen.

XI

MARKING THE BOUNDARY BETWEEN LIFE AND DEATH

In the vernacular of the lighthouse historians it is stated that the Marblehead, Ohio, lighthouse is the oldest continuously operating light on the Great Lakes. This single statement has enough loopholes and qualifiers to make any lawyer proud. It implies that the light was never taken out of service since it's establishment in 1821 and has operated during every navigation season thereafter, while other lights on the lakes established in the same year have not. It is quite likely that this is true. After all, this part of western Lake Erie has always been a key to regional commerce and activity in one way or another. During the War of 1812, critical sea battles were waged in the waters off this lighthouse. In the Civil War, prisoners of the Confederate Army were held on nearby Johnson's Island. Cut stone used to build the towers of lighthouses such as Stannard's Rock and Spectacle Reef was quarried near the Marblehead Lighthouse. For many decades and into modern times, essential cargoes of coal were shipped from Sandusky Bay at the foot of this light. Today, the area is Great Lakes wine country, and tourists flock to the region for the spirits of the grape. In short, the lighthouse has always been active, because the region itself has always been active, so the whole of the Marblehead area can be called "the oldest continuously operating place on the Great Lakes".

Driving out to visit the Marblehead Lighthouse, visitors will find themselves on a two-lane blacktop highway that stretches to the east. For a time, it is hard to tell if this road is taking you deep into farm country or out to Lake Erie. Without warning, old stone buildings constructed of locally mined bedrock begin to appear, and the shops and stores that sell local souvenirs begin to display lighthouse miniatures. As the drive toward the end of the point continues, the entire area turns into a delightful matrix of life near the lakes. It is not hard to obey the speed limit, simply because the setting is so pleasant that you instinctively slow your car just to make the experience last a bit longer. It soon becomes apparent that the entire community at Marblehead revolves around one local item—the lighthouse! Every place you look there are images of the Marblehead Light, even the local police cars sport the image of the lighthouse on their doors. Each autumn the peaceful community suddenly becomes packed with lighthouse buffs as the annual lighthouse festival takes place. The wait to visit and enter the old

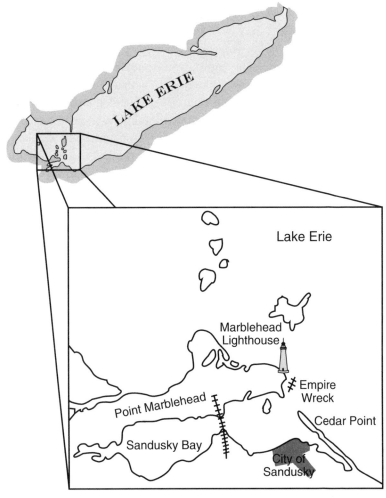

light tower can be as long as one and one-half hours with long lines of tourists paying their respects to one of the oldest of the lakes beacons.

The point of land on which the Marblehead Lighthouse is located divides Sandusky Bay from Lake Erie. Stretching a half dozen miles to the east, the point provides a natural breakwater, and without doubt its mass has provided shelter to countless mariners. The tip of the point was a natural site to locate a lighthouse and, in later years, a lifesaving station. To this day, the United States Coast Guard maintains a station at the Marblehead location. In 1822, the powers that be activated the lighthouse at Marblehead for the first time. Made of hand-laid stone, the conical tower elevated the lamp to the point where it was given a focal plane of about 52 feet above Lake Erie's surface. To stand up against any force that the lake may dish out, the lighthouse was given walls that were five feet thick at the base. The tower was constructed to have a 25-foot-diameter base with a taper to a 12-foot-diameter top. According to published Marblehead Lighthouse historian, Betty Neidecker, the contract for the building of the light was awarded to Stephen Wolverton who in turn subcontracted the work to William Kelly. Contractor Kelly, a noted local stone mason from Sandusky, used native limestone to build the tower. The origin of the station's lamproom is unclear, and it could have

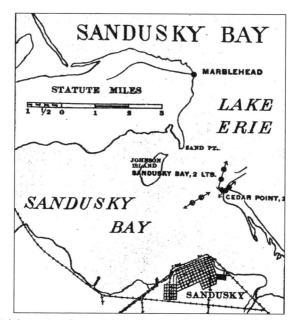

This 1896 Lighthouse Board map shows a closeup of the Marblehead Light and its later companion lights on Cedar Point.

In this detail of the Marblehead Lighthouse it can be seen that the lamp is a plastic beacon which has replaced the original optic. (Pat Snider photo)

been constructed by either the tower builders or the lamp builder. Within the lamproom, an optic which used 13 lamps and reflectors was constructed by Winslow Lewis. Some sources say that the following year the keeper's quarters were finished and later occupied. Although the same sources say that the original keeper's dwelling was located three miles from the lighthouse, others imply that the quarters were actually on the lighthouse grounds. If the quarters were indeed three miles away, by 1823 standards it was far closer to civilization than was the lighthouse itself. By the beginning of May, 1857, civilization was not yet encroaching on the Marblehead light as her beacon patiently flashed waiting for mariners to be guided and warned.

As the lakeboats started the 1857 season, lake commerce was beginning a boom which would continue nearly unchecked for the next 120 years. Granted, there would be the occasional financial "panic," and the decade-long "Depression," but after each of these there was always a recovery and the factories and industry that was fed by the lakeboats always came roaring back. In 1857, the new locks at Sault Sainte Marie would see their second full season of operation having been opened on June 18, 1855. The following year, 1856, would also be significant because it would be the year that the Bessemer method of steel production would be perfected. This method of shooting hot air through a mixture of iron ore, limestone and coke, mixed within a blast furnace, would remove impurities and leave behind molten steel. Originally, Bessemer called his blast furnace a "converter," which would have been appropriate for what the process would soon do to the Great Lakes maritime industry. The making of steel, and the nation's thirst for that product, helped to fuel the industrial revolution and converted the Great Lakes maritime fleet from hauling passengers and sundry packaged goods to hauling raw materials for making steel. This boom would result in the Great Lakes becoming the most active waterway on earth. Indeed, as the 1857 season began, everyone involved in lakes commerce stood on the threshold of an expansion that none of them could imagine.

On May 3, 1857, the 350-ton Canadian barque *Empire* was moored at the Toledo, Ohio lumber dock of J. W. Russell. Being loaded aboard the boat was a cargo of "shaped" or "squared" timbers. These squared timbers were different from the normal lumber planks in that they were long sections of a given tree that had simply had their bark cut off making them into a long square piece of solid wood. The lumbermen loathed this type of timber product because, much like peeling a potato by simply cutting it to have four square sides, there was a great deal of waste in the process of squaring timber. These timbers were, however, highly popular in Great Britain and other European nations and thus there was always an export demand for squared timbers. Captain Alexander Milligan's command, the *Empire*, was specially equipped to handle squares. The barque was rigged with hoisting equipment that was moved by a state of the art two-horsepower mechanism—which was, of course, two horses. Fueled by oats, the two-horsepowered lift would load and unload the heavy squared timbers far more efficiently than any gang of dockwhollopers. Seeing that the *Empire* was fully capable of loading and unloading under her own power, this may have been one of the first examples of a self-unloader on the lakes. One of the horses was brand-new to the job, but the other was a longtime veteran of the Great Lakes, having seen many a storm and bitter cold day of work. Today's cargo was bound to Tonawanda, New York, at the east end of Lake Erie, but to the veteran mariner horse this made little difference.

He simply pulled at the line attached to the rig when directed. When the work was over, so was the pulling—then it was time for oats.

Also aboard the *Empire* was a crew of a dozen mariners. First Mate Thomas Marsh kept a close watch on the cargo and loading operations, as was his duty. Second Mate Alexander McLane probably worked right along side the other members of the crew, as his rank had little other privilege other than higher pay and standing an additional watch. Other members of the able-bodied crew included John Maloy, Robert Moore, George Poasock, John Skelton, Edward Macaby, William Irvine, and Patrick Flanery, all Canadians who had shipped from Port Robinson. There were Ship's Cook James Adams and Crewman John Albors, who had a bond that none of the others aboard the *Empire* could share. These two had common ground in the fact that they were among the small number of black men working the lakes in 1857. Lastly, there was young "Thomas," the orphan cabin boy from Port Robinson, who had shipped aboard under unrecorded circumstances. In all, the *Empire* was a fairly unique vessel with a rather unique crew that could easily have come from a Dickens tale. When Captain Milligan guided the *Empire* out of the Maumee River, Lake Erie was waiting for them, and the lake was not in a good mood.

Although there is no official record as to the direction of the storm winds which churned the lake that spring day, the collective accounts seem to

This photo was taken during the "Holy Thursday" spring gale of 1998, and shows the waves breaking at about the same location as Keeper Keyes and his crew launched their rescue boat. It is into waves just like these that they launched to attempt the rescue of the crew of the Empire. *(Pat Snider photo)*

prove that the blow was a nor'easter. On Sandusky Bay, west of Marblehead Point, the tracks of the Cleveland & Toledo Railroad crossed the waters in a sort of railroad causeway. So strong was the storm that blew in from Lake Erie, that the waves swamped the railroad tracks and the evening trains were unable to pass across the bay. Around the western end of Lake Erie the frail vessels, which were the best that the era had to offer against the lake, were sent fleeing from the storm. Small wooden steamers such as the steambarge *Bay City* and the passenger and package freighter *New York*, although considered to be substantial lakeboats in their day, suddenly found themselves nearly overwhelmed by the blow. At 372 tons, the *Bay City* was still no match for Lake Erie's temper and was forced to run for shelter at Put-in-Bay on South Bass Island. Rolling the length of the lake, powerful seas had boarded her nearly from the time that she had departed Detroit bound for Sandusky. By the time she had neared Put-in-Bay, her master decided that he could not make the run of just over a dozen miles to get to the shelter of Sandusky Bay. Shortly after the *Bay City* came to her original shelter, the winds and waves shifted and forced her to run over to Kelleys Island where she rode out the rest of the gale. Likewise, the 184 foot *New York* was pounced upon by Lake Erie and mauled. The steamer's massive oak rudder was practically bitten away by the waves, but she too managed to make the shelter of Kelleys Island.

Sailing out in this spring madness, the *Empire* was making bad weather of it as her load of heavy square timbers weighed her down. Along with the *Empire*, the sailing vessel *Mary and Lucy* was also being tossed by the storm. At some point in the maelstrom, both Captain Nickerson of the *Mary and Lucy*, and Captain Milligan of the *Empire* concluded that there was not a prayer of making any headway in the storm and decided to turn and run for Sandusky.

Ashore, on Marblehead, the seas came exploding over the beach and expended themselves as flood waters upon the point. Keeper Jared B. Keyes knew that now his job was of its greatest importance. With the prevailing weather conditions, desperate mariners would likely be running for Sandusky Bay, and his light alone would mark the boundary between life and death. The clockwork mechanism that made the panels rotate and caused the beam to flash had to be fully wound, the whale oil which fueled the wicks of the 13 Argand lamps had to be kept filled and the light trimmed. Outside of the lighthouse the waves were stone gray in color and capped with sharp peaks of white foam as they came rolling toward the tower. The wind screamed and beat at the stones of the lighthouse and everyone associated with the station realized exactly why the building specifications had called for the tower to be five feet thick at its base.

There is little doubt that in such a storm all of the members of the keeper's family pitched in to insure that the station continues to function. Likely to have been on hand at that time were the keeper's wife, Arvilla, his son, Robert, and his new son-in-law, William Clemons, as well as daughter Alvira Clemons. Alvira Keyes had done fairly well in her selection of a husband. When looking at an 1872 map of Marblehead, no less than seven parcels of land and two stone docks belong to the Clemons Family. On the other hand, any historian will tell you that one of the positions of greatest social accomplishment in 1857 was that of lighthouse keeper, so probably it was William Clemons who did well for himself by being wed to the lighthouse keeper's daughter. William and Alvira were wed in January 1, 1856 at the lighthouse in what was no doubt a big social event on Marblehead. Now, just over a year later, the lighthouse was hosting a marriage of a different sort. This was the wedding of wind and waves, and it was about to deliver a very special wedding gift onto the point at Marblehead.

From out of the spume of the gale appeared the silhouette of a storm-battered sailing vessel. It was 10 o'clock on Monday morning, the fourth day of May, 1857 and soon every soul at the lighthouse was alerted to the floundering vessel just off shore. The vessel, it turned out, was the barque *Empire* and her unique crew of men and horses. As the residents of the lighthouse watched, the crew aboard the vessel scrambled to reset their canvas and tack back against the storm. At first their efforts appeared successful as the boat rounded and came up close to the wind. Lake Erie, however, was prepared for such a maneuver and sent a sudden burst of wind to smite the boat. The wind carried away the forward stay and the jib sail reefed loose and then was lost. Without her jib, the vessel was unable to put her heels to the wind and the waves grabbed her. In short order, the *Empire* was cast into the trough of the seas and broached with the waves washing over her beam. Cascades of gray lake water ran freely over the cargo and deck of the *Empire* as the waves shoved her toward the lighthouse and across the boundary between life and death. In desperation, Captain Milligan ordered both anchors dropped, and all hands went at the task of dropping the hooks knowing that their lives depended on it. Nearly as soon as the anchors went down, they took hold and the *Empire* swung about with her head to the wind and apparently safe.

Even with her anchors holding the bottom, the *Empire* was not in a safe position by any standard. A number of things could happen and cause the vessel to wreck and all of the residents of Marblehead knew it. Her anchor chains could part, her seams and planking could work open, her deck could swamp and her hold flood, her cargo could shift or her anchors could drag— all of these possibilities were discussed by those gathered at the lighthouse as they kept watch over the boat. The year 1857 was a full decade before professional lifesavers would be stationed on Marblehead Point and so if any assistance was going to be needed by the crew of the *Empire*, it would have to come from the local residents. Being the only official government maritime authority on the point, Keeper Keyes wasted no time in mustering a crew of volunteers to man a rescue surfboat. By early afternoon Keyes, his son, Robert, and his son-in-law, William Clemons, had been joined by J.A. Spencer, Richard Tichman, John Meacham, George Clark and John Burns as all of them waited for the worst to happen to the *Empire*.

When standing on the boundary between life and death on the Great Lakes, it normally does not take long for the lake to cross the line. So it was

As of this writing, the Marblehead Lighthouse has warned mariners for a remarkable 172 years! (Pat Snider photo)

151

that the wait for the volunteers at the Marblehead Lighthouse was not long at all. By three o'clock that afternoon, it became apparent that the storm was intensifying. With that escalation in the violence the crowd ashore began to see that the *Empire* was again being forced toward the rocks of the point. Her anchors were dragging and the relentless seas were now washing clean over her decks. For the next 50 minutes she wallowed toward the point, but 1,850 feet before the rocks could get her, the waves finished the 350-ton ship. Finding its way into her hold, the lake waterlogged the boat and she rolled onto her side. In an avalanche of heavy shaped timbers her cargo cascaded over and through her sides into the seas. The two horses were cut loose and left to swim among the churning waves of ice water. The crew who had not been killed in the sliding cargo, or by their initial submergence in the lake, scurried into that part of her masts and rigging that still remained above water. Lake Erie, however, was not finished with the *Empire* and continued to shove her to the southwest.

Seeing the vessel make her final roll, Keyes and his band of would-be lifesavers went about launching their lifeboat. Placing a large lifeboat into the teeth of the storm was no easy task. To make matters worse, the water had only recently been thawed from winter's ice and the temperature was close to freezing. By placing themselves in the lake's grip, the amateur rescuers put themselves into the same peril as the mariners who clung to the wreck of the *Empire*. The only difference was that the *Empire's* crew had started out with 350-ton barque and the rescuers were about to challenge the lake in a small surfboat. It is also important to note that these amateur lifesavers were not trained, nor were they practiced in the art of lifesaving. They had no special equipment such as protective suits, cork life belts or regularly inspected equipment. Their challenge of Lake Erie was either pure bravery or pure madness. Still, there was no way that those ashore could stand by and watch as the crew of the *Empire* perished. It was clear that some of them were already dying and dropping from the vessel into the lake.

Nearly as soon as the lifeboat was launched with Keyes at the steering oar, the lake began to demonstrate the folly of the effort. As the lifeboat breached the first set of breakers, one of the crew's dry rotted oars snapped in his hands. Quickly, Keyes gave that crewman his steering oar and the boat continued ahead. Before the little rescue craft had cleared the breakers, the lake had bitten away two more oars and the crew was forced to turn back. Lake Erie was not about to let the rescue gang get away that easily. With a large breaker the lake reached out and tossed the lifeboat end-over-end as it approached the beach and tossed its occupants into the surf and upon the

Tapering from a 25-foot diameter at its base to a 12-foot diameter at its top, the Marblehead Lighthouse was constructed to withstand the worst that Lake Erie could deliver. (Pat Snider photo)

rocks. Bruised, soaked and shivering uncontrollably, the rescue crew all managed to drag themselves ashore and then did the same for their lifeboat. A call was sent out for additional oars, and was soon answered. Before anyone could be warmed completely by the bonfire that Arvilla and Alvira had built on the beach, the rescue boat was again launched. Seeing that the future held a number of soaked and freezing men, the two ladies of the lake went about gathering as much dry clothing and as many dry blankets as they could find, then waited by the bonfire which they continued to fuel.

A line was strung from the shore and, by way of the lifeboat, was attached to the wreck. Using that line the rescue team managed to keep their tiny surfboat under control and succeeded in removing the two crewmembers of the *Empire* who remained alive. Captain Milligan remained alive and able to get aboard the lifeboat. Crewman Robert Moore was still alive but in an insensible condition. Using the rope to the shore for stability, the lifesavers pulled the two castaways back across the boundary between life and death and toward the dry clothing and warm fire that Arvilla and Alvira had prepared. The exact location of the wreck is unclear. All that is recorded is the vessel went over on her side "...110 rods from the lighthouse..." and it was "...in deep water..." It is also recorded that the storm continued to blow the wreck "...further down the shore." Just how far it went or where it ended up is unknown.

Shortly after reaching the shore, the entire group was warmed and freshly clothed by Arvilla and Alvira. After being given "restoratives," Robert Moore made a full recovery and the task of collecting the spilled cargo and dead bodies was started. There was, however, one additional survivor of the *Empire's* wreck. The eldest of the two deck horses managed to swim ashore and found a home on Marblehead Point. There is no record as to what happened to the horse, but the animal showed itself to be more than a match for Lake Erie.

Later that week the sailing vessel *Mary and Lucy* tied up at a Sandusky dock. Captain Nickerson reported that from the dock through his marine glass he could see the remains of the *Empire* as she slowly went to pieces in the waves. Both the *Mary and Lucy* and *Empire* had attempted to make Sandusky Bay at nearly the same time, but seeing that it was not possible, Captain Nickerson directed his boat north toward Put-in-Bay, and found shelter there. The *Empire* had continued south and found only Marblehead Point and destruction.

A steady stream of visitors come to the lighthouse at Marblehead during the fair weather months and throngs of lighthouse buffs crowd the place during the autumn lighthouse festival. Standing at the foot of the lighthouse they gaze out across the beautiful waters of Lake Erie and ponder the setting, never realizing that they are standing on boundary between life and death. Few, if any, know the tale of the *Empire's* wreck, whose bones rest within wading distance of where they are now standing. For those who do know the story, or who have read this version of it, there is just one unanswerable, nagging question that runs through the mind as you tour Marblehead, "I wonder what ever became of that horse?"

XII
VIEIRA'S PRIVATE RANGE

Sources say that the concept of the "range light" was invented in the year 1860 by Dewitt C. Brawn on the banks of the Saginaw River. The range light system consists of two lights that are mounted on towers, one being placed a given distance behind the other. These lights are located in a manner so that when aligned in the eyesight of an oncoming vessel master, they assure him that his vessel is within the navigation channel. It is said that Dewitt Brawn, the 15-year-old son of the Saginaw River Light's keeper, had the idea of hoisting two lanterns atop two towers and giving the incoming lakeboats guidance in the channel. From there, the legend says, the idea caught on and soon spread around the lakes and later the world.

As to whether or not the Dewitt legend is true it is difficult to say. Records concerning his invention of the range light are scarce and no patent exists. Some sources say that the British were using a system of ranges as early as the 1820s. As with any single idea, it is nearly impossible to put a finger on the exact moment that the concept was created. Odds are that mariners were doing things with lights which made navigation more accurate long before Dewitt's time, and if that were in the form of a range or not, the idea was the same—increase safety and aid navigation. Certainly Dewitt's homemade range was the first on the Saginaw River, but it would not be the last. That honor would go to John Vieira nearly 120 years later. Much like Dewitt's range, the records of the creation of Vieira's range are scarce. In fact, the only written account of Vieira's range system is what you are now reading and, although it is hearsay, it is worth telling.

For several decades up to the 1980s, the dredge *Niagara* slithered the length of the Saginaw River delivering her cargoes of Lake Huron's bottom to the thundering foundries that worked at the head of the waterway. The

So often did the Niagara pass up and down the Saginaw River that she almost blended into the background—much like she does in this picture. This photo was taken just 14 days before she was withdrawn from service. No doubt Captain Vieira is aboard guiding her. (Author's photo)

sand that the boat dredged from the lake bottom was used in making castings for molded auto parts and other material which needed to be manufactured from poured and formed molten metal. Construction sites of all types needed sand in their work, and that was also provided by way of Erie Sand Steamship's motor-vessel *Niagara*. From the opening of the navigation season until the last possible day the river could be navigated, the 257-foot dredge went casually about her toil. Normally, the boat made the round trip from the pumping grounds to the dock in about 36 to 48 hours, so her captain found himself bringing his vessel through the river about three or four times a week.

Often, the little green-hulled *Niagara* would blow her whistle for one of the drawbridges, and the bridge tender would let her continue much closer to the span than other lakeboats before stopping traffic and opening the bridge. After all, the crew of the *Niagara* was so good at "making" the Saginaw River's bridges that they needed far less time and room to safely complete the passage. This was of particular importance on the old Zilwaukee Bridge. This was the only drawbridge on Interstate 75, from Naples, Florida, to Sault Sainte Marie, Michigan. In later years the old drawbridge was replaced with a high-span, but in the era of the *Niagara* the "draw's" opening could back up traffic on I-75 for two dozen miles. The least offender in such backups was the *Niagara*. Her crew could push her up and the tender could drop the gates at the last moment. The little dredge would then speed through the gap and clear it practically before the first motorist became impatient.

Considering the boat's frequent passages and extended navigation season, an interesting situation developed. The crew knew every turn and shallow spot in the river, but found that in the beginning of the season they were often sailing before the Coast Guard had placed all of the river's buoys. Likewise, they often sailed the river long after the buoys had been removed at the end of each season. In daylight this was not a great concern because her pilothouse crew knew every turn and channel. When the boat was attempting to navigate in the dark, however, the story was different. Even the fabled crew of the *Niagara* could not judge the turns of the Saginaw River in the blackness of a winter night without some kind of markings. It was John Vieira, the *Niagara's* captain, who cooked up the solution to this problem.

For a long time, Captain Vieira had pondered what everyone else in the Saginaw River's maritime community had always known—that the *Niagara's* pilothouse crew knew the river better than anyone else, including the Coast Guard. On several of the passages through the river, the captain and his crew took notes on certain trees that lined up at the turns, both inbound and outbound. One day, said to be in 1978, while the *Niagara's* crane was busy unloading her cargo of sand, Vieira dispatched two of his crew to the local Kmart. They were on an excursion to purchase as many big aluminum pie plates and big red bicycle reflectors as they could find. On the next trip out, the captain assigned his two agents to proceed ahead of the boat by way of land and meet her at the critical turns. At each of these turns the coordinated an effort to nail the reflectors and pie plates to the trees on the river bank making a "range" on each turn. In the daylight, the pie plates would show up; in the dark, the *Niagara's* searchlight would illuminate the red reflectors, and by aligning the targets the boat could make every turn.

Oddly, what started out as a simple experiment soon became a useful tool. In fact, the homemade range was more efficient than the official Coast Guard buoys. So precise was the placement of the reflectors that when the navigation season opened on the river, there were instances when the crew of the *Niagara* would notify the Coast Guard when their buoys were placed in the improper locations. When the Coast Guard officials inspected the site, they found that the *Niagara's* crew was right. Scratching their heads a bit, the Coast Guard would take note and have the buoy moved. This, of course, only added to the legend of the crew of the old dredge. "Those guys really

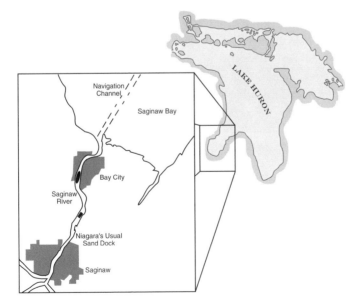

know the river," would be the utterance along the shore. No one knew that the trick was a system of pie plates and bicycle reflectors.

Another advantage to the homemade ranges was that they allowed the boat to keep her speed up when traversing the river. Normally, a strange lakeboat coming into the river has to spot the buoys and match them against the chart to thread the channels and turns. Then a specific heading has to be held in order to insure that the boat will not run into the shallows. Using his range, all that Captain Vieira needed to do was line up the reflectors and plates in the distance and "let 'er go." Also, when the winds and current were strong, keeping the range lined up in your sight insured that the boat was not drifting out of the channel. This all allowed Vieira to move his boat and his cargoes more efficiently and safely than anyone else using the Saginaw River. To his crew the homemade system became known as "Vieira's private range."

Vieira was forced to keep his private system of ranges a close secret. If the Coast Guard were to find out that an unauthorized and unapproved system was being used for commercial navigation they would surely have an "administrative cow." The result of the administrative fits would be, at the very least, the dismantling of the ranges. So the system had to be quietly used, and the crew of the *Niagara* were very good at that. Still, there were likely plenty of snickers when the range would show one of the Coast Guard's officially-placed buoys out of place—and discovered by the *Niagara*. Like most mariners on the Great Lakes, Vieira had a circle of trusted colleagues and, although his range was kept secret from outsiders, he did share it with his good friends. One of those colleagues is said to have been Captain William McCoy of the American Steamship Company. Often called by their former name "the BoCo boats" which is the Great Lakes slang for the Boland & Corneilus fleet, the American Steamship Company's boats have long been a common sight on the Saginaw River. McCoy, much like Vieira, was often at the helm as one of the big BoCo boats clawed up the river's twisting channels. Shortly after he had developed his private range system, legend has it that Vieira let McCoy in on the secret, and apparently McCoy took advantage of the range.

As the story is told, one gray and stormy day a number of vessels were wind-bound in the Saginaw River. Among the boats waiting to get out was the BoCo steamer *John J. Boland* which was McCoy's command. While the boats were waiting, some of the crews had gathered in a sailor's haunt adjacent to the river, and began debating the prospects of getting out of the river in the ugly weather. As it happened, Vieira's *Niagara* was tied up and

One yarn that is often told along the Saginaw River is that, using Vieira's ranges, Captain McCoy once backed the giant Laker John J. Boland out of the river amidst a wild storm. (D. J. Story photo)

unloading, so he happened to be in attendance at the local haunt. While the discussion raged, Vieira suddenly spoke up.

"McCoy'll be the first one otta' here," he stated flatly.

Scoffing loudly some in the crowd challenged the captain, and asked what made him so sure that McCoy could get the *Boland* away.

"Because," Vieira answered with a wink and a knowing smirk, "he knows the range."

Whether or not McCoy ever used Vieira's private range there is no record. But as the story goes, while all of the other boats were waiting for the weather to moderate, the *John J. Boland* was "backed" all of the way up the Saginaw River and out onto Saginaw Bay!

Economic trends and the powers of big business always have a far greater effect on vessels and crews than any other factor. Thus, the repercussions on the Great Lakes maritime industry caused by the recession of 1980 eventually reached as far as the little green dredge *Niagara* in 1983. All of the factors that caused the U.S. auto industry to crash also caused the need for auto parts to decline. That decline included the decline in need for engine block halves. The engine block halves were made from molten iron that was cast in molds made from the sand that had been delivered to Saginaw's Grey Iron Foundry for the past 23 years by the *Niagara*. With the need for the castings reduced, the need for the *Niagara* quickly evaporated. Contracts for larger vessels to bring giant piles of sand in on a monthly basis were signed, and the *Niagara's* daily deliveries were suddenly no longer needed. In the autumn of 1983 the dredge was withdrawn from the Saginaw River, never to return. A short time after departing the river trade, the *Niagara* was retired to the boneyard. Over the winter of 1997-98, at the age of 100, the boat was put to the scrapper's torch as historians and lakeboat buffs shook their collective heads in sorrow.

In an epilogue to this legend, we are told that shortly after the *Niagara* was withdrawn from the Saginaw River, Captain Vieira went along the river bank and removed the reflectors that were his private range. Now, all that is left are the official buoys and markers. Captain Vieira passed away a few years prior to this writing, and so all that is left to us is this tale of his clever system of ranges. It is likely, however, that when taking down his private range, Vieira did not get *every* marker. Odds are that someone with the proper amount of motivation may just be able to hike along the banks of the Saginaw River and find a tree or two with a bicycle reflector or pie plate attached. The hiker will then have located one of the most obscure light navigation systems in the world—Vieira's Private Range.

XIII
SAVING ROUND ISLAND

In the romantic movie *Somewhere In Time* the lead character, having swept back in time to 1912, finds his eternal true love and in courting the fair lady rows her to a nearby lighthouse. There they talk, pick clover, kick stones and generally swoon as theme music plays in the background. This entire scene is set near a beautiful lighthouse which serves to greatly enhance the romance of the moment. That lighthouse is none other than the Round Island Light, and if not for the efforts of a large number of individuals, the lighthouse may never have been there for the use of the moviemakers.

Within the Straits of Mackinac there are many treacherous reefs and shoals and a peppering of tiny islands making the area hazardous to shipping. Prior to 1894, the Lighthouse Board had been requesting funds for the establishment of a lighthouse on Round Island in order to augment the light established on Old Mackinac Point in 1892. Congress appropriated $15,000 for the establishment and construction of the Round Island Light in 1894, and the contract for its construction was reportedly awarded to local builder Frank Rounds—who is also said to have worked on Mackinac Island's famed Grand Hotel.

On May 15, 1896 the Round Island Light was made operational. The structure was a three-story, red brick building with an integral square tower. This building was set on a 40-foot-square pier, whose lower nine feet is concrete faced to help it fend off the wind, waves and ice that so often bangers the straits. The tower which supported the lamproom was 53 feet tall, but the focal plane of the original lamp is listed as being 53 feet, two inches, so the tower is several feet taller than 53 feet. A fourth order optic was installed in the lamproom which shows a white light with flashes of red at intervals of

20 seconds. The lamp was oil-powered but in later years the fuel was switched to kerosene. Officially, the attached keeper's quarters is listed as being two and one-half stories and consisting of a boiler room on the first floor; a kitchen, dining room, living room and bedroom on the second floor, and a service room plus three bedrooms on the third floor. The only thing missing from the station was a water closet—or what we would call today a bathroom. Keepers and their kin stationed at the lighthouse had to use an outhouse, or "privy." Oddly, the Detroit River Light, with others constructed a full decade earlier, had indoor toilets and running water. Just why those who built the Round Island Light decided that outhouses were better is unknown.

One of the first keepers of the Round Island Light was Chester Marshall, who was a kin to Keeper William Marshall of the Spectacle Reef Lighthouse. The tragic story of Keeper Marshall's itch was told earlier in this book. Apparently, the Marshall family was a light-keeping lot and many of their clan served on nearly every lighthouse on the Mackinac Straits at one time or another, so it is only natural to find one of then assigned to this light which was so close to home.

As with so many lighthouses, the decline of the Round Island Light began with it's automation. In 1924, the lighthouse board elected to auto-

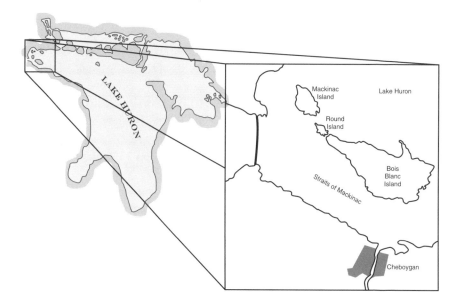

mate the station and remove its full-time keepers. By 1947, the U.S. Coast Guard had taken control of the lighthouses and declared the Round Island Station to be unneeded. A modern light-on-a-post had been built on the breakwall at Mackinac Island and the lighthouse was simply abandoned. Eleven years later, the whole of Round Island, including the lighthouse, was made a part of the Hiawatha National Forest. This lofty designation, however, did not spare the lighthouse from the scourge of vandals. Over the next two decades, the interior of the lighthouse was completely gutted and the outside was rapidly deteriorating. Then, on of October 20, 1972, there came what should have been the deathblow for the old lighthouse. A vicious autumn gale swept across the Great Lakes, and the resulting waves exploding against the lighthouse was more than the old, hollow structure could stand. The gale bit away one corner of the building and left a massive gap as if a sea monster had slithered up and taken a piece. Now the winds and waves would have free access to the lighthouse and would become the allies of the vandals—surely, the Round Island Lighthouse was now doomed!

The ways of the Great Lakes are often strange, and the results of one disaster often lead in a direction that is totally unexpected. So it was with the Round Island Light. The sight of this lighthouse that all of the local residents had grown up knowing as a beautiful landmark—sitting there in the straits with a giant bite taken out of it—was enough to shock the local residents into action. Oddly, what should have been the death stroke for the lighthouse was what that got the wheels of its restoration moving. Using funding that had been diverted from the Mackinac Island Historical Society, the "Save the Round Island Lighthouse Committee" was formed. Nearly parallel to the save the lighthouse effort, the "Friends of Round Island Lighthouse Committee" was also formed. Over the next year, the Mackinac Island newspaper, the *Town Crier,* highly publicized the effort to save the lighthouse. Finally, in late 1973, the tables started to be turned on the vandals and the lake. Loads of rip-rap stone were dumped all around the lighthouse intended to sap the energy from the waves as they approached the lighthouse. The following year, the lighthouse was placed on the National Register of Historic Places which lead the way to federal funding of the effort to save the site. Local friends of the lighthouse began to raise funds by selling photos, buttons and lithographs of the lighthouse and raised more than $12,000, but it was not going to be nearly enough money.

Saving the lighthouse was going to be a daunting task and restoration seemed impossible. The breakwall near the lighthouse needed to be rebuilt; a new roof was needed on the keeper's quarters; all of the walkways, brick

Although restored on the outside, much of the inside of the Round Island Lighthouse is a mess of fallen plaster and gutted walls.

With the help of Scout Troop 323 the inside of the Round Island Lighthouse is being cleaned and prepared for restoration. Note the brickwork above the window on the left.

For too long the Round Island Lighthouse has had cobwebs in place of its lamp. As this view shows, the site is fortunate to still have its original lamp room.

Looking down the stairway of the Round Island Lighthouse, some of the remaining woodwork can be seen. (All Mark Fowler photos)

walls and exterior woodwork was in an advanced state of decay; the interior was a clutter of debris, and the building needed to be secured against vandals. The estimate of repair costs was $90,000, and the Federal Government balked at the price tag. In fact, the U.S. Forest Service said that the lighthouse may have to be destroyed as a safety precaution, and as early as 1955 a Coast Guard survey had declared the lighthouse to be an "eyesore" and recommended that it be demolished. Fortunately, the Advisory Council on Historic Preservation, an independent arm of the Executive Branch of the U.S. Government, stepped in and ruled that they had oversight of the lighthouse, and that the Forest service had not made an adequate attempt to secure funding for its preservation. The sum of $125,000 was budgeted for fiscal year 1977 to save the lighthouse, and it was given a new lease on life.

When the people from Hollywood arrived in 1980 to film *Somewhere in Time,* the federal funds, combined with the amazing dedication of the people involved in the restoration of the lighthouse, had worked a magic that not even the moviemakers could have imagined. The exterior of the lighthouse was nearly restored, the foundation and surrounding property had been stabilized and, from the outside, the lighthouse appeared whole again. By the time that the stars took their places, it was becoming clear that the Round Island Lighthouse was on the road to preservation. Still, the lake was not going to be easily robbed of this delicious tidbit, and in 1987 abnormally high water levels undermined the out-structures, collapsed the foundation of the privy and damaged other buildings. Truly, the effort to preserve the site would be an unending task.

For the pursuit of such a task, there is the requirement for unending resources. Enter Scout Troop 323 and the Great lakes Light Keepers Association. The Great lakes Light Keepers Association, the umbrella organization dedicated to the preservation of all of the lights on the lakes, offered an ever-expanding broad base of members who were now aware of the plight of the Lighthouse. Scout Troop 323 offered the endless energy of its youth and countless hands willing to pick up, clean up, repair, paint and guard the lighthouse. Lead by lighthouse enthusiast Mark Fowler, Troop 323 invaded Round Island like ants and attacked the job of cleaning the station in a way that only scouts can manage. Meanwhile, the Great Lakes Light Keepers Association took plaster and paint samples from the walls and ceilings of the interior and had them analyzed so that the original colors could be matched.

As of this writing, the effort to save the Round Island Lighthouse goes on and is far from being finished. Each summer the scouts return to the lighthouse in an excursion that takes them far from their homes in Freeland, Michigan. The Great lakes Light Keepers Association still extends its efforts toward saving the Round Island site, and the growing number of members donate time, money and skill. Yet, the lighthouse is only restored on the outside, and the interior remains nearly gutted. Looking around it is possible to find some remains of the original woodwork, but for the most part the lighthouse is a hollow shell. To the throngs of tourists who pass the lighthouse on their way to and from Mackinac Island, it is one of the highlights of the trip. The lighthouse has always added a touch of beauty and mystique to the Mackinac Straits experience. Thanks to the efforts and dedication of countless lighthouse enthusiasts, this once-endangered structure will continue to exist and serve its new role as a beacon of tourism, the fastest growing industry on the Great Lakes.

Round Island Lighthouse before restoration. (Mackinac Island State Park Commission photo)

Round Island Lighthouse after restoration. (Mackinac Island State Park Commission photo)

XIV
THE HARDWARE TO PROVE IT

With the rest of the lifesavers of the Cleveland Station, Frederick T. Hatch climbed back aboard the surfboat and the whole crew pulled for shore. The only exception to those leaving was Surfman John Eveleigh, who remained aboard the distressed vessel to help handle the line that they now planned to fire from shore to the boat. The trip out to the schooner had been a hard pull, and most of the surfmen were nearly exhausted as they headed back, but that was the way of the Lifesaving Service—keep going in spite of the cold and exhaustion. They hadn't rowed more than 100 feet before the waves came over the stern and completely swamped the boat. Now, as the surfmen worked at bailing their waterlogged surfboat, she became nearly impossible to control, and drifted well south of the harbor entrance. On that side of the harbor there were the two Lake Shore Railroad harbor piers which were made up of tall piles. The waves were exploding through their telephone pole-like legs and making an awful roar. If the surfboat were to drift into them, it would be smashed into splinters and the surfmen would be beaten to death. Between the two piers, however, was a narrow stretch of beach, and Keeper Charles T. Goodwin told his crew of surfmen that they would make for that stretch of beach. Along with his comrades, Hatch pulled at his assigned oar as he had so many times before, but the swamped lifeboat was almost impossible to row. Then suddenly Hatch discovered that he was under water even though he was still tugging at his oar. The sting of the bitter cold lake coated his face like a million angry hornets, and the burn of water shooting up his nose overpowered his senses as he released the oar and instinctively clawed to regain the surface. Fortunately, what Hatch could not do with his thrashing arms, his cork life belt did for him and after what seemed like an eternity he found himself popping to the surface. The waves had capsized the surfboat, just as Keeper Goodwin had feared. Like the other surfmen, Hatch turned to his training and attempted to regain the surfboat. Lifesavers practiced capsizing and then quickly righting their surfboats, but this time the seas were wild beyond anyone's imagination or training. Now Lake Erie would thwart Hatch, and every time that he got a grip on the surfboat, the lake sent a towering wave of ice water over him. The story was the same for the other lifesavers and soon they were all so benumbed by the cold that no one could grip the boat. In fact, they were so stricken by the cold that they soon could not even swim and were left simply bobbing in the breaking surf buoyed up by their life belts—and being carried toward the piles of the pier and a churning frigid death. The relentless waves kept coming, and shoving the now-helpless lifesavers closer and closer to the piles and the thunder beneath the pier. Hatch wanted to swim but his legs were numb and cramped. He could see the other fellows in the darkness, but no one could raise a voice over the surf. Indeed, Lake Erie had him in its grip, in fact—it had them all. It was November 11, 1883, and it surely looked like the end for the storm warriors of Cleveland, Hatch included.

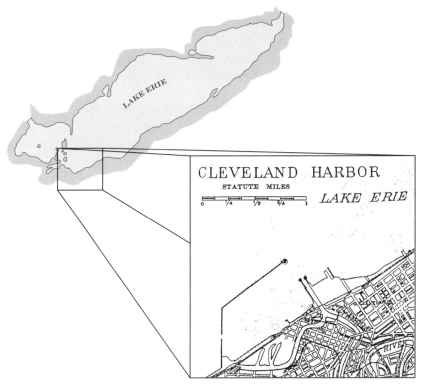

In later years, whenever storm winds blew across the surface of Lake Erie, Hatch, who was now the keeper of the West Breakwater Lighthouse at Cleveland, looked across the lake's distance with a special eye of consideration. He knew firsthand that the shallowest of the Great Lakes could easily bring disaster his way. Prior to taking the assignment as keeper of the breakwater lighthouse, Hatch had been a member of the United States Lifesaving Service and had often done battle with the angry lake. In fact, Hatch was one of few individuals who had done it all. He had been shipwrecked, been a heroic lifesaver and a lighthouse keeper—all in the immediate vicinity of Cleveland. So, when the storm winds howled, it did not matter if it was a summer squall or an autumn gale, Hatch squinted out toward the incoming waves with the eye of an expert—and he had the hardware to prove it.

Duty at the Cleveland West Breakwater Light probably suited Hatch quite well. It was a tough and lonely spot for most of the season where the keeper was normally cut off from the rest of the harbor by the rough seas. Yet, the lake vessel traffic was thick and always in a bustle at the harbor mouth of Cleveland. Normally, just getting from the West Breakwater Light over to the main light, which was located on the corner of Water and Main streets, was a chore. The simple task of traveling from the mainland light to the breakwater light to shuttle supplies meant a trek of a mile and the use of a rowboat. Often that put the lightkeeper in a struggle with the wild ways of the lake. All of this was probably just fine with Hatch. You see, Hatch had made a career out of tempting Lake Erie, and he always seemed to win. Stored in a safe place was the proof that Hatch was better than Erie, and the odds are good that he sometimes took the time to open the box and look at the shining gold symbol of his bettering of the lake. Surely, on occasion the callused fingers of the mariner Hatch would run across the gold medal that had been awarded to him for bravery in the act of lifesaving. This was the "hardware," the proof, the symbol that said that Lighthouse Keeper Hatch was better than Lake Erie. He had earned it in his previous employment as a lifesaver at the Cleveland Station and, although his current duty as a lighthouse keeper did not require lifesaving, he still knew that he was in a contest with the lake itself. Each time that the lake tried to swamp his light or snuff out his fog signal and he kept them going, he had saved lives and defeated the sweet water sea. In the act of tending the light he had accomplished that task many times over. His duty now was just as important as his duty had been at the lifesaving station. Still, every time the lake began to churn, Hatch turned his watchful squint toward his old nemesis and remembered the previous conflicts with its icy grip. Surely, this station, where it was just

Frederick T. Hatch the most decorated mariner, lightkeeper, and lifesaver on the Great Lakes. (From the Dennis L. Noble Collection, used with permission.)

Hatch against Lake Erie, was just fine with this lightkeeper. Yes, the West Breakwater Light suited him just fine indeed.

Although there are no records to the exact movements of Keeper Hatch on the stormy Sunday morning of October 26, 1890, we can envision his routine with just a bit of our imagination. The winds had been blowing a classic October gloom from off of Lake Erie through the night, and by the time that the morning church bells rang out their call, the bluster simply carried the tones away unheard. From the West Breakwater Lighthouse Hatch could see the lookout at the Cleveland Lifesaving Station, poised atop the station and scanning the lake. Hatch knew the routine at the station very well, and although his former commander, Keeper Goodwin, would be giving his lifesavers their Sunday day of rest, the lookout was still required to be posted atop the station. So, with the first light of the dawn, the scheduled surfman was sent aloft to stand out in the weather and keep a close watch on the lake. Remembering back to his days in the Lifesaving Service, Hatch had to be glad that he had made the move into the Lighthouse Service. Now, rather than standing watches atop the station or walking the nightly beach patrol, Hatch was required to simply maintain his light and fog signal in the warmth of the lighthouse's buildings. The coming of the dawn meant the end of Hatche's workday, rather than the beginning. While the winds whistled past the lighthouse windows, Hatch prepared to take his rest. No doubt that if this weather kept up, he would have a busy Sunday night with the light. He had no idea that in the hours to come he would meet Catherin Hazen and earn even more hardware in that encounter. As the exhausted lightkeeper drifted off into his well-earned sleep, those winds may just have foretold exactly how busy that upcoming night would be. They did so by reminding him of how he had earned that gold hardware. Only the moan of the winds from off the lake, and the crash of the surf upon the breakwall could spin his memory back to that fateful day almost seven years before.

Those pre-slumber images took Keeper Hatch back across the years and months of his career to another stormy autumn. Back his mind spooled, back across thousands of pounding waves and as many hours of his life dedicated to thwarting the lake, back to a point slightly before this story began. It was the last day of October in the year 1883 and he was the number five surfman at the Cleveland Lifesaving Station under the command of Keeper Goodwin. The United States Lifesaving Service was the forerunner to the modern Coast Guard and had stations located at strategic points around the Great Lakes as well as the shores of the rest of the nation. Each station was equipped with a battery of lifesaving equipment ranging from self-bailing lifeboats to breeches buoys. As we have noted, these stations were each manned by a crew of professional lifesavers called "surfmen" commanded by the station keeper. Maintaining a 24-hour-a-day watch over the lake from the opening of navigation in April until the close of the season in December, these storm warriors were oath-sworn to risk their lives in the effort to save mariners in distress. It was a job that they took very seriously, and there were occasions when entire station crews were killed while attempting to battle angry seas to save the mariners. This was a calling of honor and valor, and it was one that Frederick Hatch was selflessly committed to.

Ranked according to numbers sewn upon their uniform sleeves, each surfman had his own place and duty during a given rescue situation. Hatch knew that his position in the deploy of the beach cart was on the left front; that he was on the shovel when the sand anchor needed to be buried, and that he was to pull on the weather side of the whip line when hauling the hawser out to set the breeches buoy. These positions and tasks were practiced each week, in all weather, until each surfman knew them as second nature, and Hatch could do his job with his eyes closed. There were, however, times when the carefully orchestrated rescue procedures had to be tossed aside and improvisation was the order of the moment. When that moment comes, all of the practice in the world would do no good. Each surfman would have to function on his individual valor alone. For all of the crew of the Cleveland Lifesaving Station, and the future keeper of the West Breakwater Light Frederick Hatch in particular, such a moment was fast approaching.

Blasting from out of the northwest, a powerful Lake Erie gale was ripping around the Cleveland Station. From that same station the lookout spotted a three-masted schooner headed toward the harbor from off the slate-gray horizon. She was the 636-ton schooner *Sophia Minch*, under the command of Captain Bates and hauling a bellyful of Marquette iron ore. It was just before seven o'clock in the evening and, with the wind at her heels, the *Minch* should have been able to sail a perfect line into the protection of the breakwater. Rather than entering the port, however, she suddenly dropped her hooks and stood outside the harbor. Recognizing that something was probably amiss aboard the schooner, the surfman on watch alerted Keeper Goodwin. By the time Goodwin got a glass on the *Minch*, she was showing a signal of distress. Tooting her whistle, the tug *Peter Smith* answered the schooner's signal and headed out toward the reluctant schooner. Before departing, the *Peter Smith* stopped at the lifesaving station located on the end of the west entrance pier and picked up two of Goodwin's surfmen.

Their assignment was to help handle lines and evaluate the schooner's condition. As it turned out, the following seas on the open lake had disabled the *Minch's* giant oak rudder, and she was not able to make the entrance to the harbor on her own. The crew of the *Smith* offered to take the big schooner in with them, but giving thought to the dense load of ore aboard his boat and the current weather conditions, Bates refused to go in with just one tug. He requested a second tug and sent the *Smith* back. Returning to the harbor, the captain of the *Smith* enlisted the help of the tug *Fanny Tuthill*. Additionally, all but one of the lifesavers went aboard the *Smith* and headed out to the *Minch*. A single surfman was left behind to tend to the station while the rest went out to aid in bringing in the schooner. Among the surfmen aboard the *Smith* was Frederick Hatch, clad in his oilskins and cork life belt. To him, this was just another routine run out to aid a troubled vessel. It was the kind of job that the surfmen participated in on a regular basis.

Before the *Smith* had gotten away from the breakwater, the first of Lake Erie's waves came exploding over her bow, showering the tug with an ice water spray. Hatch squinted at the waves marching toward him from the gloomy distance. Still, he was sure that this would be just another routine assistance to a troubled lakeboat. There would probably be some pumping of the hand bilges, some handling of lines and perhaps some shoveling of cargo—all of which would be done in the bitter rain and sleet. For a lifesaver it was all a part of the job. Several hours of work, and Hatch and his comrades would rob Lake Erie of another victim and then they would be back within the warmth of their station. As the tug *Smith* came bumping alongside the *Minch's* oak hull, Hatch waited his turn and then scrambled as best he could over the schooner's rail. The wind was lashing at his hands as he took a grip on the slick wooden rail and tumbled aboard the stricken schooner. Keeper Goodwin was already in a huddle with Captain Bates as Hatch stood by waiting for his next order. Some of the surfmen turned their backs to prevent the wind from blowing under their Nor'easter hats, but Hatch turned to face the lake as if asking for the worst that it had. Remaining aboard the *Smith* to handle lines, the number one surfman, Lawrence Distel, also awaited the plan from Goodwin. In short order, the captain and the keeper had their plan. The lines would be set to the two tugs, both forward, and then the anchors of the *Minch* would be hove up. Once her anchors were secured, the tugs would bring her in. Quickly the orders were given and the surfmen set to the task of assisting the schooner's crew with the lines and windless.

Just being glad to finally have a task to do, Surfman Hatch leaped to his work of helping the crew of the *Minch* in the effort to bring the boat safely into Cleveland harbor. The act of raising the anchors in itself required a great deal of manpower. The windlass was a giant wooden double spool with a locking ratchet and the massive 1,200-pound anchors had to be hoisted by hand. So, the help of the lifesavers aboard the *Minch* was more than welcome. As everyone went to their assigned tasks, the lines to the tugs were made good and the anchors were hove. No sooner were the *Minch's* hooks free of Lake Erie's bottom than the wind took hold of the boat. In a matter of minutes the lines to the tugs snapped and the schooner was firmly in the grip of the gale. In harmony, both Captain Bates and Keeper Goodwin ordered the anchors let go once more. It was too late, the lake had set its desire toward the *Minch* and it was going to have the schooner. Now the waves began to wash the decks and the water found its way into the hold as the anchors simply dragged in the sandy bottom. Deeply laden with iron ore, the schooner was riding low in the water and the waves burst over her side and swept waist-deep over the deck. The crew were ordered to the pumps, but most of the men found themselves fully occupied with the task of simply trying to keep from being washed overboard. Again the captain and the keeper consulted. Goodwin knew that the shallow region over which they were now floating had a sand bottom, but in a short distance there were rocks. He convinced Bates that if he were to scuttle his boat now, it would likely stay intact, but if she pounded on the rocks later, the *Minch's* oak hull would quickly break up. Bates agreed and sent a team forward to auger holes in the boat's wooden bottom and scuttle her. It would take the sinking of the *Minch* to save her!

Shortly after the holes were drilled, she began to rapidly settle. Within a few minutes her keel scuffed into sand bottom and the *Minch* was scuttled. She went from being a ship to a shipwreck, and all aboard her were now in danger. Foaming waves of ice water now broke cleanly across her deck and swept everything overboard. Taking to the standing rigging the schooner's crew, and the Cleveland lifesavers climbed as high as they could to escape the waves. Goodwin and Bates along with all but two of the people aboard the schooner went up the forward mast's rigging. Finding themselves cut off amidships by the breaking waves, one surfman and the boat's mate were able to climb the mizzen rigging.

In one of the oddest circumstances in the history of the Lifesaving Service on the Great Lakes, nearly the entire crew of the Cleveland Station were now stuck aboard a shipwreck of their own making. Now, the question could be asked, who was going to rescue the rescuers?

Fortunately, Surfman Distel had been left safely aboard the tug *Smith* which turned and, along with the *Tuthill*, ran for shelter inside the breakwall as soon as the towlines parted. Now it was up to him to formulate the rescue of the 16 souls aboard the *Minch*. By the time that the *Smith* landed Distel back at the dock, it was after two o'clock in the morning, and mustering a crew of volunteers to man the needed equipment would not be easy. Time was short, the waves could knock down one of the masts aboard the *Minch* and with it the lake would claim the lives of everyone in the rigging. Amazingly, Distel, with the surfman left at the station, managed to secure the assistance of Customs Inspector Bates, keeper of the Cleveland Land Lighthouse, George H. Tower, and three local fellows whose names are recorded only as "Messrs Pryor, Duffy and Tovat." Tovat offered the use of his team of horses to pull the apparatus cart with the lines and beach equipment aboard. One of the aspects of the number one surfman's job was that he was normally in training so that one day he could get a station of his own and serve as keeper. Thus, Surfman Distel was fully acquainted with the firing of the Lyle gun and shooting a line to a wreck. The Lyle gun was a tiny cannon and into it would be a cast iron projectile with a line tied to one end. the gun was then fired to drop the line over the wreck. The shipwrecked crew would then set the line so that they could pull out a heavier line and a breeches buoy. This breeches buoy, which was a slur of the descriptive term "britches buoy" was actually a large canvas pair of pants-like britches sewn into a life-ring and attached to an overhead pulley. The shipwrecked persons would simply step into the britches and be pulled across the lines to safety. All that Distel truly needed was a crew to help him set up the beach rig and he could surely pull his fellow lifesavers to safety along with the crew of the *Minch*.

Once the rig was set, Distel fired the line toward the sunken *Minch*. The shot was perfect, and the line fell directly across the forward mast. In short order the skilled hands of the lifesavers in the rigging had the lines fixed, and the breeches buoy was sent out. The breeches buoy sent from the lifesavers has always been a welcome sight to many a stranded mariner. On this occasion, it was the lifesavers themselves who welcomed the sight. Keeper Goodwin was the first to get into the britches and be hauled ashore so that he could direct the rest of the rescue. Soon everyone on the forward mast was safely ashore with the exception of Frederick Hatch. This left only three people aboard the *Minch*, two crewmen on the mizzen mast and Hatch on the foremast. The problem now was how to get to the two men on the mizzen rigging. The lines that worked the breeches buoy were attached to the foremast and moving the whole rig was nearly impossible.

Between Keeper Goodwin and Surfman Distel it was decided that Distel would climb into the breeches buoy and be pulled back out to the *Minch*. Once at the boat, Distel and Hatch would decide on a plan to rescue the people in the boat's mizzen rigging. Amid the whipping winds of the gale, Distel swung madly as he was pulled out to the wreck. Once at the *Minch* he and Hatch discussed the dilemma and tried to find the best way of saving the two men in the mizzen. It was Hatch who came up with an audacious plan. He would set out hand-over-hand and foot-over-foot along the schooner's gaff boom and then would lead the two men back over the way that he had come. If it was not possible to lead the castaways back to the forerigging, he would wait with them until Keeper Goodwin could put a shot to him on the mizzen.

"If I don't come back in a reasonable time, you can figure that I can't get back," Hatch told Distel. "Then you go back and tell Goodwin what happened."

With that, Hatch set out along the gaff. The waves were slapping at the gaff and it swung like a funhouse ride under his boots. In the pitch-black of the night each step could have been the end for the defiant lifesaver. The telephone pole-sized wooden boom had its surface slickened by the rain and seas and the sail rigging was strewn beneath Hatch's every step. This trek would appear just short of insanity to most people, but in the eyes of Hatch, it was simply his way of outwitting Lake Erie's treachery once again.

As the lake roared and spit in protest all around him, Hatch reached the mizzen rigging. Once there, however, he saw that the gaff boom, without his weight on it, was swinging so violently that there was simply no chance to get back upon it. He had no choice other than to wait for Distel to get the idea that he was not coming back and then to report back to Goodwin. Still seated in the breeches buoy, Distel waited a reasonable period of time and then signaled to the men ashore to draw him back. The lifesavers would have to fire another line out to the *Minch* and hope that Hatch could be reached.

After Distel reached dry land, the whip block was cast adrift and the line to the *Minch* was hauled ashore. Goodwin repositioned the Lyle gun and inserted another projectile. Just firing the projectile toward the people on the wreck was a dangerous operation. The projectile itself was a 19-pound, cast iron bullet that had an eyebolt screwed into one end to which the whipline was tied. If the shot was off target, the people out on the wreck would find a huge cast iron bullet coming their way from a cannon. Having practiced the firing of the gun once each week through the entire navigation season,

Goodwin was an expert at putting a line exactly where he wanted it over any ship's mast. This time, when the gun was discharged the shotline arced gracefully into the night using the bluster of the gale to aid its course. In a demonstration of perfection the shotline fell directly across the mizzen rigging and nearly into Hatch's hands. In minutes, Hatch had rigged the communication and the three remaining people of the *Minch* were hauled ashore in the breeches buoy. Last to leave the *Minch* was Hatch himself, and the rescue was complete.

Escorting the seven survivors back to the Cleveland Lifesaving Station, Frederick Hatch walked in squishy socks, soaked to the skin yet too numbed by the cold to feel the discomfort. He knew, however, that he had outmatched Lake Erie through little more than courage. All of the lifesavers settled into the warmth of the station for a hot meal and some well-deserved rest. The castaways from the *Minch* would stay at the station for the next day and dry out. They too settled into the cozy station's comfort while the citizens who Distel had recruited headed back to their homes with a good story to tell.

In less than 12 hours after the rescue of *Minch's* crew had been accomplished, the three masted schooner *John B. Merrill*, hove in off of the stormy lake, was bound for Cleveland. Like the *Minch*, the *Merrill* was a large vessel and she had a cargo hold packed with iron ore. Bound down from Escanaba, Michigan, the *Merrill* was making good weather of it as she neared the harbor and signaled for a tug. Steaming out in response came the tug *James Amadeus* and shortly she was clear of the breakwater and pounding her way toward the waiting schooner. In a routine played out countless times on the Great Lakes, the tug met the schooner and a towing hawser was made secure between the two. Hauling with all of her power, the tug nearly had the *Merrill* under the protection of the breakwater when the strain on the hawser caused it to part. In an instant the same wind that caught the *Minch* now took hold of the *Merrill* and began to drive her toward the beach. Maneuvering in a manner that only a tugboat can manage, the nimble *Amadeus* spun about and quickly returned to the *Merrill's* side. Again the towline was made secure and the two boats made for the harbor entrance. The position of the schooner at that time was such that a course made for the harbor entrance put the boats directly into the sea trough. Soon the *Merrill* began to roll severely, and the stress brought upon the towline was too much. Snapping for the second time, the towline's parting now left the schooner nearly in the breakers, and in a position where the tug could not dare to reach her. Captain J. H. Coleman, the *Merrill's* master, ordered the

Projectile →

Although poor in quality, this photo shows a practice firing of the Lyle gun and also shows the "projectile" in mid-flight (arrow). The crew is from the Harbor Beach Station. (Author's photo)

anchors dropped, but the drifting schooner simply had too much inertia and the hooks just dragged in the sand. The boat was headed for the shallows and nothing on earth would stop her.

Watching all of this the lookout of the Cleveland Lifesaving Station realized the danger and sounded the alarm. Again, for the second time in 24 hours, Frederick Hatch was called to battle against his old foe—Lake Erie. Being joined once more by local citizens Tower, Bates and Tovat, the lifesavers readied the beach gear which was still wet and sandy from the *Minch* rescue. The darkness of night was again upon Cleveland, as the lifesaving team headed out. This time on their way, the crew was joined by Assistant Lighthouse Keeper Reed of the Cleveland Land Lighthouse. Hauling their beach cart across the massive structure of the Lake Shore Railroad bridge, the band of storm warriors hurried as best they could. It was a strange sight as the lifesavers cloaked in their oilskins and cork life belts, trudged across the bridge high above the Cuyahoga River while the wind whistled through the structure. Calculating that the *Merrill* would fetch up off of the Lake Shore Railroad freight house, Keeper Goodwin intended to establish his beachhead near that spot. Taking the route of the railroad was the most direct way to get there.

Aboard the *Merrill*, Captain Coleman felt her keel strike the sand bottom as the boat drifted outside of the *Minch's* wreck. The *Merrill's* master knew that the end was near and ordered her hatches opened. He figured that the waves that were now boarding the schooner would find their way into her hold and effectively scuttle the boat before she would reach the rocks. He was correct, and the *Merrill* soon settled onto the bottom in the sand. Like the *Minch*, the *Merrill* now had a fighting chance against the breaking waves. Like the *Minch*, the crew of the *Merrill* took to the boat's rigging. All ten of the boat's crew took to the mizzen rigging and awaited the lifesavers.

Once more, the beach apparatus was deployed and the Lyle gun was fired and for the second night in a row a shotline arced into the darkness from nearly the same spot on the Cleveland shore. It was just after eight o'clock in the evening and this time, many of the city's people had turned out to watch the spectacle. Once the whipline was sent and the breeches buoy was rigged, Keeper Goodwin asked for a volunteer to ride the line out to the wreck and help the survivors with the evacuation. Sending anyone out to a shipwreck is risky, but having a skilled lifesaver at the other end to manipulate the breeches buoy is preferable. Without a heartbeat of hesitation, Surfman Hatch stepped forward and volunteered to go out to the *Merrill*. Moments later he was being conveyed out to yet another mizzenmast, but his effort resulted in having the entire crew of the *Merrill* safely ashore in less than 45 minutes! As soon as the castaways were landed lifesaver Hatch came in, riding the breeches buoy and swinging in the gale's bluster as if having fun. Again he had outmatched Lake Erie and robbed it of human souls.

In the days ahead, Hatch and his fellow lifesavers helped to pump out and refloat both the *Minch* and *Merrill*. The two wrecks were subsequently towed into the harbor and repaired. No sooner had these wrecks been removed, than the schooner-barge *John T. Johnson*, with a cargo of Escanaba ore and a crew of seven, was blown ashore in almost the same circumstances as the *Merrill* and *Minch*. On the evening of November 11, 1883, the *Johnson* was anchored off of the east pierhead and being beaten by a savage gale. Correctly figuring that the barge would soon drag ashore, Goodwin set to the rescue with his crew in the station's surfboat. Official accounts say that the seas were running so high that the East Pier Lighthouse was being swamped, and the temperatures were well below freezing. When the lifesavers, including Hatch, reached the *Johnson* they found her in a sorry state. She was being swept by the waves and her anchors were barely holding. Goodwin signaled for a tug to Lighthouse Keeper Reed, who was stationed on the pier, but when Reed put out the word, all of the tugs refused to go out under the current conditions.

Goodwin knew full well that if he were to attempt to take the surfboat in filled with the schooner's crew, under these conditions, it was likely to swamp and capsize. The lifesavers practiced being capsized as one of their weekly drills, and could easily right their boat, but if it were filled with civilians those people would surely drown. With that in mind the keeper decided to head for the station and ready the beach apparatus for deploy of the breeches buoy. He left one of his surfmen behind to aid in handling the buoy, but this time it was not Hatch. Instead it was the number two Surfman, John Eveleigh.

And so we are at the exact moment in time where this whole story began. As Keeper Goodwin had feared, the surfboat was swamped and then capsized. The lifesavers soon found themselves benumbed in the waves and being swept toward the piles of the Lake Shore Railroad pier and certain death. A large crowd had gathered on the pier and witnessed the upset of the surfboat. From the pier they tossed lines to the drifting surfmen. Half of the crew managed to grasp the lines and were pulled to safety by the citizens of Cleveland. The rest of the lifesavers drifted onto the narrow sliver of beach between the piers by holding onto the overturned surfboat. It was a narrow escape, and most of the beaten storm-warriors were too stricken by the cold to walk when they reached safety. The entire crew was taken to the office of Customs Inspector Bates at the head of the pier. A runner was sent over to the lifesaving station to fetch dry clothes and near the warmth of Bates' iron stove, the near-dead men, including Hatch, began to recover. This was later recorded as "one of the narrowest escapes on record in the Life Saving Service."

At about the same time as the crew of frostbitten lifesavers began to regain the use of their cramped limbs, the word reached the customs office that the *Johnson* appeared to be drifting toward shore. It was true. The schooner-barge's anchors had lost their grip against the power of the gale and now she was dragging toward the breakers and probable destruction. Instantly, Hatch and his fellow surfmen forgot their own pain and sprang toward the door—as if their brush with death just minutes earlier had never happened at all! Stepping again into the bitter wind, Hatch gave his defiant squint toward the enraged lake once more. Erie had knocked him down, but he was not out and now he was going to get back into the fight. In the pitch-black of the distance beyond the whitecapped surf, the faint image of the helpless *John T. Johnson* could be seen as she rocked and swayed. There was not a moment to lose. Everyone knew that she may just crumble to pieces as soon as she hit the shallows, and the only chance for her people would be the quick deployment of the breeches buoy. In a dash, the lifesavers of Cleveland made for their station and the beach apparatus stored there.

By the time that the beach equipment was set up, the *Johnson* had fetched up in the shallows. Oddly, she had come to rest in nearly the same spot as the *Sophia Minch* had 11 days earlier. The lifesavers found themselves shooting a line from the spot on the shore they had used on two previous occasions in less than two weeks. At 11:55 p.m., the bang from the Lyle gun was heard above the storm as Keeper Goodwin sent another flawless shot across another wreck. The line was actually caught by Surfman Eveleigh who, like everyone else aboard the *Johnson*, had taken refuge in the boat's mizzen rigging. In minutes, his skilled hands had the lines rigged and in less than half an hour all of the *Johnson's* crew as well as Eveleigh were safely on land.

On Wednesday, December 3, 1884, more than a year after the three dramatic rescues, the lifesavers of the Cleveland Station were finally recognized for their efforts in that stormy November of 1883. For "Rescuing the crews, twenty-nine persons of the schooners *Sophia Minch, John B. Merrill*

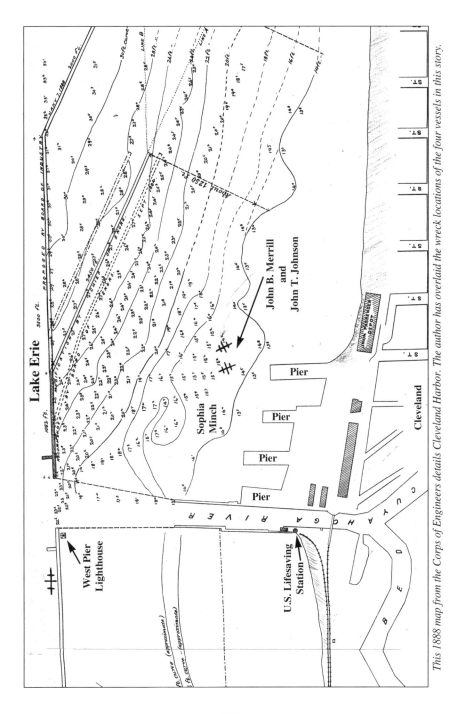

This 1888 map from the Corps of Engineers details Cleveland Harbor. The author has overlaid the wreck locations of the four vessels in this story.

and *John T. Johnson*, sunk off of Cleveland on Oct. 31, Nov. 1 and 11, 1883, respectively." Charles C. Goodwin, Lawrence Distel, John L. Eveleigh, Joseph Goodroe, William Goodwin, Frederick T. Hatch, Delos Hayden, Charles Learned and Jay Lindsay were all awarded the service's highest honor—the gold medal for lifesaving.

Perhaps it was Hatch's desire to quit while "on top" that lead to his leaving the service, or maybe it was simple economics that lead him from lifesaving to lightkeeping. Whatever the reason, it is a matter of fact that he did leave the Cleveland Station to take over command of the West Breakwater Lighthouse just before he was awarded the gold medal. Hatch took his oath of office as a lighthouse keeper on November 22, 1884, just 11 days prior to being awarded his gold medal. It is most likely that simple economics was the reason for Hatch's change of careers. In the era when he switched jobs a surfman earned about $320 per year, and was paid only during the months of April through November, when the station was active. Expenses such as uniform and meals were also deducted from a surfman's pay, dropping the annual total to about $304. One comparison showed that this wage was less than that earned by streetcar drivers. It is interesting to point out that the modern storm-warriors in the U.S. Coast Guard are also paid far less for risking their lives than civil servants are paid for driving public transportation. From Frederick Hatch's standpoint, the low wage paid to surfmen was probably quite irritating. Lighthouse keepers, on the other hand, were paid a base salary of $700 per year and received pay all year with no deductions. To become a lightkeeper, Hatch would be given an annual salary of $580, which—although not the top pay earned by the keepers at isolated stations—was a significant increase over his pay as a lifesaver. No doubt, when the job of tending the west breakwater light was offered, along with its pay bump, Hatch leaped at the opportunity. On September 1, 1885, he was officially appointed keeper of the Cleveland West Breakwater Lighthouse.

When Hatch took command of the West Breakwater Light, it was not the same light which exists today. The modern light was erected in 1910 on an extension of the original breakwater. Hatch's command was in the original lighthouse which was established in 1885. Prior to that season, the light had been a simple fixed white lamp and sixth order optic mounted at the end of the breakwater, but in the 1884 season, work commenced to establish an actual lighthouse at the site. Records indicate that the effort to construct a true lighthouse on the west breakwall was approved as early as 1868, but the process was slow. When the plan to place the lighthouse was finally put into action the tactics were very interesting. First, a 40-foot-square crib was constructed on the end of the breakwater, and then the 29-foot-deep structure was filled with crushed stone to form the foundation for the lighthouse. This was accomplished in the summer of 1884, but the structure was allowed a full year to properly "settle." Next, beginning on July 1, 1885, the crib was topped with concrete, bringing its total height to 36 feet, or about nine feet above the waterline. An octagonal "oil cellar" of eight feet in diameter, and six feet, 10 inches in depth was formed into the concrete foundation in a position such that the lighthouse would sit atop it. When it came time to place the tower, the task was one of simple transferal. The tower that was used was the iron tower from the west pier at Charlotte, New York. Rather than going through the trouble of constructing a whole new tower, the Lighthouse Board had elected to move one. How this light was moved from Lake Ontario to Lake Erie is not in the official reports, but by November of 1885, Frederick Hatch's ready-made lighthouse was in place.

The lighthouse itself was an octagonal iron tower that stood with a focal plane of 36 feet. The tower was painted brown, and had a lamproom which was black. A fourth order optic was placed in the lamproom with alternating red and white panes that rotated by a mechanical means. The light was said to illuminate the entire horizon and flashed red and white at 10-second intervals. A fog bell was removed from the Cleveland west pier facility and transferred to the new West Breakwater Light when the station was established. Additionally, there was a boathouse and appropriate launching equipment located on the west side of the tower. The lighthouse was also equipped with a bunk for the keeper, but it was intended that the full-time residence of those tending the light would be on the mainland at the site of the Cleveland Land Lighthouse. No doubt that when the weather got heavy, Keeper Hatch elected to remain in the bunkroom rather than rowing the more than half-mile to get ashore—and then walking another half-mile or more to get to the Land Light. Indeed, this was apt to be a comfortable spot for Hatch. After all, he was still doing battle with Lake Erie, but now he was in an iron fortress with a cement foundation.

Over the years the original station was added to and upgraded. A locomotive boiler was placed at the site to power the fog signal, and must have been a true pain to tend. Odds are, however, that the steam signal was better than the old bell signal. Hatch also discovered that his station's foundation was not nearly as stable as one would think. Each time that a heavy blow cooked up on Lake Erie, the whole tower would shake heavily with the crashing waves. Hatch reported that, in the winds of a heavy gale, the tower would lean so badly that the revolving mechanism of the light would grind to a stop! The keeper often had to add extra weights to keep it turning. In extreme cases he had to actually revolve the lens by hand because the tower was tilted so far from vertical. In 1888 a survey of the lighthouse showed that some of the timbers that surrounded the light's foundation were damaged allowing the stones under the foundation to be washed away. Rafts of logs that were often towed into the harbor would tend to strike the crib on the south and east face which caused some of the damage. Additionally, this lighthouse had the tendency to be struck by vessels. When the winds blew from off shore, the smoke from the heavy industry in Cleveland, and from the thousands of coal stoves that were used to warm nearly every room in the city, made for a dense smog. Often it was difficult for vessel captains to see the breakwater and its lighthouse until they were nearly on top of it. For that reason, many a vessel master had been embarrassed by colliding with the lighthouse. These collisions of logs and lakeboats caused the damage to the leeward side of the crib's timbers and the stones washed away. The crib was settling on its foundation and allowed itself to tilt and rock with the wind. To cure Hatch's teetering station, the Lighthouse Board had a series of 21 oak piles driven into the south east face of the crib to fend off the collisions. Oddly, we would think that a lighthouse such as this would be threatened by the waves and ice, but the threat turned out to be from the boats and rafts!

By the time that Hatch put his head down to rest on that stormy Sunday in October of 1890, and found his mind spooled back to his days as a surfman and the resulting adventures and awards, he was quite familiar with the ways of his light. Indeed, Hatch had become quite comfortable in his role as a lighthouse keeper, but on this Sunday his former role as a fearless lifesaver would soon be recalled. Soon his nap in the lighthouse's bunkroom and the probable recollections of the past storms and rescues came to an end. Odds are that when Hatch's daytime sleep was finished, he began the toil of tending to his light. Darkness would soon set in around the southern shore of Lake Erie, and the weather was quickly deteriorating. Hatch's light would be greatly needed by the mariners this night, and that was certain. Unknown to Hatch, four mariners who would need much more than the guidance of his lighthouse were currently headed his way from off the wild lake.

Downbound from Lake Superior and the port of Ashland, Wisconsin, came the big wooden package freighter *John M. Nicol* headed for Cleveland. In tow of the 280-foot *Nicol* was the 1,400-ton schooner-barge *Wahnapitae* loaded with nearly two million board feet of lumber. Both of these vessels

This is Frederick T. Hatch's command, the West Pierhead Lighthouse at Cleveland. This lighthouse was moved from Charlotte, New York in 1885. The fog horn, fog bell and boathouse are clearly seen here when viewed from the lake. The small rowboat seen in the foreground is probably the same one used by Hatch in his daring rescue of the crew of the Wahnapitae. (The Great Lakes Historical Society photo)

were substantial in their size and strength and were well able to take nearly any dusting that Lake Erie may choose to cast upon them, but the lights of Cleveland would still be a welcome sight on this storm-raked autumn night. Although the *Nicol's* burden was bound for Cleveland, the *Wahnapitae's* load of lumber was consigned to the harbor of Fairport, some 28 miles up the coast. In 1888 a new east breakwater had been constructed to shelter vessels from exactly the kind of wrecks for which Hatch and the Cleveland lifesavers had been awarded their medals. Now Hatch's lighthouse marked the gap that was the entrance to a truly safe harbor. Tonight, the plan of the inbound steamer and her consort was to haul the barge inside the protection of the breakwaters and drop her off, thus allowing the *Nicol* to navigate the twisting Cuyahoga River more freely. Once the *Nicol* had assumed her Cleveland cargo, she would pick up the *Wahnapitae* on her way out and continue on to Fairport. Aboard the barge was a crew of eight mariners, seven men and a female cook who was also the wife of the boat's captain. This lady of the lakes was named Catherin Hazen, and as she finished the chores in her galley she was sure that soon the *Wahnapitae* would be safely sheltered behind the Cleveland breakwater. Mrs. Hazen had never met Frederick Hatch and she had probably taken very little notice of his lighthouse when her boat passed it on previous occasions. The light on the end of the west breakwater was simply another of the countless lights that the *Wahnapitae* passed in any given season. Somehow, they simply seemed to melt together and become a part of the landscape. As the *Nicol* and *Wahnapitae* drew near enough to see the alternating red and white flashes of west breakwater's lighthouse, the last person looking for the light would have been Catherin Hazen.

Winds that night were blowing a perfect gale from due north, and both the *Nicol* and the *Wahnapitae* were taking the seas on their heels. Even with the waves occasionally breaking over their stern rails the two lakeboats were making good weather of it as they pressed toward Cleveland. The problem came in getting the two vessels safely between the ends of the two breakwaters. The shore on which the city of Cleveland is located does not run due east and west, rather it angles on a course that is about 37 degrees off of a true east-west line. Considering that the waves were being driven by a due north wind, they were cutting across the entrance at an angle of more than 50 degrees. This would make the task of safely pulling the heavily burdened *Wahnapitae* through the entrance nearly impossible. Wisely, the *Nicol's* captain elected to drop the barge on the open lake and allow the nimble harbor tugs the chance to pull her inside. Such was common on the lakes and a matter of routine in most cases, so even Keeper Hatch watched with only a passing curiosity as the lights of the two vessels separated, and the *Nicol* passed his lighthouse tooting her whistle to gain the attention of the harbor tugs. It was just after eight o'clock on what would become a deadly evening.

Answering the whistle signals from the *Nicol*, the harbor tugs *H. L. Chamberlin* and *Tom Maytham* came steaming toward the gap in the breakwater. As they reached the open lake the two tugs found the seas rolling high and each began to take solid water over their bows. All along the breakwater the lake was bursting and often the seas were sweeping cleanly over the riprap stones and swirling into the harbor on the other side. Out on the *Wahnapitae*, Captain Hazen had decided to drop only one of the barge's anchors thus allowing the boat to be more quickly tugged into the harbor. The act of maneuvering these huge anchors, each weighing nearly a ton, was manual labor and was always very time consuming, so Hazen gambled that a single hook would hold them until the tugs made a line secure. As the tugs approached, all hands mustered at the task of getting a line fastened between the barge and the two tugboats. Like all of the Great Lakes, Erie waits for anyone to make just one mistake, and not dropping both of the *Wahnapitae's* hooks was Captain Hazen's one and only allowed mistake. Each time that the crews attempted to pass the lines, the lake reached out with her wind and foiled their efforts. All hands were completely preoccupied with working the lines until someone discovered that the *Wahnapitae* was dragging her hooks. In fact, it is likely that the boat had been dragging her hooks the entire time. Immediately, Hazen ordered the other anchor dropped, and all hands scrambled to that task, but it was already too late. Lake Erie had the *Wahnapitae* in its stormy power and would now destroy her.

No sooner had the crew dashed to the anchors than those aboard the tugboats realized that the *Wahnapitae* was going to be smashed against the west breakwater and about to take them with her. Both tug captains headed back inside the breakwall and on the way began to blow their boat's whistles in an effort to alert the lifesavers. Again this action was too late, because the station lookout had noticed the schooner-barge's drift long before anyone on the three boats and had already rang the alarm. Keeper Goodwin and his crew of storm warriors were already on their way in the station's lifeboat. From his lighthouse, Hatch had a front row seat to the unfolding disaster. In one direction he could see the lifesavers pulling hard at their oars and headed in his direction. In another direction he saw the two tugboats steaming in through the breakwater. Out on the lake he saw the *Wahnapitae* heeled hard over and being blown directly toward him. At that moment no one on earth could have felt more in the middle, and more helpless than Hatch.

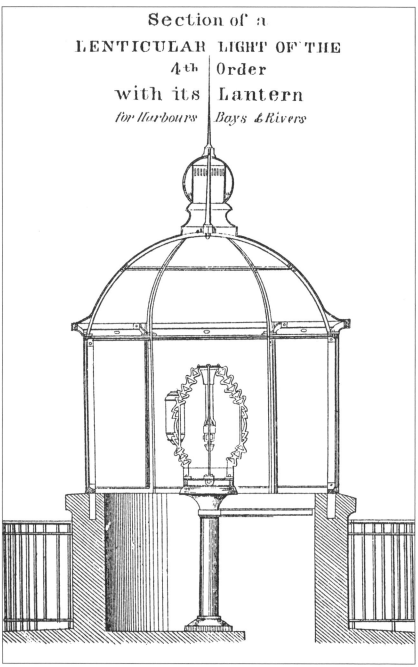

Section of a
LENTICULAR LIGHT OF THE
4th Order
with its Lantern
for Harbours Bays & Rivers

This cutaway of a fourth order optic and lamproom is very similar to the lamp in Frederick Hatch's Cleveland West Breakwater Light. (Lighthouse Board Annual Report *1852*)

Sounding like a thousand giant oak trees all being felled at the same time, the 1,400-ton *Wahnapitae* and her nearly two million board feet of Wisconsin lumber were planted upon the west breakwater. The boat crashed several times against the riprap stone of the breakwater and then began to grind into splinters with the help of the waves. She had fetched up just about 100 feet west down the breakwall from Hatch's lighthouse, and her crew knew instantly that she was going to pieces. All eight of the crew took no time at all to decide to make a leap for the breakwater, and remarkably, they all made it. Lake Erie, however, was not about to let her prey escape with such ease, and sent her ice water waves to take them away forever. Hatch knew instinctively and from firsthand experience that the lakes can rob its victims of life when they are within reach of safety. Without a moment's hesitation he dashed from the lighthouse and onto the breakwater. Within arms' reach, Hazen and two of his crew pulled them from the wash of lake-water that was swirling over the breakwall and forced them toward the open door of the lighthouse. Hazen was nearly in a panic indicating that his wife was still out there on the breakwater. Turning toward the frothing waves that now carried with them thousands of torpedoes that once were the boards of the *Wahnapitae's* lumber cargo, Hatch checked the lake's destruction with a special eye of consideration. A cascade of frothing water garnished with sharp edged lumber swirled between him and the rest of the survivors. Suddenly a massive sea exploded over the breakwater and the three most distant of the castaways were simply swept away as he watched. Now only the captain's wife and a single crewman were left upon the breakwall. At that moment, Hatch switched his career back from lightkeeper to lifesaver. He knew that no one else on earth could save those two people. Quite simply it was him alone against his old foe, the lake.

Grabbing a long, thin piece of line, Hatch tied one end to the cribwork near the light tower, and the other end he attached to himself. Next he bounded into the station's rowboat, and struck out toward the luckless souls left on the breakwater. Doing his best to stay in the lee below the breakwater, and to avoid the waves and lumber that were dumping over the wall, Hatch pulled toward the two survivors. As he approached, they began to crawl down the jagged riprap rocks toward him. Both Catherine Hazen and the other poor retch who had been stranded with her climbed into the rowboat. Hatch turned and began to row back toward the lighthouse, but he had hardly started on his way when the lake turned its sights on him. In that single moment he was vulnerable, there was no breeches buoy to hold him above the waves, no cork life belt to keep him afloat, and no oilskins to protect him from the cold. Lake Erie, at long last, had Hatch right where she wanted him. A massive wave came leaping clean over the breakwater and slammed directly onto the tiny boat. In a heartbeat the craft was slammed over and all three of its occupants were in the water. Instinctively, with one arm Hatch grabbed the small rope he had tied around himself and the cribwork, and managed to get hold of Mrs. Hazen with the other arm. Using that rope alone, he pulled both of them to the safety of his lighthouse. Soaked, shivering, and bruised, Hatch and Catherine Hazen gained the warmth of the lighthouse and were safe from Lake Erie.

Rushing from the lifesaving station the surfmen pulled their lifeboat under the lee of the breakwater searching for survivors. They found only one. The crewman that had been tossed from Hatch's rowboat managed to get back and find a ladder attached to the breakwater and was clinging there waiting to be rescued. As he was taken aboard the lifeboat, another giant wave came pouncing over the breakwall and again nearly toppled the rescuers. Elsewhere in the harbor both the tugs *H.L. Chamberlin* and *Tom Maytham* each had picked up one survivor. When the lifesavers rowed past, the tugs reported their saves and when the storm warriors pulled past the lighthouse, Hatch shouted that he had four people in his care. On the outside of the breakwater the *Wahnapitae* continued to disintegrate in the surf and spew her lumber over the breakwater and into the harbor. The lifesavers headed back to their station with their lone save, and the storm blew on.

On the morning after the storm, the lake had simmered down to just a rude chop. Launching their lifeboat from the station, the lifesavers headed toward the west breakwater lighthouse. In every direction, the harbor was a blanket of new lumber and the station lifeboat had to work through it as if breaking ice. As far as the eye could see the beach was littered for miles with lumber in mute avowal to Lake Erie's power. The tugs had dropped off their survivors at the lifesaving station the night before, and now the storm-warriors were out to pick up those left at the lighthouse. During that process it was discovered that in all of the confusion one soul had not been accounted for. Crewman Orla W. Smith of Oswego, New York, was missing from the group rescued. In fact, Smith remains missing to this day, as reports indicate that his body was never found. Thanks in large part to Frederick Hatch, however, Smith was the only death in the entire event. Oddly, some modern sources say that Mrs. Hazen was the only survivor of the wreck, and that the wreck occurred on the east breakwater. Those sources are in error as official records give the story as it has been related here.

So it was that on February 26, 1891 Lighthouse Keeper Frederick T. Hatch was awarded the gold bar from the United States Lifesaving Service for a "second service" of heroism in the case of the *Wahnapitae's* wreck. He was the first and only person in the annals of Great Lakes history to receive two gold awards for lifesaving on separate occasions. He is one of only three persons to receive double gold awards during the existence of the Lifesaving Service itself from 1876 to 1914, after which the service became the U.S. Coast Guard. In all of those years only five double awards were given, two silver and three gold.

Looking back across time, and reviewing this story, the reader may want to call Frederick Hatch the bravest person in Great Lakes history. Making such an assumption would be a mistake. There are hundreds of stories of valor just like Hatch's which I have discovered, and countless more yet to be researched and written. It can bring one to ponder that Hatch's was a time when valor was true and instinctive, not "spun" and "dramatized" or considered foolish. In this we can take a lesson from people such as Frederick Hatch. He may not have been the bravest person on the lakes, but he was among those at the top. Still, he was more than a match for Lake Erie, and he certainly had the hardware to prove it.

There is no way for the reader to visit the site of this story other than by reading the story itself. As was noted earlier, the west breakwater light was demolished around 1910 and replaced with another lighthouse which is located on an extension of the breakwater about 30 yards from the place where Hatch's light stood. The bones of the *Wahnapitae's* wreck have been covered over by the shoring up of the riprap stone, or washed away by the waves—although an adventurous historian may venture to that spot and perhaps find something among the rocks. Such a trek would not be recommended and would be done at one's own peril. All of the other vessels involved are now long gone to scrap or distant shipwreck. The *Sophia Minch*, having outlived her usefulness, was towed from Toronto "about 1927" and scuttled in deep water in Lake Ontario. Both the *John B. Merrill* and *John T. Johnson* were lost to shipwreck on Lake Huron. The *Merrill* sank on October 14, 1893 off of Drummond Island, and the *Johnson* stranded and went to pieces on North Point Reef near Alpena on November 28, 1904, and is a sport diver's target today. So, although none of the players in the preceding drama exist any longer, there is their story and the inspiration that it may have provided.

XV
GUARDIANS OF THE GUARDIANS

A book such as this must end with a true tale of the people whose single interest is the preservation of the historic lighthouses of the Great Lakes. These people operate on many different levels, using many different methods, all with the same goal in mind—the restoration and guardianship of our historic lighthouses.

One such restorationist is a "phantom" of sorts. This person works outside of the rules, beneath the shroud of secrecy and beyond the grasp of the official organizations, groups, associations and committees. Often those groups scorn his methods and berate his results with accusations of slipshod work, yet he works on. A "Lone Ranger" of lighthouses, he is often mistaken as one of the bad guys, yet his absolute resolve is toward the preservation of the endangered lighthouses. Avoiding the limelight and publicity is essential to his efforts, and so his name will not appear here. But his methods are just too intriguing to resist putting into these pages.

Whenever a Great Lakes lighthouse is in danger, the Lighthouse Lone Ranger is ready and willing to put his own personal assets to work in the effort to charge to the rescue. He has often told a concerned lighthouse group, "you won't know where or when I'm gonna do it, but I'll be there and it will get fixed" It is a method that can really make an organized lighthouse association smolder. Bypassing the committees, red-tape, official channels and self-proclaimed persons in power, he simply goes to the lighthouse with his helpers and does the work, then quietly departs. His effort is often not to exactly duplicate the facility as it was when operational. Rather, he performs a sort of lighthouse first-aid. This can buy the facility a decade or two free of decay and allow the "official" preservation groups and committees the time to finish their motions, votes and other procedures and get on with the work of preservation.

Additionally, the Lighthouse Lone Ranger concentrates on the offshore sites that are beyond the access and capability of many lighthouse preservation groups. Recently, he has been haunting the most famous of the haunted Great Lakes lighthouses, the Waugoshance Light. Erected to replace a lightship in 1851, this lighthouse was one of the earliest to be constructed well off shore. For the era, the project was a major undertaking, but the lighthouse was constructed using somewhat inferior stone and mortar. In 1910 it was abandoned because the Lighthouse Board considered the White Shoals Light to be its replacement. As we have seen, the real reason for the site's abandonment may have been the pesky ghost of John Herman, a former keeper. Apparently, no one could be found who wanted to staff the facility as long as the hauntings went on. In later years, during World War II, the abandoned light was used for target practice by Navy fighter-bombers. Such a lighthouse scorned is just the kind of site that attracts the Lighthouse Lone Ranger. He has spent a great deal of time and effort on attempting to stop the deterioration caused both by nature and by man.

His most recent accomplishment was a number of healing fixes applied to the Squaw Island Light. Established in 1892, the light has been long abandoned. The only thing that has kept the site from being totally devastated by vandals has been its remote location in the western Straits of Mackinac on northern Lake Michigan. In May of 1993, when the owner of the site discovered that someone was secretly performing maintenance to the lighthouse, he set out to capture the rascal and run him off.

When the Lighthouse Lone Ranger leaves a site, he does not leave behind a silver bullet. Rather, he leaves a logbook and an open door so that legitimate visitors who truly are there to appreciate the site can log in. This tactic is also one that sets the established lighthouse groups on edge, because it is the philosophy of most preservation groups that securing a site's integrity equates to isolating it from public traffic. On off-shore sites, it is the theory of the Lighthouse Lone Ranger that such visitors actually help to secure the light from those who would seek to vandalize it. The presence of lighthouse enthusiasts at an abandoned light is more effective than a uniformed security guard.

Another avenue of salvation for Great Lakes lighthouses comes in the form of official preservation organizations such as the Great lakes Light Keepers Association. By getting people involved through membership, such groups put an "official" stamp to the efforts of preservation. Additionally, they spread the word among the lighthouse public that certain sites are in great need of rescue. These organizations give a legitimate collection point where donated funds may be properly dispensed to the efforts of saving the lights. Also, these official groups find ways to share the historic lighthouses with the public while controlling the access and thus minimizing the impact of people visiting the site.

Some of the official lighthouse preservation groups have started to organize and conduct local "lighthouse festivals." These events attract thousands of people and become a true boon to the local economies. Venders come from all around the nation to visit the festivals and sell their crafts, books, photos and other lighthouse related goods.

Lighthouse organizations also sponsor tours by boat of previously inaccessible sites. These are an outstanding way to guard the lights by bringing the public to them in a controlled manner. Nothing scares away the vandals better than a tourboat packed with camera-armed lighthouse buffs. Educating the public is one of the best ways that lighthouse organizations guard the guardians. Once the damage done by the vandals or the neglect of the government is exposed to the public, and they are educated to the historical significance of these lighthouses, all who hear the stories can not help but become involved in the guardianship of the lights.

Above all, the greatest asset in the effort to guard the guardians is found in you, the reader. You are a member of the army of consumers who wear the lighthouse shirts, display lighthouse knickknacks, drink from lighthouse mugs, send lighthouse postcards, take lighthouse photos, shop in lighthouse gift shops, read lighthouse books and generally admire the old lighthouses themselves. This is an army that is growing exponentially in members and enthusiasm. With it grows the general atmosphere of protection and preservation that will keep the lights safe and mend the lights that are in decay. Recently, I was in a discussion with the keepers of a lighthouse about to be deactivated by the Coast Guard, and that person worried what would happen to the property when the sight was deactivated. It was my opinion that there should be no fear at all, because in this day and age the thought of demolishing any lighthouse has become so repugnant that no one would dare to attempt it. Indeed, as soon as the Coast Guard vacates any lighthouse on the Great Lakes, the problem may actually be in the number of preservation groups fighting to gain control of the site!

Every time consumers purchase anything relating to lighthouses they make the cottage industry of lighthouse goods more attractive of the retailers to enter. That market raises the demand for new products. One result is the research and production of books such as this one! Items of lighthouse interest are then exposed to the general public and upon sampling them, new lighthouse enthusiasts are born. Readers should never underestimate their role in this critical chain of events. You start a cycle that leads to the expansion of such material, the education of the public, and the preservation of lighthouses. Thus, if you did not know it previously, you are an important guardian of the guardians, and you have done it by simply obtaining and reading this text. So, as you sit in your easy chair, or in your car on your way along the highway, or strapped into your airline seat, or on the beach near the lake or even tucked snugly into your bed, you can close these pages and know that you are one of the guardians of the guardians. Across all of the Great Lakes, at this moment, the old lighthouses and the spirits of those who dedicated their lives to tending the lights, turn to you and give a well-deserved sigh of thanks.

ABOUT THE AUTHOR

W. Wes Oleszewski was born on the east side of Saginaw, Michigan, in 1957. He attended Nelle Haley and Webber public schools there through grade 9. His family then moved to Freeland, Michigan, where he graduated from high school in 1976.

Through most of his youth, Wes had an interest in the vessels of the Great Lakes second only to his fascination with the space program and areas of aviation. When accepted for enrollment at the Embry-Riddle Aeronautical University in 1977, Wes' career turned toward aviation leaving time for a deeper diversion into Great Lakes maritime history. Such diversion was

often needed during the 10 years of difficult work and mundane employment required to pay his way through the university. By 1987, Wes had earned a Bachelor of Science Degree in Aeronautical Science, with pilot certification through commercial pilot with multi-engine instrument rating. He also earned the Student Leadership and Involvement Award, served on the university's Precision Flight Demonstration Team, leaving as the team's Chief Pilot. He collected awards and honors for 10 years of outstanding service to the university, and worked as the editorial cartoonist for the *Avion* the student newspaper, from 1978 until his graduation. Wes paid for his entire education through earnings and student aid—sometimes working as many as two jobs at one time.

This, however, was not enough to keep Wes' creative urges occupied. In the summer of 1986, he was earning money to return to school by working days as a film delivery driver and nights as a part-time clerk at Land and Seas Gift Shop, in Saginaw. While there he noticed that every book on the shelf was already in his personal library. With that in mind, Wes sat down the next day during his lunch hour and began writing his first book on a legal pad. No one ever told him how it was done or that he couldn't do it. For the next year he assembled the true stories of the obscure adventures of the lake mariners—the tales that everyone else had overlooked. Over the summer of 1987, while Wes attended college classes in a doubled effort to graduate, his soon-to-be wife, Teresa, transferred the handwritten text into computer text. That same summer, Wes sent the text to a well-known Great Lakes publisher, who promptly rejected it. In 1990 the same text was sent to Avery Color Studios who promptly published it as *Stormy Seas.*

Since that first book hit the shelf, Wes has written and Avery has published *Sounds of Disaster, Ice Water Museum, Ghost Ships, Gales and Forgotten Tales,* and *Mysteries and Histories: Shipwrecks of the Great Lakes.* Avery also has published his books on lighthouses: *Great Lakes Lighthouses, American and Canadian* and *Lighthouse Adventures.* Wes has written more than a quarter of a million words about the maritime history of the Great Lakes. Currently he has more than 100 stories in research and can produce a book every year if he desires. As of this writing he is busy at work on his next book, which deals with the true tales and ghost stories of the lighthouses of the United States. Aside from writing, and working at his other job as an airline transport pilot, Wes finds time to travel around the Great Lakes region visiting bookstores to sign copies of his work, researching local maritime history, and his favorite side-trip—speaking to classrooms of students beginning at the elementary level. Often the enthusiastic boat-nut can find Wes perched on the canal wall at Duluth, or shooting videotape under the Bluewater Bridge at Port Huron, or hanging out on the west observation platform at the Soo locks. Like most professional pilots, he gets around!

This professional pilot and author, as of this publication, has logged more than 5,000 hours of flying time, most of that in airline category aircraft. Currently, he holds the highest pilot certification issued by the FAA—the Airline Transport Pilot Certificate, and has achieved the rank of airline captain. He is presently living on the East Coast and employed as a professional pilot.

For those who wish to contact the author or sample his other work, Wes maintains a web site at: www.lighthouses-lakeboats.com.

BIBLIOGRAPHICAL SOURCES

Keeper Marshall's Itch

United States Life Saving Service Annual Report, 1883, 1908

Annual Report of the Activities of the Lighthouse Board, 1872,1882, 1884, 1894

The Northern Lights, Hyde

National Parks Service 1994 Inventory of Historic Lighthouses

National Archives microfilm box M1373 Register of Lighthouse Keepers

Great Lakes Historical Society web site- www.inlandseas.org/ispage3.htm

It Was Called "Stannard's Rock"

Annual Report of the Operations of the Lighthouse Board, 1882, 1892, 1896

Haunted Lakes, Stonehouse

The Northern Lights, Hyde

Dave Swayze data base

National Archives microfilm box M1373 Register of Lighthouse Keepers

E-mail from Fred Stonehouse, 5/19/1998 concerning the date of the official name change of the Stannard's Rock lighthouse

Lake Superior Shipwrecks, Wolff

In Search of John Herman's Ghost

Annual Report of the Operations of the Lighthouse Board, 1852, 1910, 1911, 1912, 1913, 1914

List of the Lights of the United States, Embracing the Atlantic, Gulf, Lake, and Pacific Coasts, 1857

Treasury Department, Lighthouse Board, Form 313, National Archives microfilm box M1373 Register of Lighthouse Keepers

E-mail from Dave Swayze, 12/17/1998

Detroit Free Press 10/13/1883

Meeting with Mark Fowler, 5/11/1997, 11/27/1998, Freeland, MI

Meeting with Bernard Hellstrom, 11/29/1998, Port Huron, MI

Phone conversation with Jack Edwards 12/10/1998

E-mail correspondence with Bernard Hellstrom 12/3/1998, 12/12/1998

Shipwrecks of the Straits of Mackinac, Feltner

Great Lakes Lighthouses American & Canadian, Oleszewski

Haunted Lakes, Stonehouse

The Northern Lights, Hyde

E-mail from Dave Swayze 12/17/1998

Phone conversation with Ann Sindelar 6/12/1988, 12/14/1998

Phone conversation with PS3 J. Richards USCG 11/22/1998

Meeting with Dave Allen, Greenbush, MI, 8/19/1998

Phone conversation and mail contact with Leo and Sue Kuschel 10&11, 1998

Phone Contact, National Archives, Chicago Branch, 12/17/1998

Andrew Shaw's Concern

United States Life Saving Service Annual Report, 1882

Lake Huron, Landon

Michigan Lighthouses, Penrose

The Northern Lights, Hyde

Author's visit to Pointe aux Barques lighthouse 7/20/1996

Steaming Through Smoke and Fire 1871, Donahue

Treasury Department, Lighthouse Board, Form 313, National Archives microfilm box M1373 Register of Lighthouse Keepers

Pointe aux Barques lighthouse file-box, misc. papers and letters, National Archives

Record of Lights-Keepers' Names, Birthplace, National Archives microfilm box M1373 Register of Lighthouse Keepers

Disaster On The Doorstep

Duluth Evening Herald, 9/1,2,4,5,6,/1905

Bay City Tribune, 7/26,27/1900

Saginaw Courier Herald, 7/27/1900

Davidson's Goliaths, Cooper & Jensen

Ships Built on the Saginaw, Swayze, Roberts, Comtois

The Unholy Apostles, Keller

Lake Superior Shipwrecks, Wolff

A Traveler's Guide to 116 Western Great Lakes Lighthouses, Penrose

The Northern Lights, Hyde/Mahan

Fresh Water Whales, Wright

Titanic, Bonsall

Freeman's Dunking
Oswego Daily Times, 12/23/1851
E-mail from Richard Palmer, Lake Ontario research historian, 1/25/1998
Lake Ontario, Pound
Great American Lighthouses, Holland
New Coast Pilot for the Great Lakes, 1896
The Bay of Dead Ships, Reich
America's Lighthouses, Holland
National Archives microfilm box M1373 Register of Lighthouse Keepers

Yarn of Disaster
Buffalo Express, 12/10, 11/1909
Bay City Tribune, 12/9,12,14,/1909
Beeson's Marine Directory, 1910
Annual Report of the Operations of the Light-House Board, 1892, 1909, 1910
Dive Ontario Two!, Kohl
Shipwrecks of the Lakes, Bowen
Ghost Ships of the Great Lakes, Boyer
Shipwreck!, Swayze
Great Lakes Ships We Remember Vol. II, Van der Linden
Namesakes 1900-1909, Greenwood
Queen of the Lakes, Thompson
Freshwater Whales, Wright
Namesakes II, Greenwood
Phone conversation with research diver Roy Pickering 9/24/1996
Phone conversation with research diver Cris Kohl 9/16/1996
E-mail from Brendon Baillod 10/30/1998
Runge File, Milwaukee Public Library

Spirits of The Point
Author's visit to the Point aux Barques lighthouse, 7/20/1996, 11/29/1998
Phone interview with Pamela Kennedy, 8/26/1998, 11/3/1998
Phone interview with Martha Janderwski, 8/26/1998, 11/3/1998
Internet Public Library, Carter

United States Life Saving Service Annual Report, 1876 to 1913 (all volumes searched in this effort.)

Lake Huron, Landon

List of Light-Houses and Floating Lights, 1880

National Archives microfilm box M1373 Register of Lighthouse Keepers

List of the Lights of the United States, Embracing the Atlantic, Gulf, Lake, and Pacific Coasts, 1857

Strange Adventures of the Great Lakes, Boyer

Lake Huron's Ghostly Surfboat, Wreck and Rescue, No.9, 1998, Stonehouse

Traveler's Guide to 116 Michigan Lighthouses, Penrose

Sounds of Disaster, Oleszewski

Wreck Ashore, Stonehouse

The 100 Best Great Lakes Shipwrecks, Vol. I and Vol. II, Kohl

U.S. Life-Saving Service, Rescues and Architecture of the Early Coast Guard, Shanks

A Keeper's Nightmare Comes True

Soo Evening News, 4/28, 30/1909 5/1, 4/1909

Duluth Evening Herald, 5/1, 3/1909

Marquette Daily Mining Journal, 5/1, 3, 7/1909

George Nester file, Institute for Great Lakes Research

Dave Swayze data base

Lake Superior Shipwrecks, Wolff

Great Lakes Lighthouses, Roberts and Jones

Annual Report of the Operations of the Lighthouse Board, 1882, 1890, 1896

United States Life-Saving Service Annual Report, 1909

Namesakes 1900-1909, Greenwood

Namesakes 1920-1929, Greenwood

E-mail from C. Patrick Labadie concerning the spelling of the name of the captain of the *George Nester*, 5/11,18/1998

America's Lighthouses, Holland

Lake Superior Shipwrecks, Wolff

Great Lakes Lighthouses American & Canadian, Oleszewski

Ice Water Museum, Oleszewski

State of Michigan Aeronautical Chart, 1988

Internet search of telephone records, call to Dubeau residence 12/4/1998

The Lakeboat Vs. The Lighthouse

Annual Report of the Operations of the Light-House Board, 1885

List of Light-houses, Lighted Beacons, and Floating Lights, United States Lighthouse Board, 1880

Great Lakes & Seaway Shipping, web site.

Soundings, Vol. 17 Number 4, March 1998, Vol.18 Number 9, August 1998

Port Huron Daily Times, 9/19/1872

Marking The Boundary Between Life And Death

Detroit Free Press, 5/8, 10/1857

Correspondence with Dave Swayze by e-mail and letter 8/10, 15/1998

Dave Swayze shipwreck data base

The Marblehead Lighthouse: Lake Erie's Eternal Flame, Neidecker

A Traveler's Guide to 100 Eastern Great Lakes Lighthouses, Penrose

National Park Service 1994 Inventory of Historic Lighthouses

The World Almanac, 1988, Journal

Encarta 98 Encyclopedia, Microsoft

Author's visit to the Marblehead light, 10/9-10/1998

America's Lighthouses, Holland

Vieira's Private Range

Shipwrecks of Lake Huron, Parker

The Northern Lights, Hyde

The New Namesakes of the Lakes, Greenwood

Saginaw News, 6/12/1984

Phone conversation with Ralph Roberts, 12/6/1997

Letter from Ralph Roberts, 12/11/1997

Saving Round Island

Annual Report of the Operations of the Light-House Board, 1894, 1895, 1896

Interview with Mark Fowler, Freeland, MI. 11/27/1998

Compilation of material on the Round Island Lighthouse intended for the light's centennial celebration, dated 1/18/1996, compiled by Jack Edwards.

Shipwrecks of the Straits of Mackinac, Feltner

National Parks Service 1994 Inventory of Historic Lighthouses

Shipwrecks of the Straits of Mackinac, Feltner

A Traveler's Guide To 110 Michigan Lighthouses, Penrose

Deep Six Those Cheap Plastic Imitations, Great Lakes Cruiser, Vol.5, Issue 11, November 1998, Edwards

Phone conversation with Jack Edwards, 12/10/1998

The Hardware To Prove It

United States Life-Saving Service Annual Report, 1883, 1891, 1908

America's Lighthouses, Holland

Annual Report of the Operations of the Lighthouse Board, 1872, 1868, 1886, 1888, 1889, 1892, 1893, 1896, 1899

Lake Erie, Hatcher

Wreck Ashore, Stonehouse

Treasury Department, Lighthouse Board, Form 313, National Archives microfilm box M1373 Register of Lighthouse Keepers

Phone conversation with Ann Sindelar, Western Reserve Historical Society, 6/17/1998

A Pictorial History of the Great Lakes, Hatcher & Walter

Namesakes 1900-1909, 1920-1929, Greenwood

National Parks Service 1994 Inventory of Historic Lighthouses

A Traveler's Guide to 100 Eastern Great Lakes Lighthouses, Penrose

Lighthouses & Keepers, Noble

Dave Swayze shipwreck data-base

Annual Report of the Chief of Engineers, U.S. Army, 1888

Guardians of The Guardians

National Parks Service 1994 Inventory of Historic Lighthouses

Shipwrecks of the Straits of Mackinac, Feltner

A Traveler's Guide To 110 Michigan Lighthouses, Penrose

Interview with Bernard Hellstorm, Port Huron, MI. 11/29/1998

E-mail from Bernard Hellstorm, 12/3/1998